The Textile Industry

Lexington Casebook Series
in Industry Analysis

The Textile Industry

An Industry Analysis Approach to Operations Management

Richard Paul Olsen
IMEDE Management
Development Institute

Lexington Books
D.C. Heath and Company
Lexington, Massachusetts
Toronto

Library of Congress Cataloging in Publication Data

Olsen, Richard Paul.
  The textile industry.

  1. Textile industry—Management—Case studies. 2. Textile industry—United States. I. Title.
HD9856.O47   658'.97'7   77-9167
ISBN 0-669-01807-4

Contents

List of Figures

List of Tables

Preface

This book is one of a series published by Lexington Books, D.C. Heath and Company. Each book focuses on a selected industry through a general background description and specific cases directed at the operating programs and policies of companies within the industry. For the purposes of this series of books, an *industry* may be defined as a set of firms in competition, producing goods or services of a like function and nature.

Part I has been designed to provide a general background for individuals who are unfamiliar with the industry. Such readers might include students, members of the financial community, and members of government. Also, these sections have been included to help members of the industry who may be functional specialists, or those whose careers have been confined to one subsegment of the entire industry. Part I and Part II also serve to define the use of terminology and provide reference material that will be useful in considering individual case studies.

The third portion of the book describes actual company situations and management decision-making processes in case studies. We stress the fact that these are actual cases, drawn from the experiences of real managers. They are not fabricated illustrations. We have disguised some names where it was appropriate, but all cases are used with the approval of the companies involved and with their agreement that the cases are a fair portrayal of the situations they faced, in all their complexities.

The cases have been selected to be representative of the vital decisions that influence the overall competitiveness of these firms. Most of these cases were developed as a response to a question posed to management: "What are the most important decisions that you have made in the recent history of your company? By and large, the responses we received to this question, and consequently the selection of case studies included in this book, have focused on the issue of operating policy.

The approach of this book may be novel to some readers. Basically, we are presenting an inside look at an industry through "situational analysis" rather than the more conventional "theoretic construct" approach. We present the situation and the views of managers, but we leave the final analysis and conclusion to the reader, rather than present the actual outcome or "textbook" solution. By working through each of the case studies presented here it is possible to derive general principles of good management in this industry. Furthermore we believe that such an outcome is *only* possible by treating the book as a unit—considering all of the case studies together. The principle underlying this belief is that good decisions relating to one area within a company can only be made with reference to a comprehensive understanding of the goals and operations of the entire company, and that decisions by a single company cannot be taken independently of consideration of that company's role and position within the entire industry.

This approach is derived from the teaching methodology developed at the Harvard University Graduate School of Business Administration. These books were originally intended as texts to teach the elements of industry analysis, and, so far as is feasible, to place the students in the industrial climate so they could draw upon their own knowledge and simulate the decision-making process that might be expressed in the climate.

Our principal reason for making these books generally available is based on our observation, primarily through executive programs, that others have also benefited from this approach.

In the industry approach, the reader should examine the technological and economic structures of the set of competitive firms producing goods or services in the industry. If an industry is not integrated to any extent from the final product back to the intermediate or raw materials, the executive does not need to know a great deal about the economic and technical aspects of stages preceding or following the particular phase in which he or she is engaged.

In the Harvard Business School approach to industry analysis, students are directed to study an industry to determine what characteristics are unique to it. What elements are within the control of the manager? How can the manager affect the outcome of a firm in the industry? We have found that the following questions or topics are often useful in approaching this task. Of course, not all topics are equally relevant or important to each industry. However, the following list has proven to be a reasonable point of departure.

Economics of the Industry (at Each Level of the Industry)

1. Labor, burden, material, depreciation costs
2. Flexibility to volume changes
3. Return on investment, prices, margins
4. Number and location of plants
5. Critical control variables
6. Critical functions (maintenance, production control, personnel, etc.)
7. Typical financial structures
8. Typical costs and cost relationships
9. Typical operating problems
10. Barriers to entry
11. Pricing practices
12. The concept of maturity of an industry
13. Importance of economies of scale
14. Importance of integrated capacities within corporations
15. Importance of balance of equipment

16. Ideal balances of equipment capacities
17. Nature and type of production controls
18. Government influences

Technology of the Industry (at Each Level of the Industry)

1. Rate and kind of technological changes
2. Scale of processes
3. Span of processes
4. Degree of mechanization
5. Technological sophistication
6. Time requirements for making changes

Competitive Situation in the Industry (at Each Level of the Industry)

1. Number and type of companies
2. Nature of competition
3. Marketing approaches
4. Job of the operating vice-president
5. Degree of linked or coupled operations
6. Possible strategies
7. Task of the operating function
8. Diversity of product lines
9. Interindustry sales and relations
10. Public policy towards the industry
11. Social expectations of the industry
12. Foreign competition
13. Competition from other industries
14. Historical and current problems
15. Company comparisons

Acknowledgments

I am grateful to John G. McLean who is credited with the conception and early development of the industry approach at the Harvard Business School in 1947. This concept was developed into the course "Manufacturing Policy" which is still taught at Harvard and other business schools. A substantial contribution to the concept and course structure were made by Wickham Skinner and David Rogers, who coauthored a five volume manufacturing policy series.

I am especially grateful to Wickham Skinner, who as a teacher and colleague has been a source of encouragement and inspiration. Parts I and II are structured after the industry process note and reference note written by Professor Skinner and Edward Graham in 1970.

I wish to thank several people for their contribution to the material in this book. First, Robert S. Merkel and Marshall Field, who as research assistants, contributed substantially to the researching and writing of Parts I and II respectively. The WestPoint-Pepperell and Texfi cases were written by Wickham Skinner.

I have received assistance from Bob Leone who helped support the writing of Parts I and II through his Water Pollution Abatement Research Project under contract #WQ4ACO14 from the National Commission on Water Quality.

We are grateful to the president and fellows of Harvard College, by whom the cases and notes included in this book are individually copyrighted. These cases are published here with their permission.

Introduction

This volume is designed to provide a basis of understanding of the textile industry to three groups of people. The first group encompasses those individuals who are entering the textile industry for the first time in some operating or management capacity; the second group of individuals are those managers and analysts embarking on some relationship with the industry, either as suppliers of goods and services to or investors in the industry; the third group are those individuals within the industry whose previous jobs have limited their necessary knowledge and interest to a specific area of the industry or operations within the industry but who are entering a phase of their career that requires a broader understanding of overall industry strategies. To accomplish its goal this text is divided into three parts. Part I deals with the various manufacturing processes in the textile industries. It describes the structural elements of the total process: fibers, yarn, fabric forming, and finishing. Within each of these structural elements, alternative manufacturing processes are described, for example, weaving, knitting, tufting, and nonwoven processes of fabric forming. The process structure, technology, and the microeconomics of the processes are described in lay terms. Part II describes the structure of the industry in terms of size of firms, competitive positions, and vertical and horizontal integration.

Thus, Parts I and II provide the foundations of understanding the process technology and market structure of the industry. The understanding developed in the first two sections are applied in Part III. Part III contains four cases that present a cross section of issues dealing with managing a firm within the textile industry. The first case, Seneca Mills, Inc., focuses on the issues and problems of mill operations. It is designed to develop in the reader an understanding of the microeconomics and other management issues of plant operation. The second case, WestPoint-Pepperell, Inc. (B), focuses on the issue of capacity expansion. The reader is asked to examine and evaluate two expansion proposals. The first involves adding capacity to an existing plant while the second is directed at adding a completely new mill. The third case, Carpetex Industries, examines decision making in the rapidly changing technological and competitive environment of the carpet industry. Issues present in this case include a 50 percent increase in required capacity for the same quantity of output, rapidly increasing material costs, and increased competition resulting from low barriers of entry. The fourth and final case, Texfi Industries, Inc., deals with the overall evaluation of a company's position within the industry and an evaluation of its competitive strategies.

The cases present the facts and managements' evaluations of the situations. The cases are designed to allow the reader to sharpen their managerial skills by applying the knowledge of the first two sections to the problems presented in the third section.

Part I:
Manufacturing
Processes in the Textile
Industry

Introduction to Part I

The textile process encompasses the total manufacturing process from the manufacture of raw materials to the fabrication and service of industrial and consumer goods. There are four distinct stages in this process: fiber and continuous filament manufacturing, yarn and fabric forming, finishing, and apparel manufacturing. Each of these stages have a different dominant technology. The first stage, fiber and filament manufacturing, is dominated by two distinctly different technologies: agriculture and large-scale physical chemistry processes. The second stage, yarn and fabric forming, is dominated by mechanical processes. The third stage, finishing, is a chemical conversion process with greater scale economies than the fabric forming stage but not as great as the fiber production stage. The fourth stage, apparel manufacturing, is to this day dominated by small-scale, labor-intensive artisan manufacturing.

The first stage, or fiber and filament stage, involves two quite different processes and also two quite different sectors of the economy. These are the agricultural production of cotton, wool, and silk fibers and the chemical manufacture of synthetic or man-made fibers and filaments. The second stage of the process, textile mill production, converts the fibers and filaments to yarn and weaves, knits, tufts, or otherwise forms the yarn into various types of fabrics. The third stage, finishing, is often integrated with the second stage in a single manufacturing process. The finishing stage dyes and chemically treats the fabrics to change its color, texture, and mechanical properties. The final stage converts the textile mill products into usable industrial and consumer goods such as clothing, draperies, sheets, wrapping materials, and screening materials. Although each of the four stages performs distinct tasks and utilizes very different technologies, there is often some overlap. For example, such consumer goods as towels, sheets, and hosiery are produced in a fabric forming mill. To understand the entire process in all its variety, we will treat the industry as consisting of these four stages and note any overlap and/or integration.

Yarn Preparation Processes

Fiber and Filament Production

Fibers and filaments are the raw materials of the textile industry. These raw materials can be classified into two principal groups: natural fibers and man-made fibers and filaments. Table 1-1 lists the names, types, and sources of textile fibers. Figure 1-1 shows prices of major fibers and yarns.

Natural Fibers

Textile industry raw materials are selected for processing with consideration of fiber cost, fiber availability, fiber properties, and end-use requirements. Among natural fibers, only cotton and wool remain as major raw materials for the textile industry. Silk, hemp, and jute are still utilized but in insignificant quantities. As total U.S. and world consumption of textile fibers has increased in recent years, the proportions accounted for by cotton and wool have decreased as man-made fibers have become the major source of raw material for the industry. In 1973 U.S. cotton fiber consumption was 3.66 billion pounds, and wool fiber consumption was 153.8 million pounds out of a total mill fiber consumption of 12.55 billion pounds.

Sixty million pounds of U.S. wool consumption in 1973 was imported. The world price of wool has been very variable in the last several years, with the price declining from about $2.45 per pound in August 1973 to $1.78 per pound in March 1974. Natural fibers, both animal and vegetable, are produced in the agricultural sector, harvested from the plant or animal source, baled, and sold to textile yarn mills with little or no preparation of the fibers.

American upland cotton is by far the most important of the several cultivated species of cotton. In the United States it is grown as an annual crop across all the southern United States as far as the southern edges of Virginia, Illinois, and Nevada. An acre of cotton yields just over one bale of cotton fiber (approximately 480 pounds net weight) after mechanical harvesting and separation of the fibers from the seeds by ginning. The price of cotton in the early 1970s was very sensitive to world economic conditions, with the most common quality grade and length reaching a low of 25.7¢/lb. in October 1972 and a high of 80.5¢/lb. in September 1973.

Cotton is classified by staple length, color and grade, growth, and fineness.

5

Table 1-1
Classification of Fibers

Type	Name of Fiber	Source or Composition
Natural fibers:		
	Cotton	Cotton boll (cellulose)
	Linen	Flax stalk (cellulose)
	Jute	Jute stalk (cellulose)
	Hemp	Hemp or abaca stalk (cellulose)
Vegetable	Sisal	Agave leaf (cellulose)
	Kapok	Kapok tree (cellulose)
	Ramie	Rhea or China grass (cellulose)
	Coir	Coconut husk (cellulose)
	Pina	Pineapple leaf (cellulose)
	Wool	Sheep (protein)
Animal	Silk	Silkworm (protein)
	Hair	Hair-bearing animals (protein)
Mineral	Asbestos	Varieties of rock (silicate of magnesium and calcium)
Man-Made fibers:		
	Rayon	Cotton linters or wood
Cellulosic	Acetate	Cotton linters or wood
	Triacetate	Cotton linters or wood
	Nylon	Polyamide
	Polyester	Dihydric alcohol and terephthalic acid
	Acrylic	Acrylonitrile (at least 85%)
	Modacrylic	Acrylonitrile (35%-84%)
	Spandex	Polyurethane (at least 85%)
Synthetic, long-chain polymers	Olefin	Ethylene or propylene (at least 85%)
	Saran	Vinylidene Chloride (at least 80%)
	Vinyon	Vinyl chloride (at least 85%)
	Vinal[a]	Vinyl alcohol (at least 50%)
	Nytril[a]	Vinylidene dinitrile (at least 85%)
	Fluorocarbon	Tetrafluoroethylene
	Lastrile	Acrylonitrile (10%-50%) and a diene
	Alginate[a]	Calcium alginate
Mineral	Glass	Silica sand, limestone, and other minerals
	Ceramic	Minerals
Metallic	Metal	Aluminum, silver, gold, stainless steel
Rubber	Rubber	Natural or synthetic rubber
Protein	Azlon[a]	corn, soybean, etc.

Source: Adapted from J. Potter and C. Corbman, *Textiles: Fiber to Fabric* (New York: McGraw-Hill, 1967), p. 4.
[a]Not presently in commercial production in United States.

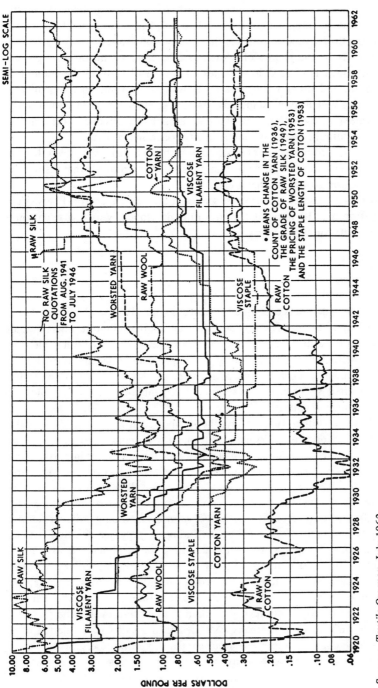

Figure 1-1. U.S. Fiber and Yarn Prices, 1920-1962

Source: *Textile Organon*, July 1962.

Note: This graph is plotted on a semi-log or ratio scale. Data was not accumulated after 1962, price ranges for 1970-1975 period were (per pound): wool, $1.40-$1.80; cotton, $.34-$.59; man-made fibers, $.96-$1.40.

1. *Staple length* is the predominant length of the cotton fiber. Domestic cottons vary in staple length from 3/4 to 1 3/4 inch. In general, the longer staple lengths are used for making the finer cotton fabrics.
2. *Color* refers to the degree of whiteness. There are six major color groups, each of which is divided into *grades* to cover variations in the amount of leaf, trash, and other foreign matter as well as variations in the quality of the ginning preparation. Standards for each grade are kept in a vault in the Department of Agriculture. Samples are available to anyone in the industry and constitute the basis for commercial transactions in cotton.
3. *Growth* refers to the geographic area in which the cotton was grown. Cotton from different areas will have certain physical characteristics that distinguish it from cotton grown in other areas.
4. *Fineness* is a measure of the cross-sectional area of the cotton fibers. Very fine cotton may be immature, or not fully developed. Very coarse cotton is only suitable for coarse yarns.

Man-Made Fibers

By 1973, man-made fibers accounted for over two-thirds of total fiber consumption in the United States. The broadest division is into cellulosic fibers that are regenerated from natural polymers (rayon and acetate fibers are both made from wood cellulose or other natural sources of cellulose) and noncellulosic synthetic organic fibers made primarily from petrochemicals. Rayon and acetate production in the United States in 1973 was about 1,357 million pounds. Polyester and nylon fibers alone accounted for 80 percent of synthetic fiber production in 1973, with several other types of synthetic fiber such as Acrylic, Modacrylic, Olefin, Vinyon (polyvinyl chloride), and Spandex (an elastic polymer) making up the rest. Fiberglass, although a small portion of the market, is important for a restricted group of end uses: reinforced composites, tire cord, and insulation.

Man-made fibers are made by extruding a viscose chemical solution through tiny orifices in thimble-like objects known as spinnerets. There are three basic methods for extruding fiber: It may be *wet spun* by extruding polymer solution into coagulation bath, *dry spun* by extruding a polymer solution into an evaporation zone, or *melt spun* by extruding a molten plasticized solid into a cooling zone. The major purpose of all three processes is to solidify and draw a chemical mixture into a fiber with various length, thickness, texture, and structural and mechanical characteristics. The structural and mechanical characteristics result from orientation of the polymer molecules during the extrusion process. The polymers are normally extruded into lengths of a fraction of an inch to many inches to form *staple fiber* similar to natural fibers. Stable fiber is extruded from spinnerets with many holes to form bundles of large filaments known as *tow*. The tow is draw-stretched, may optionally be crimped (i.e., eliminate the straightness of the fiber) by passage between gears or by forcing it into a small heated *stuffer box* chamber. The staple fiber is then cut into the desired length ranges (some fiber-to-fiber length variation is preferable), subjected to mechanical separation, and packaged. The tow itself, after surface treatment and draw-stretching, could be packaged for shipment to a textile plant for conversion into staple yarns alone or blended with cotton, wool, or other types of synthetic fibers.

The polymer may also be extruded as a continuous filament. This continuous filament may then undergo a number of processes, such as (1) treatment with a fiber lubricant or surface finish, (2) draw-stretchings, (3) twisting, and (4) texturing before wound onto large aluminum or cardboard tubes, called *purns,* to form large spools of yarn called *cheeses.* This filament yarn is then ready to be used (with little or no further processing) as textile yarn.

Apart from generic class (e.g., nylon, acrylic), man-made fibers are classified by staple length, fineness (weight per unit length), luster, presence or absence of crimp, and other properties. A specific "type" of man-made fiber has a certain array of properties. A specific "merge number" represents a particular production lot whose properties should be identical throughout.

Fiber Structure and Properties

Fibers are constructed from *high polymers* that are long chains of molecularly bonded *monomers,* or single molecules. A polymer may be constructed from a single type of monomer or several different types of monomers. The structure of the polymer (such as the type or types of monomers, how the monomers are chemically bonded to form the polymer, and the geometric structure of the chain) determine the mechanical properties of the polymer (the length of the polymer, *crystallinity*—the relationship between polymers—and the orientation of the chains to the fiber axis). The mechanical properties of the polymers in turn determine the mechanical properties of the yarn, such as wrinkle and dyeing characteristics. Permanent press garments are constructed from yarns with high elasticity of recovery. This yarn property results from a strong interpolymer bonding that allows temporary slippage between polymers (otherwise the yarn would be too stiff) but prevents permanent slippage between polymers that would cause wrinkles. Dyeing rate is effected by crystallinity. A high crystalline structure (i.e., a strong relationship between polymers resulting in a compact fiber structure) results in very slow dyeing rates that can only be increased by chemical or temperature treatment during the dyeing process.

The effect of polymer structure on fabric characteristics (e.g., dyeing rate) has led to a proliferation of man-made fibers. The cellulose polymer of natural cotton has very high molecular weight and a high crystallinity that interferes with dyeing. By contrast, rayons are made from cellulose of much lower molecular weight in order to achieve desirable extrusion characteristics in its manufacture; the resultant fiber characteristics are improved dyeing rates. Poly*esters* were developed to give improved dyeing characteristics to fabrics. Because of the manner in which the *ester* polymer is constructed, they are more easily dyeable with so-called basic or cationic dyes than other synthetics.

With few exceptions man-made fibers have been designed to fit into the same yarn manufacturing and fabric forming processes as their natural counterparts—cotton, wool, and silk. Synthetic fiber manufacturers have sought to design fibers that meet the needs of the industry without greatly disrupting in-place textile equipment. The required changes have been minimal in the mechanical process (spinning, weaving, and so forth), for example, modification of tensions and speeds on existing equipment. The changes in the chemical processes (dyeing and finishing) have been more extensive, for example, changes in chemicals used, operating temperatures, and so forth. Some changes in fiber have been made in the past that have led to major changes in the textile manufacturing process. The prime example is the use of continuous filament fiber that eliminates the yarn manufacturing process; another example is the development of longer length stable fiber for carpet tufting of higher quality tufted carpets at higher speeds. More recently there has been some more coordinated developments between fiber manufacturers and equipment manufacturers that are leading to major changes in the textile manufacturing processes, for example, texturized continuous filament yarn for use on high-speed water jet looms. Most of the in-place systems are modifications of the traditional natural fiber manufacturing systems. These will be the basis for describing the yarn manufacturing and fabric forming processes.

Yarn Manufacturing Processes

Historically, the cotton, woolen, worsted, and silk yarn manufacturing industries each had different equipment adapted to the specific production requirements of their raw materials. Each industry employed equipment suitable for fibers of certain length and diameter and for producing yarns with certain characteristics. The major ways of producing staple fiber yarns today are still based on the traditional cotton, wool, and worsted systems, but employ both natural fibers and synthetic fibers with similar dimensional characteristics. The cotton spinning system is used for fibers near one inch in length, the woolen spinning system for making very fuzzy yarns from fibers up to two inches in length, and the worsted and long fiber spinning systems for fibers over two inches in length. Even though individual textile mills may include both spinning and fabric manufacturing, they usually possess equipment for only one type of spinning system. Mills that utilize continuous filament yarns ready for processing into fabric, eliminate the need for yarn manufacturing; however, there remains a vast scope for filament yarn modification by such traditional spinning processes as twisting, texturing, winding, and dyeing.

Cotton Spinning System

Cotton system yarn mills receive raw fiber in bales or boxes, spin them into yarn through a series of process operations, and wind the yarn into various package configurations according to the needs of the fabric forming processes. A typical cotton manufacturing system is diagrammed in Figure 1-2; the cotton spinning system includes the steps from input of raw cotton through winding. This process is used for both cotton and cotton-type synthetics (example polyester). The fabric forming and finishing steps will be described in later sections.

Opening and cleaning are the initial operations performed on the incoming raw materials. The incoming raw fiber is so tightly compressed together that mechanical action is needed to separate clumps of fiber small enough for further processing. Raw cotton, in addition, contains a significant percentage of unwanted leaf and trash from the cotton plant. If synthetic fibers are to be blended with cotton, they may be mixed before processing by a blender-feeder but are usually processed separately for the first few operations because they require less cleaning than the cotton.

The opening line is used to break up the fiber mass into small clumps and to do part of the cotton cleaning. The raw fiber from bales or boxes is fed manually in large clumps onto one or more feed aprons or conveyors that carry the fiber to the *opener*. Each machine in the opening line is equipped with one or more rotating beaters with coarse teeth to shred small tufts of fiber from the incoming mass of fiber as it is fed between pressure rolls. Stock caught on the teeth of a beater is brushed against grid bars where dislodged pieces of trash may fall. Beyond the opening line, stock is pneumatically transported to the feed hoppers of two or three pickers. The opening line proper may consist of only one machine for synthetic fibers or two or even three different machines for cotton. Some newer mills have installed bale plucker machines that automatically pluck or tear fiber clumps from several entire bales of cotton at once.

The *picker* includes a hopper feed section with provision for controlling the weight of material fed per unit time. Most pickers then have two very similar sections consisting of a feed apron, knurled pressure rolls, a beater working against grid bars, and a pair of open-work cylinders with suction to trap the fiber when it leaves the beater. Older pickers compressed the output layer of fiber into a "lap" about half an inch thick and about four feet wide that was rolled up for delivery to carding machines. Specialty yarn mills continue to make picker laps, but most of the commodity yarn mills, on the other hand, have converted to automatic systems in which the fiber output from the picker is conveyed pneumatically to chute feed units behind several carding machines.

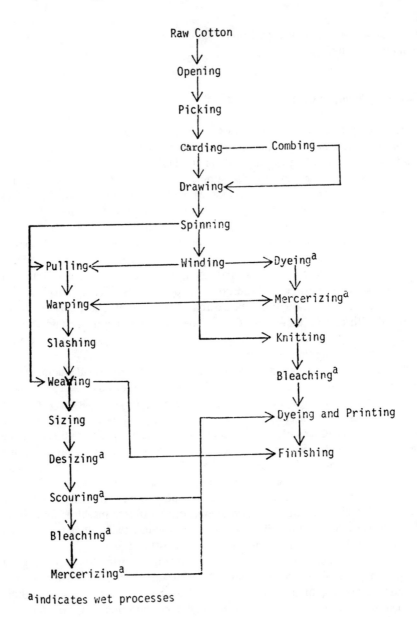

ᵃindicates wet processes

ᵃIndicates wet processes.

Figure 1-2. Cotton Textile Manufacturing Process

Carding completes the separation of the original fiber mass into individual fibers, continues the process of trash removal, and converts the material to a ropelike *sliver.* While an opening line may produce well over 1,000 pounds of opened fiber per hour and the production of each picker is the range of 300 to 500 pounds per hour, individual carding machines operate at only 25-50 pounds per hour. Whether from lap or chute, the incoming fiber layer feeds through a pair of knurled feed rolls into the working zone of a toothed roll, the "licker-in," which brushes the fiber tufts against grid bars. The fibers then are carried around on a very large cylinder, usually 50 inches in diameter. This main cylinder of the card is surfaced with close-set windings of toothed wire similar to a band saw blade. Its rotational speed is so high that a veritable fiber-to-fiber separation of the fed clumps is achieved. The fibers brush against wire-surfaced *flats* that tend to trap some short fiber and trash, which they transfer to a smaller *doffer* roll. A vibrating comb or a pneumatic mechanism removes a tenuous web of fiber from the doffer. That web may go through a pair of crusher rolls (for cotton), which tend to fragment any remaining vegetable trash, and then into a "condenser trumpet" to form the sliver that is finally coiled into a sliver can.

Usually, slivers are processed twice through the next type of machine, the *drawing* frame. Either six or eight slivers are fed together through four pairs of *drafting* rolls arranged so that each successive pair turns at higher speed. The total speed change, or draw ratio, is generally equal to the number of slivers. The web of fiber emerging from the front rolls is condensed into sliver again and coiled into a can. An electronic feedback mechanism, or autoleveler, monitors the uniformity of the material being processed and adjusts the roll speeds to maximize the uniformity of the output sliver. Not only does fixed drawn sliver have improved uniformity but also the fibers are much more aligned in parallel by the drawing operation. The most common method of blending cotton with man-made fibers (e.g., polyester) is to feed card slivers of the different blend components at the first drawing operation. In most cases sufficient blend uniformity is achieved between that point and yarn spinning to prevent any "barber pole" effects in the yarn after dyeing.

In the manufacture of combed yarns, two extra process steps are added to the drawing sequence prior to drafting. *Lapping* produces a rolled layer of fiber about eight inches wide, the "sliver lap." The second is the combing itself. *Combing* is literally a process in which some shorter fibers are rendered extremely parallel. The processes maximizes the strength and luster of resulting yarns and is usually applied to naturally long-fibered cottons such as those from Egypt and the Pima varieties grown in the United States. One use of combed yarns is in fine men's shirts. Six combed sliver laps can be produced on one combing machine, or drafter, and coiled into a can. *Noils,* the waste fiber from combing, contains much spinnable short fiber that can be used in noncombed cotton.

Although some sliver-to-yarn spinning machines have been used in the industry, in cotton spinning, a *roving* is always made from the final drawing sliver or combed sliver. Each of the 96 processing positions on the roving frame is fed with a single sliver, or occasionally two slivers. The sliver passes through three pairs of drafting rolls turning at increasing speed so that the output strand is perhaps half the thickness of a pencil. The emerging roving passes through a rotating flyer to the winding point on a bobbin. The bobbin itself fits over a rotating spindle whose speed is controlled so that the speed of the bobbin always differs by a fixed amount from the speed of the flyer. The effect is to insert enough twist into the roving to give it adequate mechanical strength for feeding into the spinning frame. Having open, cleaned, and blended the raw materials and oriented the fibers into even narrower slivers through carding, lapping, drawing, and roving, the fibers are now ready to be spun into yarn by means of ring spinning or newer open end spinning methods.

In *ring spinning,* bobbins of roving are suspended over spindles of a ring spinning frame. The roving feed passes between pairs of drafting rolls traveling at increasing speed to draw the roving before twist insertion. Because length uniformity of yarns is very desirable, much inventive effort has gone into the twist insertion technology of the spinning frame. Each spinning spindle, carrying a bobbin for the yarn, rotates at a speed of 15,000 rpm or more. Above the rail holding the row of spindles, there is a vertically movable "ring rail" with circular apertures through which the spindle bobbins project. Each aperture, about 3 inches in diameter, holds a flanged ring around which moves a tiny, C-shaped wire traveler. Yarn emerging from the drafting rolls passes around the traveler and hence onto the bobbin. During the time that an inch of yarn emerges from the front rolls, the spindle may rotate thirty times. Almost all the rotation inserts twist into the yarn because during that time the slower speed of the traveler will allow just one inch of yarn to wrap onto the bobbin.

During spinning, the entire ring rail moves vertically in a programmed way to wind the yarn onto the bobbin in an optimum configuration. Most modern spinning frames are equipped with automatic mechanisms, or doffers, to remove the bobbins and replace them with empty bobbins when the spinning cycle is complete. After doffing, a winding operation is required to transfer the yarn from the small spinning bobbins to cardboard cones holding 2-3 pounds of yarn for use in the fabric forming operation or to even larger cheeses for shipment to other plants.

Open end, or break, *spinning* refers to any staple yarn manufacturing process in which there is a break in continuity between the feed material and the end of the forming yarn. Fibers travel individually between the feed and the yarn end. They may be guided by centrifugal force and air currents, as in the commercially successful rotor spinning units first developed in Czechoslovakia in the 1960s, or other methods—such as air or liquid vortexes, static electricity (which also aligns the treveling fibers in parallel), and various mechanical arrangements—may be used.

Open end spinning grew rapidly in the 1970s at the expense of ring spinning. The cost per spindle, at $800, was ten times that of a ring spindle (the cost per spindle of ring spinning machines reaches $120 with autodoffer) while the production rate at about 0.15 pounds per hour for an average cotton yarn was only about five times that of ring spinning. However, the open end spinning machine is fed with sliver instead of roving and the open end spun yarn appears to have advantages in some important end uses. Another advantage of the open end machine is that it produces a large package of yarn, thus reducing the frequency of doffing and often eliminating any need for rewinding. The most rapid growth of open end spinning is in the manufacture of coarser yarn sizes where the doffing and rewinding costs are greatest.

Ring *twisting* frames are similar to spinning frames but without drafting rolls and with provision for feeding more than one yarn to a spindle. Hollow spindle twisting frames are used to wrap covering yarns about a core yarn to form plied yarns. Novelty attachments on twisting or frames can be used to insert various sized bundles of fiber (called "nubs," "slubs," "slugs") that will be used to form fabrics with unique textures. Ring twisters are used to make two-ply or multi-ply yarns including sewing threads, as well as fancy twisted yarns with loops or other irregularities.

Mill Organization. A cotton system spinning mill designed to make average-sized yarns may have one or more complete sets of equipment, starting with an opening line and adding subsequent machines to handle the product of that opening line. Figure 1-3 is a summary diagram of the major pieces of equipment in the spinning system. The outputs and inputs of a textile system are usually measured in pounds of fiber, yarn, and fabric. Output of a spinning system is determined by the linear speed of production and the weight or fineness of a yarn. The fineness of a yarn is designated by its count, which is the number of hanks of yarn in one pound. A hank of yarn is a coil of 840 yards. Thus, the finer the yarn the higher the count. If a yarn has a count of 1 it takes only 1 hank, or 840 yards, to make a pound of yarn; if the count is 60 then there are 60 hanks, or 50,400 yards per pound. A plied yarn would be designated by its final count and the number of yarns (plys) in its construction. Thus, 60/2 yarn is 2-ply yarn that contains 50,400 yards per pound and is made up of two 30 count yarns.

Manufacturing costs of cotton system yarns vary from 10¢ to 15¢, and the published prices for carded cotton yarns vary from 80¢ to $1 from coarse to fine counts. Most ring spinning systems involve at least two and often in-process storage points (picker lap, card sliver, first drawing sliver, second drawing sliver,

16

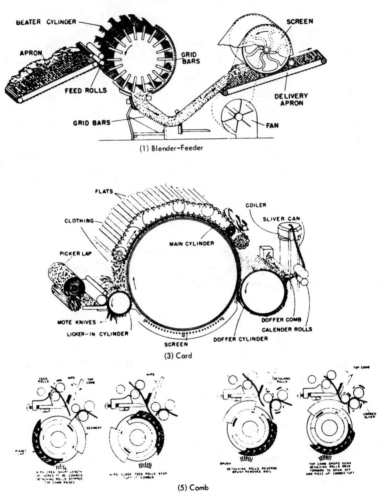

Selected Flow Chart of the Cotton Textile Industry

BEATER CYLINDER

SCREEN

APRON

GRID
BARS

FEED ROLLS

DELIVERY
APRON

GRID BARS

FAN

(1) Blender–Feeder

FLATS

COILER

CLOTHING

SLIVER CAN

PICKER LAP

MAIN CYLINDER

MOTE KNIVES

DOFFER COMB

LICKER–IN CYLINDER

CALENDER ROLLS

SCREEN

DOFFER CYLINDER

(3) Card

(5) Comb

Figure 1-3. Major Processes in Yarn Spinning

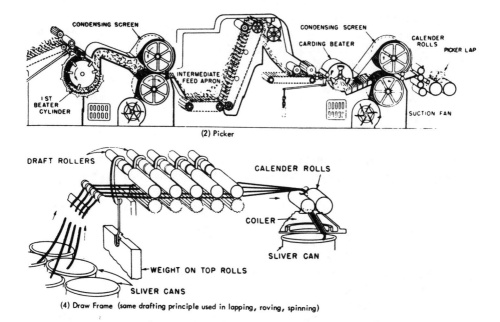

CONDENSING SCREEN · **CONDENSING SCREEN** · **CARDING BEATER** · **CALENDER ROLLS** · **PICKER LAP**

INTERMEDIATE FEED APRON

1 ST BEATER CYLINDER · **SUCTION FAN**

(2) Picker

DRAFT ROLLERS · **CALENDER ROLLS**

COILER

SLIVER CAN

WEIGHT ON TOP ROLLS

SLIVER CANS

(4) Draw Frame (same drafting principle used in lapping, roving, spinning)

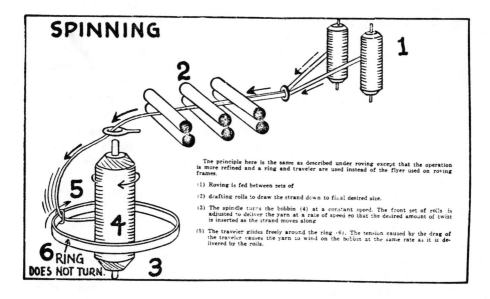

SPINNING

1

2

The principle here is the same as described under roving except that the operation is more refined and a ring and traveler are used instead of the flyer used on roving frames.

(1) Roving is fed between sets of

(2) drafting rolls to draw the strand down to final desired size.

(3) The spindle turns the bobbin (4) at a constant speed. The front set of rolls is adjusted to deliver the yarn at a rate of speed so that the desired amount of twist is inserted as the strand moves along

(5) The traveler glides freely around the ring (6). The tension caused by the drag of the traveler causes the yarn to wind on the bobbin at the same rate as it is delivered by the rolls.

5

4

6 RING DOES NOT TURN.

3

Figure 1-3 (cont.)

roving), while open end spinning systems are usually balanced to require only a single interruption (picker lap) in the process.

A typical woven cotton mill is the 316,000 square foot Columbia Weaving Mill (see Appendix 1A). Built in the early 1960s, it produces 659,000 square yards of "80 square" print cloth per 144 hour week. Selected yarn mill improvements from 1945 to 1969 are shown in Appendix 1B.

Woolen Spinning System

The distinctive soft and bulky woolen-type yarn can be made from almost any fiber, though hand and esthetic characteristics may not match those of real wool. In fact, by 1974 nearly 75 percent of the fiber processed in woolen and worsted mills was man-made. Figure 1-4 diagrams the woolen and worsted manufacturing processes. These processes are used for both wool and synthetics with wool fiber characteristics. The major differences from the cotton system are cleaning and chemical processing steps.

Sheep's wool varies from long, straight, and coarse at one extreme (carpet wools) to short, highly crimped, and fine at the other. Wool impurities can run as high as 80 percent (by weight), with 50 percent impurity content being common. These impurities are of four general types: (1) suit, or sweat residues, consisting mostly of water soluble salts; (2) wool grease (from the animal's oil glands) containing lanolin; (3) dirt and sand; and (4) vegetable matter, such as burrs. Wool scouring establishments are often located in producing areas such as Texas and Australia; in addition to scouring, these establishments may perform a sorting operation to separate wool fleeces into quality grades, a mechanical opening, a scouring operation, and baling for shipment to yarn mills. Scouring may be done in water with a weakly alkaline detergent solution or with organic solvents. The aqueous scour, with mechanical agitation, efficiently removes all but the vegetable impurities. To remove vegetable matter the wool is passed through a burrpicker and may also be carbonized. Carbonization is a treatment of the wool with strong acid, followed by heating to a temperature at which the vegetable matter decomposes. Carbonized wool must then be passed through crushing rolls and a *duster* that separates out the decomposed vegetable matter in the form of dust.

When baled fiber arrives in a wool yarn mill, it requires opening and blending prior to the carding and spinning operations. There is so much variety in woolen mill equipment that it is difficult to provide a general description, but one more-or-less typical set of equipment would include an opener, an oiling unit, and a woolen picker (somewhat similar to a cotton picker). The woolen picker blows loose fiber through a distributor into a mixing room where the stock forms a large pile. From there, the fiber is removed and often baled to allow for storage prior to blending and carding.

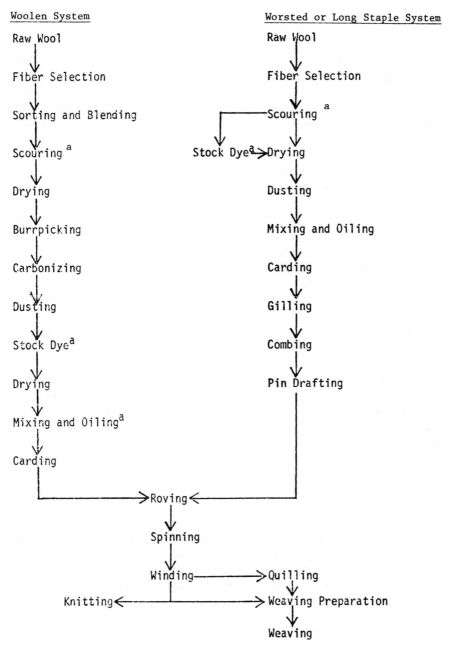

aIndicates wet processes.

Figure 1-4. Woolen and Worsted Manufacturing Processes

Unlike cotton, much woolen yarn is made from fiber dyed various colors while it is still in this loose stock form. Blending of these dyed stocks yields attractive heather effects in the finished yarn. With synthetic fibers, fibers of varying dyeing characteristics may be blended in yarn manufacture and then dyed to a heather effect after fabric manufacture.

The woolen card is a much more massive piece of equipment than the cotton card and may contain up to four large cylinders. Some woolen cards have arrangements for crosslaying fiber stock from a first section onto a feed table leading into the next section. Woolen cards also feature pairs of counter-rotating small rolls called *workers* and *strippers* to further improve the blending of the stock. The web of fibers doffed from the last cylinder of the woolen card passes into a tape condenser between many pairs of narrow tapes. These tapes oscillate from side to side so that each strip of web is rolled into a roving or roping (as it is normally referred to in a wool spinning system). A number of rovings are wound side by side onto a small beam or *jackspool.*

The woolen roving is drawn from a jackspool through a back pair of drafting rolls into a rotating tube that has wire fingers attached to the interior surface. These wire fingers catch the roving and the rotating action of the tube, imparts a temporary, or false, twist on roving. The twisted roving then passes out through a faster front pair of drafting rolls that draw and feed the roving into the spinning ring where a true twist is applied to the yarn as it passes through the traveler and is wound onto the bobbin.

Open end spinning, twistless spinning (which adds an adhesive to the fibers to hold the yarn together), and so-called self-twist spinning are alternatives to ring spinning for making woolen yarn. The self-twist or Repco spinning system combines two single yarns that are false twisted in alternating clockwise and counterclockwise directions and then immediately combined so that opposite-twist sections twine around one another.

Worsted or Long-Staple Spinning Systems

Like the cotton system with its combed cotton, the woolen spinning system also has a process for long fiber processing. This process produces *worsted* yarns by removing the short fibers or *noils* and parallelizing the fibers and twisting them into a smooth compact uniform yarn. The worsted system is similar to the woolen system up through carding. After carding the worsted system requires three additional steps prior to roving (see Figure 1-4). These steps, *gilling, combing,* and *pin drafting* are designed to sort out short fibers and parallelize the fibers and form a combed sliver called a *top.* The sliver is taken from the cards and doubled (two slivers are fed together) into the gill that contains a set of comb like bars between drafting rolls. The action of the gill simultaneously draws and combs the doubled sliver. The gilled sliver is then washed, dried, and combed to remove the noils. Finally the sliver is delivered into a pin drafter to be further drawn and combed. The resulting top is delivered to the roving and spinning operations to produce the final yarn.

Semiworsted and Coarse Long-Staple Systems. Traditional, heavy wool yarns (such as those used for carpets) were made on the woolen spinning system. The advent of man-made fibers (with their much greater mechanical strengths) an endless number of abbreviated processing sequences have developed to produce coarse long-staple yarns with variations of worsted machinery. Such systems, now designed primarily for man-made fibers, are variously called mid-fiber systems (2-3 inch staple lengths), long-staple systems (4 or more inches), or generally semiworsted systems. They may use worsted-type cards or for shorter staple lengths, cotton-type cards. A typical semiworsted sequence includes blending, carding, and several processes of gilling, roving, and spinning. One variation is the heavy roving system where carded sliver passes through two or three gilling operations and then an autoleveler-equipped drawbox to make the roving for a high draft spinning frame. Some open end spinning machines have been designed to give high production of carpet-type yarns made on the semiworsted system. The production rate per rotor is four to five times as great as the production per spindle on a worsted ring spinning frame, and yarn packages as large as seven pounds each are obtained directly from the machine.

The very substantial carpet segment of the textile industry has been and continues to be an area of strong competition among yarn manufacturing methods. Not only are conventional woolen carpet yarns still in production, but also there is an endless variety of wool-synthetic and all-synthetic staple fiber blends in staple lengths from 2 inches to 6 inches or more made on many different machinery installations. In addition, the man-made fiber producers themselves have been in the market for a number of years with three dimensionally crimped continuous filament yarns of nylon and polypropylene.

Filament Yarn Processing

The typical process for manufacturing fabrics from filament yarn is shown in Figure 1-5. The only natural filament yarn is silk. Raw silk is constructed from two filaments combined with a somewhat gelatinous coating and is exceedingly fine—much finer than the sizes of yarn usually used for weaving or knitting even the finest fabrics. Thus, the finest silk yarn is a combination of a number of silk filaments. The first stage of combining silk filaments takes place during the reeling process by which the silk is recovered from cocoons. The reels of raw silk yarns are shipped to *throwsters* who throw, or combine and rewind, the reeled silk filaments into desired yarn sizes, twist the yarn to whatever extent desired, boil off the gelatinous coating, and perhaps dye it. In the 1970s, small quantities

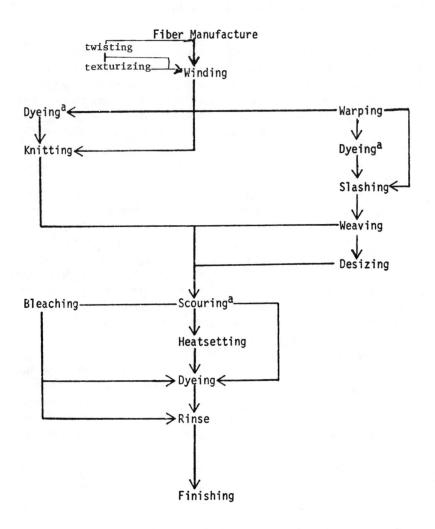

Source: John J. Porter et al., *State of the Art of Textile Waste Treatment* (Clemson, S.C.: Clemson University, 1971), p. 35.

[a]Denotes wet processing.

Figure 1-5. 100 Percent Synthetic Fabric Manufacturing Process

of silk are still used in neckties and high fashion women's wear fabrics, but the majority of the filament is cellulose acetate, polyester, and nylon.

The majority of the modern throwsters purchase filament from synthetic fiber manufacturers in sizes usually expressed in terms of total denier[a] and filament count. Filament yarn processing depends on subsequent process requirements and can include rewinding onto larger or smaller packages, texturing, twisting, dyeing or chemical treatments, and production of specialized and fancy twisted yarns. Of these, texturing is by far the most important. Others either are similar to operations already described or are too specialized to be of general interest.

Texturing is a method of deforming the smooth continuous filament yarn to provide the softer spun texture found in stable fiber yarns. The process permanently deforms the individual filaments of a filament yarn out of their original straight and parallel arrangement. Six methods of filament deformation have contended for commercial success over the years:

1. False twisting,
2. Air jet bulking,
3. Stuffer box crimping,
4. Edge crimping,
5. Knitting followed by deknitting,
6. Gear crimping.

False twist texturing dominates the field and accounts for nearly 90 percent of all texturing. All the other methods are used primarily in specialty products. Although this breakdown of production by method and yarn type is expected to change only slightly in the short term, there is still a great ferment within the industry as the new technology of draw-texturing (i.e., using a feed yarn that is only partially oriented by the fiber manufacturer and completing the draw-stretching process just before and during the texturing operation) alters the competition between trade texturers and the fiber producers. Some of the latter are supplying yarns in textured form. In 1972 fiber producers accounted for 10 percent of textured filament yarn production and could exceed 30 percent by 1977. More than three-fourths of textured filament yarn production in the mid-1970s was from polyester fiber, some one-fifth was of nylon, and the rest was other fibers such as acetate, triacetate, and polypropylene. Most textured polyester yarn (over 85 percent) goes into knit fabrics, particularly double knits for women's wear. Some 12 percent of total production is used in woven fabrics and some 15 percent of total knitted and woven fabric of textured polyester is used in men's wear.

---

[a]Denier is the weight in grams of 9,000 meters of yarn, a typical 70/34 (70 denier/34 ply) filament yarn would contain individual filaments of about 2 denier and 9,000 meters of the yarn (9,750 yards) would weigh 70 grams (2 1/2 ounces).

In air jet bulking, the filament yarn is passed, in a slack condition, into a zone of turbulent air that causes loops to form in the filaments. At the same time the yarn is twisted to lock the loops into place. Virtually all other methods of practical interest depend on deforming the filaments to the desired configuration and then fixing them there by chemical treatment or heat setting.

The conventional false twist system employs a spindle consisting of a cylindrical tube containing a bar fixed to the interior wall of the cylinder. The yarn makes one turn around the bar as it passes through the spindle. As the filament yarn passes through the spindle cylinder a twist is built up in the yarn on the feed side of the spindle. To produce a permanent twist, the yarn is heated to setting temperature and then cooled to fix the deformation into the filament *before* it passes out of the spindle. The single heater yarn that results is characterized by a high degree of stretch or retractability and hence is useful in making stretch fabrics, such as for ski pants. For many end uses, such retractability is not needed, in which case the yarn may be held under tension as it passes by a second heater after the spindle. The *double-heater* or *set* textured yarn retains most of its bulky character without the high stretch. Production costs for two-heater texturing of a 150-denier polyester yarn are about 0.125 dollars per pound for the texturing alone, of which 0.05 dollars per pound is labor. Additional costs for rewinding, packing, inspecting, shipping, and receiving would raise total trade texturing cost to about 25¢ per pound.

Yarns from Film

A recent development, which short circuits yarn preparation completely, is the emerging plastic film technology. Plastic films (e.g., polypropylene) are produced that contain minute particles of an explosive. When the films are stretched and the particles detonated, the films split up into filament-like strips that are still attached to one another. The result is an instant nonwoven fabric. Recent work on film technology has shown that highly stretched and oriented films could be induced to split or "fibrillate" merely by mechanical stressing, a process that proves to be adaptable to low-cost yarn production. Another method, split fiber or *ribbon yarn* production, has emerged in the 1970s. Ribbon yarn technology is based on controlled mechanical splitting of plastic film. The film is extruded through a narrow slit, drawn between sets of rolls, cut into narrow ribbons (each of which becomes a single yarn), treated with grooving rolls (Barfilex Process), needled rolls (Polyloom Process) or saw-toothed rolls or knives (Lenzinger Process), and wound. In some cases, part or all of the drawing is done after slitting. In other cases, drawn film may be delivered directly to a loom or knitting machine and slit into ribbon yarns just before fabric formation. From commercial beginnings in the late 1960s, polyolefin film yarns have displaced other fibers in much of the cordage market and in woven backings for tufted carpet fabrics. In both these end uses, mechanical performance at low cost is paramount. Whether or not the future evolution of film slitting and splitting processes will lead to penetration into other end uses is still problematical.

Yarn Dyeing

Because of the economies of inventorying only single-colored fibers and filaments, only small amounts of textile material are dyed prior to yarn making. However, there are a number of instances where it is advantageous to stock dyed fibers or filaments. First, heather effects in wool yarns are obtained by combining dyed stock or dyed slivers. Second, scale economies of dyeing of basic colors often offset inventory costs. Third, synthetic fiber producers often find it profitable to supply several types of yarn in black and carpet yarns in several colors that may be used by a large number of small fabric and carpet producers. Actually most dyeing is deferred until the finishing operation because dyeing of fabrics is less expensive than dyeing of fibers, filament, or yarn. Yarn dyeing is most often carried out in yarn spinning mills or texturing plants, rather than in knitting or weaving mills. The latter are usually not large enough to justify the substantial capital expense of the dyeing machines and facilities to handle the dyes, water, effluents, and yarns.

Generally speaking, dyes are dissolved or in some cases dispersed in very fine particle form in water, with added *wetting agents,* salts, compounds to control acidity or alkalinity, leveling agents to promote uniform dyeing through the package, and perhaps a carrier to increase the rate of dyeing for polyester fiber. Only certain chemical classes of dyes can be used for coloration of any particular type of fiber. Additional dye selection considerations include cost and such fastness properties as resistance of the color to fading by washing, light exposure, immersion in chlorinated water, and dry cleaning. The advent of pollution control requirements in recent years has added another set of considerations: Dyers have been forced to seek chemicals and dyeing procedures that will minimize the effluent problem or be adaptable to the available low-cost effluent purification methods.

Yarn is dyed either in wound-up package form or in skein form. The latter process is more expensive, partly because it requires skein reeling and then rewinding onto cones or tubes. Skein dyeing is essential for making bulky acrylic fiber yarns and for retaining bulk in certain other types of yarns. The *skein dyeing* process usually consists of a large rectangular vat containing a large diameter central pipe set with perforated side arms to hold the skeins. The skeins are mounted on the side arms and emersed in the dye solution, which is circulated from the bottom of the machine through the central pipe and out through the side arm perforations to provide uniform dyeing. Yarn *package dyeing* machines come in various sizes to hold from 50 to 2,000 pounds of yarn at a time. The package dyeing machine consists of a pressure vat, or *kier,* with a replaceable yarn carrier with perforated spindles. The 2-4 pound yarn package is soft wound on a perforated tube (to allow dye penetration) and mounted on the spindles (some machines can also accept single large beams wound with up to 3,000 individual yarns such as those used for weaving warp-dyed denim fabrics). The entire loaded carrier is lifted and locked into place in the kier, and the lid of the kier is closed. The kier is filled with a dye solution and pressurized. On older machines, a dye cycle could take up to four hours. Much improved utilization and dyeing uniformity is achieved with newer, fully automated machines by monitoring and controlling dye and chemical additions, temperature changes, solution flow rates, and the schedule of flow reversals to improve flow rates.

At the conclusion of dyeing, the yarn is transfered on its carrier to a unit that uses centrifuging, compressed air blowing, and hot air to complete the drying. Before shipping, the yarns must be rewound onto cones or other packages and checked for color matching and uniformity. Because the human eye is so very sensitive to color differences, color quality control is always a critical problem.

Appendix 1A:
Typical Cotton
Weaving Mill

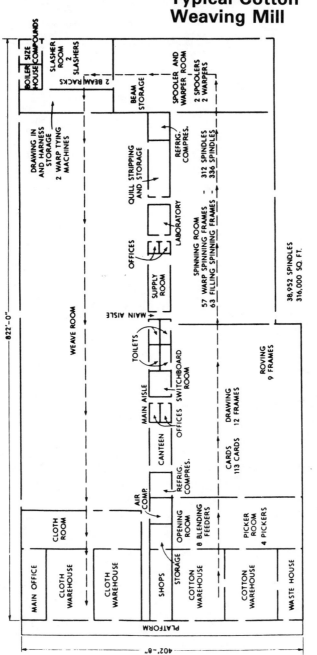

Figure 1A-1. Typical Weaving Mill, 1969

27

Table 1A-1
Estimated Production and Waste Losses at Capacity on 80-Square Print Cloth

	31's	*Pounds per* *144 Hours*	41's
Baled Cotton			
Baled cotton		180,000	
Bagging, ties, etc., waste @ 3.33%		6,000	
Open cotton		174,000	
Opening and picking waste @ 3.0%		5,220	
Picker production		168,780	
Card waste, strips @ 1.5% (metallic wire),		2,532	
fly @ 2.0%		3,376	
Card production		162,872	
Drawing waste @ .25%		407	
Drawing production		162,465	
Roving waste @ 1.5%		2,437	
Roving production		160,028	
	31's		*41's*
	91,216		68,812
Spinning waste @ 3.5%		4,001	
Spinning production		156,027	
	88,935		67,092
Spooling, warping, and slashing waste @ 2.0%		1,779	
Production before regain for sizing		154,248	
	87,156		67,092
Size regain @ 13% on warp		11,330	
Production entering weave room		165,578	
Weaving and cloth room waste @ .5%		828	
Weaving production		164,750	

Source: Company records.

Table 1A-2
Cost of Fixed Assets at Date of Acquisition

Land (1962)	$ 20,000
Grading and yard improvements (1962)	130,000
Building (1962)	3,690,000
Opening equipment	
Eight blenders @ $1,369 each (1945)	10,700
Cleaner (1962)	4,400
Auxiliary equipment and supplies (1945)	5,600
Picking	
Four pickers @ $7,711 each (1945)	30,850
Auxiliary equipment and supplies (1945)	15,000
Overhead conveyor (1962)	10,000
Carding	
113 cards @ $2,211 each (1945)	249,850
113 motors, drives (1945)	28,250
113 metallic clothing @ $820 each (1962)	90,400
Auxiliary equipment and supplies (1945)	2,000
Drawing	
12 draw frames (24 deliv. total) @ $2,800 each (1962)	67,200
2,000 cans @ $18.40 each (1962)	38,000
Roving	
Nine frames @ $20,193 each (1962)	181,737
Auxiliary equipment (1962)	15,000
97,400 bobbins @ $700/1,000 (1962)	68,000
Spinning	
57 warp frames of 312 spindles each @ $13,619 each (1962)	
63 filling frames of 366 spindles each @ $13,828 each (1962)	1,647,500
Automatic doffing (1962)	195,000
Warp tubes and 60,000 filling bobbins (inc. 30,000 reserve bobbins) (1962)	26,300
Spooling and warping	
Two spoolers, two warpers (1962)	225,000
Warp beams and auxiliary equipment (1962)	17,500
Slashing	
Two slashers (1962)	56,600
Size preparation equipment and exhaust system (1962)	8,500
Weaving	
1,205, 39.4" Draper X-2 looms @ $700 (1945)	843,500
Extra harnesses, reeds, etc. (1945)	40,000
Auxiliary equipment (1945)	6,000

Table 1A-2 (cont.)

Tying-in
  2 tie-in machines (1945)   7,500

Cloth room
  Three shearing machines @ $4,000 each (1945)   12,000
  13 inspection machines @ $1,000 each (1945)   13,000
  Folders, balers, brushers, etc. (1945)   20,000
  Overhead conveyor (1962)   5,500

Machine shop
  Two lathes, one plain miller (1962)   53,000
  Welder, gear hobber, drills, etc. (1945)   15,000

Warehouse and yard
  Truck, scale (1962)   12,600

Office (1962)   12,000
Laboratory (1962)   25,000

Source: Company records.

Table 1A-3
Labor Costs for Operations, 1969

Employees	Hourly Rate Shift		Employees Shift		
	1-2	*3*	*1*	*2*	*3*
Operation: Opening, Picking, Carding, Drawing, Roving					
Overseer	Salaried		One for 3 Shifts		
Second hand	3.16	3.30	1	1	1
Opener tenders					
Picker tenders	1.95	2.13	1	1	1
Card tenders	1.95	2.11	1	1	1
Man to tend 25 cards, strip every 60 hours, remove waste, clean cards and sweep, etc.	2.01	2.11	1	1	1
Section man to make settings and maintain cards	2.70	2.75	1	1	1
Drawing tenders	2.24	2.29	1	1	1
Roving tenders	2.40	2.45	2	2	2
Overhauler	2.45		1	0	0
Overhauler helper	1.95		1	0	0
Total			10	8	8
Operation: Spinning					
Overseer	Salaried				
Second hand	3.10	3.15	1	1	1

Table 1A-3 (cont.)

Employees	Hourly Rate Shift		Employees Shift		
	1-2	3	1	2	3
Spinners					
Warp	2.10	2.15	3	3	3
Filling	2.10	2.15	4	4	4
Roll pickers	1.90	—	2	0	0
Doffers					
Warp	2.36	2.41	2	2	2
Filling	2.36	2.41	2	2	2
Section man	2.70	2.75	1	1	1
Roving man	1.90	1.95	1	1	1
Overhaulers	2.40		2	0	0
Overhauler helper	1.90		2	0	0
Steel roll cleaner	1.90		3		
Yarn hauler	1.90	1.95	1	1	1
Traveler changer	1.90		1	0	0
Total			25	15	15

Operation: Spooling and Warping

Second hand[a]					
Section hand	2.70	2.75	1	1	1
Spooler girls	2.15		4	4	
Warper tenders	2.15		1	1	
Assistant warper tenders	1.90		1	1	
Yarn distributors	1.90	1.95	1	1	1
Total			8	8	2

Operation: Slashing and Tying-In

Slasher man	2.20		1	1	
Slasher helper	2.00		1	1	
Drawing-in-hands	2.40		1	0	0
Tying-in-hands	2.60	2.65	1	1	1
Total			4	3	1

Operation: Weaving

Second hand	3.25	3.30	1	1	1
Weavers	2.51	2.51	15	15	15
Loom fixers	2.90	2.95	15	15	15
Battery hands	2.05	2.10	10	10	10
Smash hands	2.10	2.15	2	2	2
Cloth doffers	1.90	1.95	1	1	1

Table 1A-3 (cont.)

Employees	Hourly Rate Shift		Employees Shift		
	1-2	3	1	2	3
Warp hanger (lease-out man)	2.10	2.15	2	2	2
Greaser	1.90	1.95	1	1	1
Sweeper	1.90	1.95	1	1	1
Blow-off men	1.90	1.95	1	1	1
Harness cleaners	1.80		1		
Quill stripper	1.90	1.95	1	1	1
Filling grate cleaner	1.90	1.95	1	1	1
Overhauler	2.80		1	0	0
Total			53	51	51

Operation: Cloth Room

Employees	Hourly Rate	Employees
Overseer	Salaried	
Second hand		0
Shear, brush, rolling range operator (130 yds. min.)	2.15	3
Inspectors	2.15	12
Folder operators	2.15	3
Cloth graders	2.15	4
Baler	2.15	2
Cloth man, utility helper, etc.	2.15	1
Total		25

Operation: Warehouse, Yard

Employees	Hourly Rate Shift		Employees Shift		
Foreman	3.25		One for 3 Shifts		
Supply clerks	2.25	2.30	1	1	1
Laborers	1.90	1.95	3	2	2
Total			4	3	3

Operation: Machine Shop

Employees	Hourly Rate Shift		Employees Shift		
Master mechanic-electrician	Salaried				
Machinists	2.70	2.75	2	0	0
Millwright	2.70	2.75	1	0	0
Mechanics	2.70	2.75	0	1	1
Electrician and utility	2.70	2.75	0	1	1
Total			3	2	2

I. Operation: Laboratory

Employees	Hourly Rate	Employees Shift		
4 Employees	2.20	4	0	0

aCombined with spinning or weaving.

Appendix 1B:
Yarn Mill
Improvements,
1945-1962

Table 1B-1
Description of Selected Yarn Mill Machinery and Improvements, 1945-1969

	1945	1950	1955	1962	1969
Blender-feeder					
Output[a]	200 lbs./hr.	200 lbs./hr.	200 lbs./hr	200 lbs./hr	200 lbs./hr.
Cost	$1,369	$1,775	$2,069	$3,872	$4,500
Workload	10/operator	10/operator	10/operator	10/operator	14/operator
Improvements: Improved layout and handling minimizes lot changes.					
Pickers					
Output	382 lbs./hr	382 lbs./hr.	382 lbs./hr	382 lbs./hr	382 lbs./hr.
Cost	$7,711	$12,457	$14,061	$16,501	$19,500
Workload	6/operator	6/operator	6/operator	6/operator	6/operator
Improvements: Trend to eliminate pickers with direct chute feed to cards.					
Cards					
Output	7 lbs./hr			10 lbs/hr	18 lbs./hr.
Cost	$2,211	$3,950	$3,950	$5,001	$6,000
Workload[b]	36/operator	48/operator	64/operator	88/operator	55/operator
Improvements: Chute feeds high speed cards at 50 to 100 lbs./hr. with up to 30" planetary coiler.					
Drawing (per delivery)					
Speed	100 ft/min			800 ft./min	800 ft./min.
Cost	$288	$829	$1,500	$2,800	$3,200/del.
Draft	8	8	8	8	8
Workload	40 del./opr.	44 del./opr.	32 del./opr.	28 del./opr.	38 del./opr.
Can size	12" x 36"	12" x 36"	12" x 36"	18" x 42"	20" x 48"
Can load	12 lbs.	12 lbs.	12 lbs.	40 lbs.	55 lbs.
Can price	$12	$12	$12	$14	$25[c]

Improvements: Greater versality in length fiber processed, larger cans.

Lapping

Output	150 lbs./hr	150 lbs./hr	150-190 lbs./hr	500 lbs./hr	500 lbs./hr.
Draft	1.09	1.09	1.09	2.4	2.4
Lap weight	10 lbs.	10 lbs.	10 lbs.	30 lbs.	30 lbs.
Cost	$4,956	$7,804	$9,610	$11,500	$14,000

Improvements: The 1959 lapper eliminated the sliver and ribbon lappers with the result of greatly increased output, more draft, and a smoother, evener yarn.

Combing (8 head frames)

Output	28 lbs./hr.	30 lbs./hr.	33 lbs./hr.	45 lbs./hr.	50 lbs./hr.
Speed	100 nips/min.	150 nips/min.	150 nips/min.	150 nips/min.	150 nips/min.
Lap weight	700 grains/yd.	750 grains/yd.	850 grains/yd.	1,000 grains/yd.	1,050 grains/yd.
Yield	82-85%	90-95%	90-95%	90-95%	90-95%
Cost	$3,775	$7,800	$9,882	$13,335	$14,500
Workload	36 heads/oper.	48 heads/oper.	64 heads/oper.	64-80 heads/oper.	80 heads/oper.

Improvements: The major advance came in 1958 with a unit that combined better quality with increased production and yield.

Roving (96 spindles)

Output warp	1.01 lbs./spdle./hr.	1.01 lbs./spdle./hr.	1.15 lbs./spdle./hr.	1.53 lbs./spdle./hr.	1.75 lbs./spdle./hr.
Output filling	.696 lbs./spdle./hr.	.696 lbs./spdle./hr.	.795 lbs./spdle./hr.	1.06 lbs./spdle./hr.	1.20 lbs./spdle./hr.
Speed	660 rpm	660 rpm	750 rpm	1,200 rpm	1,300 rpm

Table 1B-1 (cont.)

	1945	1950	1955	1962	1969
Roving (96 spindles) (cont.)					
Package size	46 oz.	64 oz.	80 oz.	90 oz.	96 oz.
Cost	$8,450	$9,727	$12,227	$20,193	$26,400
Workload	240 spin/oper.	288 spin/oper.	384 spin/oper.	480 spin/oper.	480 spin/oper.
Improvements: More versatile drafting, higher speeds, larger cans, and larger packages doffed.					
Spinning (288 spindles)					
Output warp	.0219 lbs./spin/hr.	.0232 lbs./spin/hr.	.0258 lbs./spin/hr.	.0347 lbs./spin/hr.	.0363 lbs./spin/hr.
Output filling	.0154 lbs./spin/hr.	.0163 lbs./spin/hr.	.0192 lbs./spin/hr.	.022 lbs./spin/hr.	.0232 lbs./spin/hr.
Spindle speed warp	8,500 rpm	9,000 rpm	10,000 rpm	11,000 rpm	11,500 rpm
filling	8,000 rpm	8,500 rpm	9,000 rpm	11,500 rpm	12,000 rpm
Cost	$4,895	$10,025	$11,576	($18,642—"K" frames) ($11,356—"N" frames)	$21,500 $13,000
Workload warp	2,000 spin/oper.	2,400 spin/oper.	2,600 spin/oper.	6,000 spin/oper.	6,500 spin/oper.
filling	3,000 spin/oper.	3,500 spin/oper.	4,000 spin/oper.	5,000 spin/oper.	5,500 spin/oper.
Improvements: Larger packages, higher speeds, better process control.					

aOutputs are for an 80-square print cloth [39" $\frac{80 \times 80}{31\text{'sw} \times 41\text{'s F}}$] although the yarn mill poundage approximates the amounts from counts five higher or lower than a 31 or a 41.

bAverages.

cWith springs and pistons.

Fabric Forming

Introduction

Fabrics may be defined as flexible sheets of material manufactured from yarns or even directly from fibers. Excluding some minor types of textile processes such as braiding and the knotting of fish nets, fabric forming can be classified into four major processes: weaving, knitting, tufting, and nonwoven. Up until the 1950s, weaving was by far the major fabric forming process, with some small specialized sections of apparel, such as sweaters, stockings, and some underwear, being dominated by knitting. In the 1950s tufting began to displace weaving as the dominant process in the manufacture of carpets. By 1975 tufting accounted for over 95 percent of all carpet manufactured in the United States and was of growing importance in the manufacture of apparel fabrics. In the middle of the 1960s, knitted fabrics, in the form of double knits, began to make serious inroads into apparel fabrics and accounted for over 30 percent of all apparel fabrics by the early 1970s. Nonwoven manufacture of fabrics directly from fibers has been considered the emerging fabric forming technology for over thirty years but has yet to become a major factor in the industry.

Weaving Process

Weaving requires an assembly of parallel yarns (the *warp*) with which other yarns (the *weft* yarn or *filling*) are interlaced one by one so as to pass over and under various individual warp yarns. This interlacing is performed by a loom (see Figure 2-1). The different patterns of interlacing are called weaves (see Figure 2-2). The warp yarns are drawn into a loom from a warp beam, while the weft yarn is drawn off *bobbins,* which move through the warp yarns, or from spools, cones, or cheeses mounted on the side of the loom.

Yarn is received at the weaving mill on cones, cheeses (short cylindrical shape), or pirns (long, double-tapered shape) depending on the type of yarn and supplier. The major subdivisions of the weaving process are warp preparation, weaving, and cloth room, where fabric is inspected and prepared for shipment.

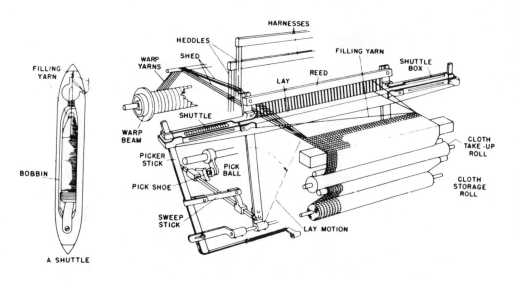

Figure 2-1. Shuttle and Loom Mechanisms

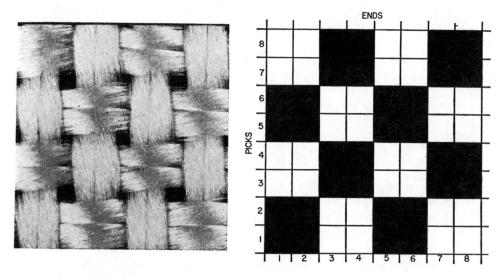

Figure 2-2. Photo and Diagram of 2 x 2 Basket Weave

Warp Preparation

The warp preparation sequence consists of *warping* or beaming, *slashing,* and either *drawing-in* (for new work) or *tying-in* (for continued work). To form the warp beam, packages of yarn are mounted on a large framework, or creel, and the yarn ends are brought together and wound onto a flanged cylinder or beam.

To avoid problems in later processing, careful attention must be paid to controlling tensions in the yarns and to obtaining a uniform windup. Man-made fiber yarns, filament yarns in particular, may exhibit color differences after dyeing when tensions vary. Even in undyed filament fabrics, excessively tensioned yarns will create shiny streaks in the cloth. Warps, even for rather narrow "broad" looms, can be made up of thousands of yarns. Thus, a warp beam may be built up in two steps. A few hundred yarns are wound onto *section beams* on the *warper.* Several section beams are then combined at the *slasher.*

The function of *slashing* is to apply a protective coating or sizing to the warp yarns. Without sizing, most staple fiber yarns would suffer excessive abrasion losses and breakage during weaving. Most filament yarns do not require sizing, but all-cotton warps are usually sized with starch solutions similar to laundry starch. Cotton-polyester blends and other blends may be sized with polyvinyl alcohol (**PVA**) or starch-PVA mixtures. The size is almost always removed after fabric manufacture in the finishing plant, thereby creating a highly polluting effluent. During the 1970s, an active search has been underway for other sizes or altered processing methods that would minimize the water pollution effect of the starch desizing effluent.

In mill practice, six or more section beams from the warper are mounted at the feed end of the slasher. From there, the yarns are passed through a size box containing a size solution, then through squeeze rolls, which remove excess sizing and control takeup of size by the yarns, and continue through a series of heated drying rolls, commonly called *dry cans.* After drying, the yarns pass through a comb and are wound up on a loom beam ready to be mounted on the feed end of the loom.

Today there are two basic types of looms: the fly shuttle loom and the shuttleless looms. "Shuttleless loom" is a generic term used for a wide variety of looms, some of which are not really shuttleless (e.g., the missile gripper loom). The basic difference between the two types of looms is that the fly shuttle loom passes a bobbin of weft yarn across the warp. This method provides a continuous strand of weft or filler yarn throughout the cloth and results in a finished edge, called a *selvage,* that prevents unraveling. The shuttleless looms draw a single length of filler yarn across the warp yarn with each pass; this method results in a nonselvage or frayed edge. Although shuttleless looms provide some advantages of speed and pattern variety, the fly shuttle loom is felt to be more reliable. The vast majority of the looms in place in the United States are fly shuttle looms.

There are three primary motions on *fly shuttle looms: shedding, picking,* and *beating-up. Shedding* is the raising of certain warp threads to form a v-shaped opening through which the shuttle containing the filling bobbin is passed. (The shuttle, shown in Figure 2-1, resembles a 12-16-inch oblong wooden box with tapered ends.) The passing of the shuttle is *picking,* while the subsequent pushing of the loose filling thread (pick) up to the rest of the cloth is *beating-up.*

Warp yarns are threaded individually into the loom through various loom subassemblies, specifically the *drop wires,* the *heddies,* and the *reed* (see Figure

2-1). The warp yarns are passed through the loom and fixed to a cloth takeup roll. Manual threading is so tedious that mechanical ways of avoiding it have been developed. If a new warp is to be threaded exactly the same way as an exhausted warp on a loom, the expedient method is to "tie-in" the new threads to the old and pull the knots through the drop wires, heddles, and reed. Automatic warp tying machines are almost always used. Drawing-in of a new warp through empty drop wires, heddles, and reed slots or *dents* is a more complex task that has been automated with only partial success. Because the setup of warp beams on the warper, loom, and (to a more limited extent) slasher is both a time-consuming and labor-intensive processes (consuming about an hour for automatic tying-in and more than a day for manual drawing-in), warp beams are wound with enough yarn to produce thousands of yards of fabric to allow the loom to operate for days or even weeks without requiring a new warp beam.

The complexity of the setup is a result of the need to individually control the tension, motion, and direction of each warp yarn. The first control on the warp yarn in the *left-off* mechanism that controls the speed at which the warp beam unwinds in order to maintain proper tension on the warp yarns during weaving. The warp yarns first pass over a *whip roll.* The whip roll, which moves vertically to apply pressure to the warp, operates synchronously with the other loom parts to minimize cyclic tension variations. Next each warp yarn passes through a *drop wire.* The drop wires are held up by the warp so that if any single yarn breaks the drop wire activites a stop motion that brings the loom to a complete stop within less than 1/100 of a minute. Each warp yarn then goes through a *heddle* in one of the *harnesses* of the loom. All yarns that pass through heddles on a specific harness are lifted together by harness to form the *shed* for the insertion of the weft yarn. Next, the warp yarns pass through *dents,* or openings in the *reed*; usually two adjacent warp yarns pass through each dent. Finally the warp yarn passes over the *lay* mechanism. On either side of the lay are *shuttle boxes.* To form the weave, picker sticks on either side of the lay throw a shuttle from shuttle box to shuttle box across the lay through alternating sheds. This action interlaces the filling yarn with the warp yarn. All mechanisms on the looms are synchronized with the picker stick, which is the controlling factor of the speed (measured in *picks per minute*) of the loom. A fly shuttle loom operates in the range of 185-210 picks per minute). This speed is determined by four factors: the type of loom, the width of the lay, the strength of the warp yarn (because of potential damage from fly shuttle), and the complexity of the pattern being woven. The older the loom, the wider the lay, the more fragile the yarn, and the more complex the pattern, the slower the loom will operate. After every filling yarn is inserted, the reed *beats-up* the newly deposited yarn against the edge, or *feel,* of the fabric. The woven material emerges out of the other side of the loom and is rolled up on a cloth takeup mechanism.

The fly shuttle carries a bobbin holding a few hundred yards of filler yarn. At one time the principle job of the weaver was to stop the loom and replace the bobbin when it was empty. Automation of this process has radically changed the labor content of weaving. Even the oldest model looms contain automatic reloading. A *feeler* senses the amount of yarn on the shuttle bobbin each time the shuttle returns to the shuttle change side of the loom. When the yarn supply has nearly run out, the feeler trips a hammer mechanism that drives a full bobbin into place in the shuttle and simultaneously forces the old bobbin out below. Most shuttle looms in the United States are equipped with Unifil loom winders. These winders require only a supply of filling yarn on a cone. Within the time a bobbin of filling is consumed in weaving, the loom winder strips any residual yarn from the exhausted bobbin, transports the bobbin to a winding station, and winds a fresh supply of yarn on an empty bobbin to be ready for insertion in the shuttle. Some older looms have *magazine loaders* that hold a supply of filling yarns prewound on a *quill winder.*

The loom assignment for a weaver is dependent on the loom stop rate (i.e., how often a loom breaks down) and the restarting time (i.e., the time required to repair the difficulty). The most prevalent breakdown is a broken yarn, which requires less than a minute to repair. The automation of bobbin reloading and incremental improvements of yarn preparation and tension control have reduced the labor content of the weave room to one weaver for as many as 60 to 120 looms without any radical change in the loom technology. Table 2-1 lists some examples of fly shuttle looms in place in the United States.

The weave patterning capabilities of a loom, apart from color, are entirely controlled by the number of harnesses and the elaborateness of their control mechanisms. The specific weave produced on a specific loom depends on (a) the warp thread drawing-in plan used to string the warp yarns through the heddles and (b) the harness lifting plan embodied in lifting cams or a programmable *dobby* mechanism. Cam looms can produce only simple weaves, but their operation is fast. Dobby looms are slower but completely versatile within the limit of the number of harnesses available. Plaids or other designs requiring fillingwise color changes must be woven on *box looms* equipped with multiple shuttle boxes on at least one side of the lay.

Types of Weaves

Weaves can be subdivided into four categories: *plain, twill, satin,* and *Jacquard.* Figure 2-3 illustrates some of the various weaves. The first three are limited to rather modest repeat dimensions in the fabric, while Jacquard patterns can be of unlimited size and complexity. Fabric effects can be varied by choosing different weaves, by mixing yarn colors in warp and/or filling, by mixing yarn sizes, and by varying yarn spacings in the fabric. Warp-direction stripes in a fabric can be

Table 2-1
Economics of Fly Shuttle Looms

	Shuttle Looms					
	X-2 (1945)	X-2 (1950)	X-2 (1955)	X-3 (1962)	X-3 (1969)	X-3 (1975)
Speed (ppm)[a]	185	185	195	212	230	170-210
Cloth width	39"	39"	45"	47.5"	47.5"	40-68"
Cost	$700	$700	$1,500	$2,000	$2,250	$8,500
Workload	60[b]	60[b]	80[b]	100[b]	100[b]	120[b]
	60[c]	60[c]	80[c]	100[c]	100[c]	100[c]

Note: The X-3 increases quality with a center fork filling motion that stops the loom on the pick that the thread breaks rather than run over a pick. The automatic let-off increases fabric uniformity, while the improved drive allows greater fixer loads. Yarn beam diameter increased from 26" to 28". The X-5 features heavier shafting and a stiffer frame for productive speeds plus simplicity of design for easy maintenance.

[a]Picks per minute.

[b]Looms per weaver.

[c]Looms per fixer.

created at warping; other effects, such as filling direction stripes and complex patterns, require specially equipped looms.

Plain weaves are made by taking each pick or filling yarn over and under successive warp yarns, with every successive pick having opposite interlacings to the previous one. There are variants in which two or more adjacent yarns follow exactly the same interlacing path. The most important such are the Oxford weave, where pairs of warp yarns weave as one, and the 2 x 2 basket weave where both warp and filling yarns are woven in pairs. Nearly half of all fabrics woven commercially in the United States are in the plain weave or its variants. Print cloth, broadcloth, muslin for sheets, and many industrial fabrics are among these.

Twill weaves give the effect of diagonal lines running across the face of the fabric. This effect is produced by raising two or more warp yarns and depressing one, with a sequence of one displaced warp yarn each time, or by passing two or more filling yarns across the warp before changing the interlace, with a sequence of one displaced weft yarn each time. Denim fabric for jeans is a 2-up, 1-down twill, in which the warp yarns are all dyed and the filling yarns are undyed. The famous shepherd's plaid is a 2-up, 2-down twill weave combined with sequences of eight colored and eight white yarns in both warp and filling. Herringbone weaves are twills in which the twill direction alternates from righthand to lefthand at intervals of several yarns. Not only apparel fabrics and furnishings fabrics, but also many heavy industrial fabrics are made with twill weaves. In general, weaves with fewer interlacings than the plain weave exhibit greater bending flexibility. Plain weaves and simple twill weaves together account for 80 percent or more of all weaving.

Satin weaves are similar to twills except that the repeat is on at least five and often more successive yarns. The effect is that the face of the fabric consists almost entirely of either warp yarns or filling yarns and does not have the noticeable twill lines. With so few interlacings, satin weaves are much more subject to damage by snagging than other weaves, but the lustrous effect of the parallel yarns is the main objective.

Jacquard weaving is performed on special looms where every single warp thread is individually controlled—that is, for each pick insertion, the pattern of interlacings can be varied at will. This method allows a variety of color and finish effects and infinite designs. Luxurious furnishings fabrics, upholstery, and some dress fabrics are Jacquard woven.

Pile or plush fabrics such as corduroys, velveteens, velvets, and terry fabrics may be produced on fly shuttle looms with specialized mechanisms on the loom or specialized treatment after weaving. In both *corduroys* and *velveteens,* filling yarns make long *floats* over several warp yarns. The warp yarns are cut after weaving to create a *pile* of cut loops. In *velvets* and other plus fabrics, the weave used and the arrangement of warps in the loom produce two separate fabrics, one above the other, that share some common warp yarns (see Figure 2-3). These common warp yarns are then cut before they leave the loom to form two plush coths. The *terry fabric* loom has a separate wrap for the pile yarns. An overfeed mechanism supplies extra yarn from the pile warp beam on every three or more picks; this extra yarn forms a loop pile (see Figure 2-3).

Recent Developments in Weaving

The current revolution in weaving focuses on faster and more efficient means of filling insertion through the use of so-called shuttleless looms, some of which can be made very wide. To compare productivity on looms of different width, filling insertion is measured in yards per minute or meters per minute or square meters of fabric produced per hour. By this measure, the fastest shuttle looms reach a limit of about 5 1/2 sq. meters per hour of fabric production. The projectile or gripper looms, various forms of rapier looms, and air and water jet looms have filling insertion rates double those of shuttle looms, and the so-called multiphase or progressive shedding looms now being developed claim production rates of more than 20 sq. meters per hour.

In a gripper loom, the filling insertion mechanism is supplied with yarn from a cone and a succession of grippers. During operation, the clamp end of a gripper closes onto the yarn end, the amount of yarn needed to span the width of the warp is metered out, the length is cut (optional—it can be cut after insertion), and the gripper is projected across the shed. At the other side, the yarn end is

Plain weave.
e.g.: sheeting

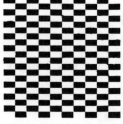

Plain weave, two ends
weaving as one. e.g.:
flat duck

Two up—one down
$\left(\dfrac{2}{1}\right)$ twill.

e.g.: drill or jean

Two up—two down
$\left(\dfrac{2}{2}\right)$ twill.

e.g.: filter twill

Three up—one down
$\left(\dfrac{3}{1}\right)$ twill.

e.g.: tent twill

Three up—one down
$\left(\dfrac{3}{1}\right)$ crowfoot satin

or broken twill. e.g.:
filament fabric for
laminating

Four up—one down
$\left(\dfrac{4}{1}\right)$ five harness

satin. e.g.: cotton
dust filtration fabric

Herringbone twill.
e.g.: work
clothing fabric

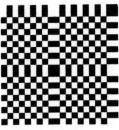

Rip-stop weave.
e.g.: filament fabric
for rubberizing

FUNDAMENTAL WEAVES

Figure 2-3. Typical Fabric Constructions

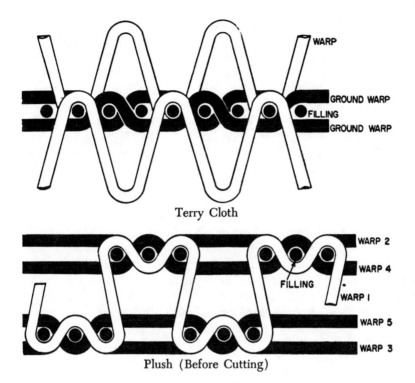

Terry Cloth

Plush (Before Cutting)

Figure 2-3 (cont.)

unclamped and the gripper is sent back for reuse. Unlike shuttle-woven fabrics, the selvages of gripper-woven fabrics consist of cut yarn ends. Between the fabric fell and the cloth takeup, those yarn ends may be trimmed to make neat edges or, alternatively, they may be turned in to form a "tuck" selvage.

Gripper looms can be made very wide, and all the simple weaves are producible on them. Often they are set up to weave fabrics that are later cut into two or even three narrower widths before takeup. Approximately 10,000 Sulzer gripper looms were operating in the United States as of 1976 to make shirtings, sheetings, print cloths, wide carpet backings, and other high volume fabrics.

Rapier looms simulate literal hand weaving. The rapier is a rigid or flexible mechanical arm that may reach all the way through the shed, or two rapiers may meet in the middle of the shed and transfer the yarn from one to the other. In the latter case, either an end or the middle of a metered yarn length can be transferred. The same sorts of fabrics that are made on Sulzer gripper looms are made on rapier looms. About 10,000 Draper DSL flexible rapier looms were installed in the United States in 1974, and a few thousand other rapier types were also in use, notably for worsted type fabrics. Although weaving labor costs are a bit higher with rapier looms than with Sulzer gripper looms and fabric quality is somewhat lower, the DSL at a price of $14,000 or so represents a much lower capital investment than a Sulzer loom at upwards of $25,000.

In jet looms, the filling yarn is effectively blown (air jet) or spit (water jet) across the shed. Through the first half of the 1970s, water jet looms have found significant application in the weaving of plain filament fabrics, with perhaps 1,000 installed in the United States as of 1974. The looms are not very adaptable to staple yarns because loose fiber can clog the jet nozzle and also the physical properties of conventional warp sizes (e.g., for cotton warp yarns) are adversely affected by water. Nissan water jet looms in commercial operation utilize about 20-25 gallons of drinking quality water per hour.

The newest development on the horizon is the Czechoslovakian Contis multiphase loom. Despite great interest, significant commercial installation had not yet appeared in the United States by 1975. Although productivity is very high on the Contis loom, it can only make plain weave fabric, which limits its application to the somewhat less than 50 percent of weaving that is strictly plain weave. By 1980 or so, the commercial role of multiphase weaving may become clear. (Table 2-2 gives examples of some of the shuttleless looms available.)

Cloth Room Processes

After the cloth is removed from the loom, the rolls are delivered to the cloth room to be inspected and packaged for shipment to the finisher. Records of fabric defects are fed back to the weaver or spinner for corrective action. Depending on the value of the fabric, certain repairable defects may be fixed during cloth inspection. Fabric mending is a common practice in traditional worsted weaving and even for cheaper fabrics. Inspectors also use solvents to remove oil and grease stains on the fabric before it goes to finishing. In some cases, bad defects may be completely cut out of the fabric in the cloth room even though the fabric then has to be sewn back together or "pieced up."

Knitting Process

The knitting process is divided into several distinct subindustries. Some knitting mills act like weaving mills in that they manufacture rolls of knitted yard goods for shipment to apparel plants to be cut and sewn. Others specialize in particular apparel such as knitted underwear, sweaters, pantyhose, and socks. These types of apparel are made on different types of equipment and usually in different mills.

The recent inroads of knitting into woven fabric markets have depended considerably on the use of textured polyester yarns and very efficient double

Table 2-2
Examples of Shuttleless Looms

	Shuttleless Looms				
	Draper DLG	Draper DGL	Draper DML	Draper DWJ	Sulzer Type E
Speed (ppm)[a]	200-285		160-325	300-500	200-300
Cloth width	26½"-66½"	26"-78"	90"-220"	50"-72"	85"-153"
Cost	$16,000	_[b]	_[b]	_[b]	$35,000
Filling Transfer Mechanism	rapier	tapes	missile	water jet	missile

[a]Picks per minute.
[b]Not yet marketed.

knitting machines capable of producing 25 linear yards of 100-inch width fabric per hour. (Compare a fast shuttle loom producing 5 yards of 45-inch fabric per hour.) Another factor has been the versatility and adaptability of many knitting machines to short runs of fabric; this is a capability made to order for the rapidly shifting fashion fabrics market. By the mid-1970s, double knits had captured more than half of the inexpensive men's slacks market and huge chunks of the women's wear, children's wear, and other apparel markets.

The basic difference between weaving and knitting is that while woven yarns are interlaced together, knitted yarns are looped together. A knit fabric is a series of interconnected loops that may be formed with as little as a single continuous yarn. Most knitting processes can be classified in three ways: (1) *weft knit* or *warp knit,* (2) performed on a *flat bed* knitting machine or *circular* knitting machine, and (3) *single knit* or *double knit.* The major portion of the growth in apparel has been in circular warp double knits.

The basic action of the knitting machine is quite simple: A hooked needle reaches through a closed loop of yarn, hooks another yarn, and pulls it through the loop forming a new loop with the first loop creating the closure for the new loop. The needle then reaches through the new loop to hook another yarn strand, and the process is repeated. The knitting is done with a row of hundreds or thousands of needles arranged in a linear position on a needle plate or in a circular position on a cylinder. The needles are evenly spaced side by side and are moved by cams. The spacing of the needles determines the gauge of the knitting machine. The gauge number refers to the number of needles in 1 1/2 inches; for example, a 90 guage machine would have 60 needles per inch.

There exist dozens of knitted fabric constructions, and these are classified by the type of stitch used and by the number of loops in each vertical row ("wale") and each horizontal row ("course") in the fabric.[a] Thus, a 40 x 60

[a]The "wale" and "course" in knitting loosely correspond to the "warp" and "fill" in weaving.

knitting construction would have 40 loops per inch of wale and 60 loops per inch of course.

Knitted fabrics are divided by stitch into two general types: (1) *weft knits,* wherein the one continuous yarn forms courses across the fabric[b] and (2) *warp knits,* wherein a series of yarns are used to form wales in the lengthwise direction of the fabrics.

In the weft knit category, there are three basic stitches and several variations on each. The basic stitches are the plain knit, the purl stitch, and the rib stitch. One variation on the rib stitch, the double knit stitch, has become very popular for the making of apparel fabrics. There are several variations on double knitting itself, most notably the double jersey and the double pique.

Warp knitting differs from the weft knitting in that in warp knitting each needle loops a separate yarn. The needles produce parallel rows of loops that are interlocked with one another in a zigzag pattern. Warp knitting is used to produce a wide variety of products ranging from light hair nets to heavy rugs. Six types of warp knit stitches are used: tricot, simplex, raschel, milanese, ketten raschel, and crochet. The tricot stitch, used in the manufacture of fabrics for lingerie, blouses, dresses, and bed sheets, is commercially the most important followed by the raschel stitch.

The two principle types of equipment are the flat bed and circular knit machines, each of which may use a single bed, or row, of needles or two beds or rows of needles. Flat bed machines produce a flat sheet of cloth with finished edges while a circular machine produces a cylinder or tube of cloth that must be cut to produce a flat piece of cloth.

There are a number of important specialized knitting techniques. Some of these techniques, which can usually employ either a weft or a warp knit, are listed below.

Jacquard Knitting. This is a knitting adaptation of the punched-card mechanism used in Jacquard weaving. It is used to produce multicolored designs.

Pile Knitting. This technique is used to manufacture imitation fur rugs and fabrics from synthetic fibers.

Hosiery Knitting. Unfinished hosiery is made directly on specialized knitting machines. Although the hosiery must then be finished, it requires no cutting or traditional sewing before being worn.

Underwear Knitting. Most underwear in use today is knitted. Although less specialized than Jacquard, pile, and hosiery knitting, several factors cause the manufacture of underwear fabric to be different from most knitting.

---

[b]All hand knitting is weft knitting.

The underwear must be soft, absorbent, porous, and exceptionally flexible, all qualities demanding specialized techniques.

Due to the enormous variations in the process and to the intricacy of the individual machines, knitting is considered by many in the industry to be a more complex technology than weaving. Despite the complexity of knitting, however, the process is generally faster,[c] more efficient, and more economic than is weaving. (Table 2-3 shows an economic comparison of knitting and weaving.)

Table 2-3
Manufacturing Cost Comparison: Woven Fabric vs. Knitted Fabric with Similar End Uses

	Woven Fabric			Knitted Fabric
	Warping, Slashing	Weaving	Total	Knitting
Labor				
Direct	$ .023	$ .094	$ .117	$ .025
Indirect	.007	.028	.035	.010
Supervision	.007	.007	.014	.002
Total labor	$ .037	$ .119	$ .166	$ .037
Overhead				
Variable	$ .003	$ .001	$ .004	$ .002
Fixed:				
Plant depreciation	.005	.015	.020	.005
Insurance & Taxes	.001	.003	.004	.001
Administrative	.002	.007	.009	.007
M & MR	—	.001	.001	.001
Total	$ .008	$ .026	$ .034	$ .014
Indirect division expense	—[a]	.001	.001	.001
Direct division area & staff	.001	.004	.005	.003
Total fixed	$ .009	$ .031	$ .040	$ .018
Total overhead	$ .012	$ .032	$ .044	$ .020
Supplies				
Operating	$ .004	$ .015	$ .019	$ .035
Other	—	.001	.001	—[a]
Total supplies	$ .004	$ .016	$ .020	$ .035
Total costs	$ .053	$ .177	$ .230	$ .094

Source: Casewriter estimates.
[a]Less than $.0015/linear yard.

[c]The speed of individual knitting machines varies from several inches to a yard per minute, but in general knitting processes produce fabric from two to ten times faster than looms producing an equivalent fabric.

Circular Double Knits

If a knitting machine is constructed with two beds of needles arranged so that alternate needles pull loops to opposite sides of the fabric, the product is 1 x 1 rib structure. The possibility exists to have groups of two, three, or more successive needles operating from one side or the other. In practice 2 x 2 and other rib structures are knitted. V-bed flat knitting machines are widely used to make rib borders for cuffs, collars, and waistbands in knitwear, but the growth area in knitting has been in the circular rib or double knit machines due to their speed and patterning capabilities.

Circular rib machines carry the second set of needles in tricks around the periphery of a flat, circular *dial* that fits just within the top of the needle cylinder. Each of the yarn feeds on the machine have stitch cams to guide the butts of the dial needles.

Although all fabrics knitted on machines with two needle beds can be regarded as double knit, or double jersey, structures, the term is usually limited to fabrics consisting of two distinct layers tied together by yarns incorporated in both. This result is possible because a machine with two systems of needles and several yarn feeds can literally produce two fabrics if all the yarns from some feeds knit only on one set of needles and all the yarns from the rest knit only on the other set of needles. Several plain double knit fabrics, some made on machines with interlock gating, and others, made on machines with rib gating, are of substantial commercial importance. These include single pique, double pique, Milano rib, and Ponte di Roma. All involve different patterns of knitting that repeat on three, four, six, or more yarn feeds. Each plain double knit structure has a characteristic appearance and stretchability. Jacquard double knitting machines utilize needle selecting devices to bring individual yarns to the face or the back of the fabric to create a color pattern on the face of the fabric.

Circular Jacquard double knit machines are classifiable according to the machine diameter (usually 30 inches); the number of needles per inch (most often 18 x 18 guage); the number of feeds (usually 36 or 48); and the type and versatility of needle selection that is provided. Versatility is measurable in terms of maximum pattern area per repeat. Machines capable of only small repeats are often called mini-jac units, while maxi-jack machines have large repeat capabilities.

A device that can be programmed with needle selection information is associated with the cylinder needles at each knitting position of a Jacquard machine. It can be a grooved disc with "pattern bits" or "jacks" set for knit, tuck, or miss positions; a drum set with removable pins; a stack of small metal discs with teeth that are left on or broken out as dictated by pattern requirements; or punched metal or Mylar film tapes that carry the pattern input. The Jacquard double knitting machine with electronic needle selection had become quite popular by 1974, even though they were priced well above comparable machines with mechanical needle selection. Intrinsic advantages of the electronic machines include nearly unlimited patterning scope, higher knitting speeds, shorter pattern change setup time, and ease of adaptation to computerized pattern preparation systems.

These pattern preparation systems are an excellent example of rapid acceptance of new technology in the knitting area. Commercial systems first appeared in about 1970. With fashionable women's wear designs changing every season, double knitters quickly found that the systems could save hundreds of hours of labor in preparing patterns for both electronic and manual machines. The former are supplied with design information via electronic controllers, while the latter can be handled with the aid of automatic machines to set, break, or punch the pattern units according to a master punched tape. Prices on contemporary Jacquard pattern preparation systems ranged in 1974 from $40,000 to well over $100,000. They include electronic scanners, light pens, CRT or TV displays, automatic color variations on the displays, mirror-imaging and dimension-changing capabilities, and automatic repeating of background patterns. They permit easy addition of design corrections, and they can be set to make designs conform to the pattern size limitations of specific mechanical Jacquard machines. By 1974, several commercial sample preparation services had sprung up to meet patterning needs of smaller knitting mills that could not afford their own patterning systems.

Double Knit Knitting Mill. In 1973, Sondra Manufacturing Company made and sold women's and children's sportswear, knitted tops, slacks, footwear, and a range of knitted yarn goods. Of Sondra's 1973 production, 25 percent was for use in its own sewing plant and 75 percent was for direct sale to various apparel manufacturers. All the double knitting machines were located in a new 50,000 square foot plant at Bethlehem, Pennsylvania, which also contained dyeing and finishing facilities. About two-thirds of the company's textured yarn requirements were met in-house. Sales of fabrics and garments together exceeded ten million dollars a year.

The double knitting department, as of the end of 1973, had 55 machines among which were several ElectroKnit 48 feed machines with mylar film pattern controls. The department was capable of producing more than 80,000 yards of fabric per week, half in men's wear patterns, from 150-denier textured polyester and a small percentage of spun yarns. The entire Bethlehem plant, including the dyeing and finishing department, employed 75 people. Since 1 operator could usually tend about 4 double knit machines, the double knitting department used 16 people per shift, including mechanics and a foreman. Table 2-4 shows the operating costs for various operating levels of the ElectroKnit 48.

Carpet Manufacture and the Tufting Process

Thirty years ago, only woven carpets were available to consumers. They were usually made of wool on slow Wilton and Axminster looms, and hence they were too expensive for mass marketing. Tufting was at that time a handcraft method

Table 2-4
1973 Estimated Operating Cost per Pound for ElectroKnit 48
($/lb)

Costs	1700 lbs/wk	1500 lbs/wk	1300 lbs/wk	1000 lbs/wk
Variable				
Direct & indirect labor	0.132	0.147	0.173	0.224
Payroll taxes and fringe benefits	0.017	0.019	0.022	0.029
Needles and maintenance	0.020	0.020	0.020	0.020
Electricity	0.004	0.004	0.004	0.004
Other (tape, oil, etc.)	0.020	0.020	0.020	0.020
Total variable costs	0.193	0.210	0.239	0.297
Fixed				
Supervision labor and taxes	0.035	0.040	0.046	0.056
Insurance	0.002	0.0023	0.0026	0.0034
Depreciation on machine	0.106	0.120	0.139	0.180
Depreciation on bldg.	0.004	0.0045	0.0051	0.0066
Property taxes	0.018	0.0204	0.0235	0.0305
Total fixed costs	0.165	0.1872	0.2162	0.2731
Other				
Interest at 9%	0.034	0.385	0.0436	0.0566
General & administration	0.092	0.1042	0.1202	0.1502
Total costs	$0.4840	$0.5399	$0.6190	$0.7829

of decorating "candlewick" or "chenille" bedspreads. Since that time the entire picture has changed. Tufting has become a high productivity method of carpet manufacture, and lightweight tufted fabrics are competing with raised and knitted pile fabrics in toys, coatings, blankets, linings, and so forth. Tufting's only major weakness has been difficulty with color patterning.

Potentialities for rapid change still exist in the carpet industry. Both circular and raschel knitting machines specifically designed for carpet manufacture have been offered commercially since 1970. Needlepunching is capturing a significant segment of the specialty carpet markets. The Blackburn "rivet head process" and the "Durcam" nonwoven pile process, both of which offer nearly unlimited patterning possibilities and economical pile yarn consumption, were at the point of commercialization in 1974. New kinds of carpet products included "Astroturf," other grasslike sports surfaces, and indoor-outdoor or patio carpets made of polypropylene flat filament yarns were growing. Carpet tiles had only a tiny share of the total market in 1974, but they represented an alternative to resilient vinyl and asphalt-based tiles.

Carpet Weaving

The *Wilton* loom is provided with several warps; some are ground or backing fabric warps and the rest are pile warps in up to five or more colors. When a particular color is to show on the face of the fabric, the yarn is raised by a Jacquard mechanism to allow formation of a loop. After the yarns for one line of pile are raised, a long wire is inserted to hold the pile loops in place until filling insertion has proceeded far enough to lock the structure together. Each wire has a knife edge at the end so that on withdrawal it cuts all the pile loops in the row. Pile yarns not needed in the surface pattern are hidden in the body of the carpet where they add to its thickness, resiliency, and cost.

Axminster weaving is more analogous to the traditional manufacture of oriental carpets, where the weaver knots tufts of pile onto warp yarns all the way across the fabric and then pushes them tight by inserting a filling yarn. In a mechanical Axminster loom, a selecting mechanism operating on the yarn supply prepares a set of tufts to go all the way across the warp; these are woven in as though they were warp yarns, but they are held by only one pick, to give a U-shaped tuft, or two picks, to give a W-shaped tuft. Spool Axminster looms receive the pile yarns on long rods or spools, each of which is wrapped with yarns in a pattern corresponding to one line of pile. Tufts for a line of pile are snipped from a spool, which is then displaced in the operating position by spool holding the next color filler required by the pattern. Gripper Axminster looms have a Jacquard mechanism on the loom to control pile yarn selection by a set of grippers, each of which places pile tufts alone one warpwise line. During an operating cycle, each gripper grasps one feed yarn end from the several available to it, cuts off the needed length, and delivers it to the weaving point. The color patterning freedom of Axminster weaving is virtually unlimited. Because of the width (9-15 ft.) and pattern complexity of Wilton and Axminster looms, they are expensive to operate and purchase. Their cost is between $150,000 to $250,000 and they operate at 20-50 ppm. Production rates range from 10 to 30 linear inches per hour.

Carpet Tufting

In *tufting,* a premanufactured fabric, the primary backing is fed through the tufting machine. Tufting yarns are fed through hollow tubes to a set of needles that are thrust by a needle bar down through the backing. A "looper" on the face side catches each pile yarn and retains it in a loop as the needles withdraw through the backing. If cut pile carpet is being manufactured, a cutter rises to press against the bottom edge of each looper hook to cut the end of the loop. Tufting machines may exceed 200 inches in width with needle spacings from 5/64 to 3/8 of an inch.

Tufting machines operate at speeds of between 600 to 800 rpm's and produce as much as 4 linear feet per minute or nearly 500 square yards of carpet per hour. Tufting machines cost around $60,000 in 1974 but could cost double that amount with special patterning features. Because of the high speed and low cost, run times of tufting machines are usually fairly low. With a 45 percent to 55 percent machine utilization rate, the cost structure for tufting is dominated by material costs of 75-80 percent, labor costs of about 5 percent, and all overhead of only 15 to 20 percent. The machine is usually tended by two people. One operator is responsible for mechanical operation and yarn supply, while the sole responsibility of the other is to inspect the carpet as it emerges from the machine. Any defects in the fabric are repaired right on the machine with a hand tufting unit capable of inserting single tufts.

The selection of *primary backing* materials for tufting is a very important consideration. Originally primary backings were a woven jute fabric. Some of that is still in use, but the two leading contenders in recent years have become woven polypropylene ribbon yarn and spunbonded nonwoven fabric. The nonwoven material possesses outstanding tuft-holding properties, but it also has exceptional resistance to needle penetration, thus requiring the use of a very heavy duty tufting machine.

A *pile yarn* for tufting should run easily through the machine and have good soil resistance, flame resistance, and antistatic properties. The yarn should also form tufts having as much resilience and covering power as possible. Continuous filament nylon in which the individual, coarse denier filaments are crimped in three dimensions along their length provide the necessary characteristics.

Because the tufts are held in place only by the resilience of the backing fabric surrounding the tuft holes, it is necessary to anchor the tufts in place before they have a chance to be pulled out. An adhesive anchor coating, a *secondary backing* fabric, and/or a foam backing is always applied soon after tufting. The backing for a tufted carpet has to be applied on a finishing range. The carpet is fed face down from a fabric feed unit, over a roller running in a trough of anchor coating material, and then under an infrared dryer. The next step may be passage under a *doctor roll* where a foam mixture is applied. The doctor roll is set a bit away from the surface of the fabric so that it controls the amount of foam mixture that remains on the back of the carpet. After foam application the carpet must be dried and the foam cured. A more common method of backing is adhesive bonding of a premanufactured foam or woven secondary backing to the carpet.

Design in Tufting. There are two dimensions in carpet design. One is through variations in pile height and the other is through variations in pile color. Pile height variation in tufting produces sculptured carpet effects. It is obtained by retarding or speeding the yarn feed to selected needles by using pneumatically operated plungers or photoelectric scroll pattern attachments. Methods of obtaining color patterns in the carpet include space dyeing of yarn and printing. Space dyeing is used to dye sections of each yarn so that a single yarn can create many different colored tufts. A process that is growing in importance is printing the entire carpet after tufting. Printing involves transferring a color pattern, which has been printed on a paper sheet, onto the carpet by laying the paper over the carpet and applying heat.

Other Techniques for Forming Fabric from Yarn

Four minor techniques for manufacturing fabric from yarn are worth brief note: (1) the *"Mali" method,* developed in East Germany in the early 1960s, (2) *braiding,* (3) *netting,* and (4) *lacing.*

The "Mali" method is a technique that constructs a fabric by placing a layer of warp yarns over a layer of filling yarns and interlocking the criss-crossed layers with a multiple needle and thread (sewing) system. The resulting fabric, in essence a hybrid between a woven and a knit, can be produced at speeds of two or three yards per minute—a rate of about twenty times that of a loom and several times faster than most knitting machines. Fabrics produced by this method do not ravel and have exceptional resistance to tear. Several European mills on both sides of the Iron Curtain are using the technique. Although it has been tried in this country, fabrics made by the "Mali" method have not been well accepted by the consumer to date.

Braiding is used to make fabrics by means of diagonal interlacing of yarns. The technique is used to make narrow fabrics, small rugs, ribbons, cords, and tapes. Tire cord is usually made by this process.

Netting is an open mesh technique of fabric construction wherein the yarns are held together by knots at points where they cross one another. The technique is used to make nets.

Lacing is similar to netting, except that the yarns are intertwined to form complex designs. The finest lacing is still made by hand. Machine-made lacing is manufactured by variations on the weaving, knitting, and braiding techniques.

Nonwoven Fabric Manufacture

"Nonwoven" is actually a misnomer. The term refers only to a fabric made directly from fibers without the use of yarn. Nonwovens were produced long before the arts of spinning and weaving were developed, but many textile industry experts believe that the age of the nonwoven fabric lies in the future.

Nonwovens are produced by laying fibers out into a mat or web and then bonding the fibers together. The bonding may be accomplished by chemical means, with or without the use of a bonding agent, or by physical means such as needling or heating. The simplest nonwoven, felt, is made by compressing wet wool or man-made fibers under heat; the resultant bonding is partly physical and partly chemical. Other types of nonwovens can be bonded with resin, by thermoplastic techniques, or by simply making the fibers so intertangled that they do not easily pull apart.

Most nonwoven products today are used for relatively low grade applications such as padding, filters, insulation, packaging, disposable napkins, draperies, towels, bandages, aprons, and working apparel. Some felts are used to make high quality products such as hats and home furnishings, but these are traditional applications. As stated before, many textile experts believe that the technology of nonwovens is in its infancy, and as newer and better nonwovens are developed, their use could become widespread and diverse.

3

Fabric Finishing and End Use Manufacturing

Newly constructed fabric from the loom, knitting machine, or other process is usually not in a form for the consumer. The unfinished (or greige[1]) fabric must undergo a number of finishing operations before it is ready for its end use.

There are quite a large number of finishing operations, many of which are quite specialized. This chapter will describe only those operations applied to most woven fabrics made of cotton or cotton substitutes. Most knitted fabrics made of cotton or cotton substitutes except underwear would undergo very similar operations. While the finishing of woven or knitted nylon and woolen fabrics is similar to that of cotton in many respects, the operations as described should not be thought of as applying to all these types of fabrics. The finishing of such specialized items as sheer women's hosiery or fancy lace goods is totally unlike what is described here.

Not all fabrics passing through finishing plants undergo all of the operations described. Neither will the fabrics necessarily pass through the operations in the order in which they are listed, although the order of listing has been arranged to correspond to a likely order for the bulk of finishing operations.

Finishing is an operation to which there is an appreciable economy of scale. Typically, a finishing plant handling woven cotton goods utilizes the output of three or more large weaving mills. The reason for this economy of scale is that finishing is inherently a chemically based operation. The cost structure of a finishing plant more closely approximates that of a chemical plant than a spinning and weaving mill: Capital costs and fixed costs are relatively high, and operating costs (other than the cost of the greige fabric) are relatively low. Most operations are economically performed on a large-batch or continuous operation basis.

Finishing Operations

Shortly after arriving at the finishing plant, rolls of fabric are sewn together end to end to form a continuous strand of material. The operations that the fabric then goes through are described below.

Singeing. The fabric is passed rapidly through gas flames. The rate of passage of the fabric through the flame is about 100 yards per minute. The flame removes fuzz, lint, and other combustible foreign objects from the fabric and produces a smooth surface that is prerequisite to dyeing.

Bleaching. This operation serves to remove all natural color from the fabric as well as to remove stains that frequently occur during fabric construction. Today, modern finishing plants bleach by means of a continuous peroxide method. The singed fabric is first run through a rapid desizing steamer,[b] washed, impregnated with a 3 percent solution of sodium hydroxide, and pulled into a large J-shaped container. The "J-box" is large enough to hold the fabric for an hour as it is run through, and the inside temperature is 212°F. The fabric is next given a hot wash, impregnated with 2 percent sodium peroxide, put through a second "J-box," washed again, and sent to a dryer fully bleached.

An older method uses kiers—that is, vessels in which up to five tons of cloth were boiled in a weak sodium hydroxide solution. This older, batch process is less economical than continuous bleaching.

Chemical bleaching tends to weaken fabric, and fabrics that must be durable are not bleached. Very high quality grades of fabric may be sun bleached, however, in a process that takes weeks but does not weaken the cloth.

Mercerizing. This operation can either precede or follow bleaching. Mercerizing is a continuous process applied to cotton fabrics to improve its appearance and feel and to improve its dye-holding capability. The fabric is passed through a 15 to 20 percent solution of sodium hydroxide and then passed through hot water sprays on a tenter frame, a device that holds the fabric flat and taut (see item on tentering). The hot water removes most of the lye, and the residual is removed by a hot water bath at the end of the tenter flame.

A variation on the process, slack mercerizing, is used to impart the property of stretch to the cotton.

Shrinking. A number of processes can be applied to control the future shrinkage of the fabric. The best known process is compressive shrinkage (trademarked "Sanforized Finish"), which reduces the residual shrinkage in cotton woven goods to less than 1 percent. It is a continuous process in which the fabric is immersed in water, stretched, held against a woolen blanket under tension, and, as the tension is released, allowed to shrink to a uniform dimension. Other similar processes can be used for rayon and cotton knitted goods.

Tentering. This process is applied at various stages of finishing. The fabric has usually been impreganted with some solution before being placed on the tentering frame, a 60- to 200-foot-long device onto which the fabric will continuously flow and pass down. The prime function of tentering is to hold the fabric to an even width as it dries while passing down the frame. An endless chain of mechanical "fingers" holds the fabric on its edges as it enters the frame,

[b]Unnecessary for knit fabrics.

and as the fabric passes down, the "fingers" gently stretch the fabric to a predetermined width.

Stiffening. Numerous processes are used to give fabric a temporary or permanent stiffness. Temporary stiffening is achieved by the application of starch. Permanent stiffening involves alteration of the structure of the fiber.

Surface Finishes. There are a number of surface finishes. The most important are briefly described below:

1. *Calendering* is basically an ironing process to add sheen to the surface of the fabric.
2. *Glazing* adds a stiff, polished surface to a fabric by means of starch, glue, or mucilage treatment. Glazing is usually followed by calendering.
3. *Schreining* is an inexpensive method that applies luster to cotton fabric by passing it under steel rollers at high pressure.
4. *Embossing* produces raised figures or designs in the cloth by passing it between heated engraved rollers.
5. *Moiréing* imparts lustrous, wavy design to the fabric by passing it under ridged rollers.
6. *Beetling* is used mostly on linens; the cloth is beaten with hammers to give it a permanent luster.
7. *Napping* is a process in which the fabric is brushed with stiff, napped prongs to make the surface fuzzy; the napped surface may be sheared to yield a smooth surface.
8. *Creping and wrinkling* can be accomplished by both chemical and mechanical processes.

Shape Retentive Finishes. These have increased in importance in the past few years. They may be broken down into three categories: wrinkle resistant finishes; wash and wear finishes; and permanent press finishes. All of these are based upon impregnating the fabric with resins or similar reactants that will chemically combine with the fabric by means of molecular cross-linking to chemically bind the individual molecules to prevent molecular slippage. The impregnation is done at the finishing plant. The cross-linking is generally done at the garment plant, by subjecting the finished garment to heat treating.

These finishes, while improving the appearance of the fabric as it is worn, generally tend to significantly reduce its tensile and tear strength and abrasion resistance.

Other Chemical Finishes. These include water repelling, finishes, waterproofing finishes, absorbent finishes, flameproofing, mildewproofing, antibacterial finishes, heat reflectant finishes, and many others. Most of these, as with shape retentive finishes, are applied by spraying the fabric with chemicals and then passing it through a tenter frame.

Dyeing. Color is added to the fabric by immersing it in a solution of dyestuffs. The dye itself may be a naturally occurring chemical or it may be synthetically produced. The actual dyeing may be performed in a number of ways, either in batches or by continuous immersion in troughs containing dye. Some types of dyeing are done under moderate pressure.

Printing. An alternative to dyeing is printing, wherein colored designs are printed onto the fabric. As in dyeing, there are numerous printing techniques, including: (1) block printing, a high-quality method using individual blocks to imprint the design; (2) roller printing, a continuous multicolor process similar to multicolor printing in the publishing industry; (3) duplex printing, a process that prints the same design simultaneously on both sides of the fabric; (4) discharge printing, a process that destroys the color on a dyed fabric—used to create such effects as white polka dots on a colored background; (5) resist printing, another process used in conjunction with dyeing—in this case, the fabric is printed with a dye repellent prior to being dyed; and (6) screen printing, essentially a mechanized silk screen process. There are perhaps two dozen more specialized printing techniques in addition to those mentioned above.

Fabrication Processes

Innumerable consumer and industrial products are made in whole or in part from textiles. Some, such as the weaving, knitting, or braiding of ribbons, tapes, fringes and other *narrow fabrics* are worlds unto themselves. They are usually produced by small specialized companies or are in internal operation of a large consumer or industrial products manufacturer. A large array of specialized equipment and process technologies existed to produce these items.

Other items such as *sheets, towels,* and *blankets* are produced in vast quantities by those few vertically integrated organizations, such as Fieldcrest and Cannon, that have come to dominate the business. Sheets, woven on extra-wide looms and then finished, dyed, and/or printed, must be cut to correct length and then hemmed at both ends. Automated sewing, folding, and packaging equipment is used. Bath towels and most of the other sizes are woven directly on the loom to the correct width and with flat woven or fringed ends. Many types require only cutting and folding after they have been finished. Cut ends of blankets are usually covered with tape that is folded over the edges and sewn. Bedspreads require only the addition of long fringes or finishing to the edges. Curtains and drapes can be made with turned ends for rods, or if they are to be hung on hooks, specially woven curtain header tapes are sewn on.

The major portion of fabrics are used by the *apparel industry*. The apparel industry is made up of establishments whose main or sole business is cutting, sewing, and pressing fabrics into garments: underware, shirts, blouses, skirts, pants, jackets, coats, and so forth. The industry is very much labor intensive, so efficient personnel utilization is a key management responsibility.

Apparel Manufacturing

The apparel manufacturing process can be classified into three main subprocesses: (1) piece making through laying, marking, and cutting; (2) joining through sewing or fusing; and (3) shaping through pressing or molding. Although there are many variations in these three processes, the major types will be described here.

Piece Making

Piece making involves *laying* the material out, marking it with a pattern outline, and cutting out the patterns. The material is delivered to a spreading table that consists of a framework to support a roll of fabric, a mechanism to unroll fabric onto the table, and clamps to hold each fold of fabric in place. The fabric is unrolled and cut in lengths with a number of lengths being layered together on the table. To avoid distortion and shrinkage in the garment parts, the cloth roll is positively driven to maintain low tension on the fabric. Electronic edge guides are used on newer machines to give accurate alignment of successive layers. Where the fabric being spread has a definite face and back, or a pile on one side, the fabric is cut after each ply is laid down.

The total thickness of fabric layers depends on the limitations of the fabric, the capacity of the cutting equipment, and the production requirements. Cutting heights of wovens can exceed 10 inches, with 4 to 7 inches (10 or more layers per inch) being more typical for knit fabrics. Fabrics that are tough to cut or slippery are cut in low piles. Sometimes lubricating papers or scrap fabrics are inserted once every several layers to improve cutting characteristics.

Fabric spreading personnel are expected to watch for defects. In some cases the defects are cut out during the spreading; in others the defects are marked with strings so that each marked piece can later be examined and replaced if necessary. Rolls of incoming fabric are grouped by shade whenever roll-to-roll color differences are visible. The likelihood of visible color differences appearing in garments can be minimized by making sure that the parts for an individual garment all come from the same cut piece of fabric.

There are several *marking* methods. Heavy paper cutouts of the different pieces may be placed on the lay and oversprayed with a removable dye or chalk to define the outlines of the pieces on the top layer of fabric. A marker paper need only to be placed on top of the lay and held there with weights, staples, nonpermanent adhesive, or clamps that also hold the lay itself. Heatseal marker papers adhere to the top fabric layer after ironing. Several photographic, hectographic, and carbon paper methods of duplicating paper markers are also in use.

Optimizing *marker making,* or the layout of pieces to be cut, can yield substantial savings in fabric utilization; perhaps two more suits can be cut from a roll of fabric with a good marker layout as compared with an inefficient one. Many apparel manufacturers make miniature markers at 1/5 scale so they can experiment with various placements of fabric pieces, lengths of the lay, or mixes of garment sizes. Once a good arrangement is found, the marker is scaled up photographically to full size and replicated as needed. By the early 1970s computerized marker making was on the way to commercial realization.

Straight, rotary, and band knives are all used in *cutting* lays, with die cutters often used for small parts. The rotary knife is the fastest but is more-or-less limited to straight cuts. More typically a straight knife is moved by hand through the layered material (much like a saber saw) by a highly skilled operator. A machine just reaching commercial use in the mid-1970s was the laser cutter. This highly automated and computer-driven machine cuts only a single layer of fabric at a time, but the beam is so fast and accurate that the total spreading and cutting time can be less than that of conventional cutting. The high capital investment for laser beam units compared with ordinary cutting machines limits their application to the larger firms in the industry. Since one slip of the knife or a poorly layed pile of fabric can destroy fifty or a hundred pieces at once, cutting knife maintenance, cutting room operator training, and all aspects of fabric handling in the cutting room are critical to controlling costs in piece making.

Joining

Once cut, the pieces are ready to be assembled by *sewing* or *fusing.* One cutting machine provides parts for as many as fifty to a hundred sewing machines. Cut parts are usually bundled and delivered to the sewing room for the various assembly operations. Efficiency is obtained in commercial apparel manufacture by using specialized sewing machines for different specific tasks. There are literally hundreds of different types of industrial sewing machines, with each producing only a narrow range of stitches. A sewing machine consists of three basic functions: fabric control, thread control, and stitch forming. Special presser feet and other attachments automatically guide the fabric, fold over edges, align zipper tapes, make buttonholes, create puckers, add trim, and so forth.

The sequence of sewing operations vary. The securing of fabric edges by overcast stitching and/or taping is always done early in an assembly sequence.

Zippers are usually sewn in, and buttons and buttonholes for shirts are added early. Button and buttonhole sewing in jackets and coats, however, are normally the last operations. The usual rule is to insert nonfunctional decorations such as embroideries early, while functional decorations are added when required by the functional purpose. In making garments that hang from the shoulders, assembly of the internal parts, such as interlinings, have to be completed before the shoulder seams are closed. Many types of sleeves are attached after shoulder closing. For pants and skirts, it is usual to assemble the basic garment pieces first, then finish the top waistband area, and finally finish the bottom.

The amount of hand manipulation required in sewing is so great that the average industrial machine only runs for 20 percent of total work time. Such low machine efficiency has been a powerful incentive in the search for ways to reduce or at least deskill sewing labor. Sewing jigs, for example, can be designed to hold the pieces for pocket flaps, ties, collars, or cuffs, or to set pockets in garments. The operator loads the jig, engages it with a specially adapted feed dog and presser foot, and starts the machine. While the jig automatically tracks through the machine to create the desired seam, the operator can unload and reload another jig. Profile stitchers featuring partial automation of fabric placement have recently come on the market. Although the potential savings with such machines are great, the initial investment puts them out of reach for all but the largest apparel firms.

Major alternatives to sewing for assembling garment parts are adhesive and thermal seaming. To date, neither has had a major impact on the industry because of the uncertainty of adhesive durability. Thermal seaming or "seam welding" machines use contact heat and radio frequency and ultrasonic energy sources, but they are limited to thermoplastic fabrics or others with thermoplastic threads placed between them. Both adhesive and welded seams tend to be stiff and show poor stretch properties. Thermal joining, or fusing, for laminating fabric pieces together in garment assembly has achieved much more success. Fusible fabrics, usually interlinings, are woven or nonwoven fabrics having dots or specks of heat-activatable adhesive on one or both sides. The fusible interlining goes between the outer shell fabric and the inner lining in jackets, collars and other garments parts to replace interlinings that were formally sewn into place. By 1973 fusibles had taken over half the interlining market in Europe and 15-20 percent in the United States. Substitution of the fusing press for a sewing machine to join three layers of fabric allows a reduction of skill requirements and frequently results in better product quality because further cutting and sewing is usually much easier.

Shaping

The traditional manufacturing sequence for men's wool suits include *pressing* or *molding* after virtually every sewing operation as well as in garment finishing.

The use of wrinkle-free and shape-retaining synthetic fiber fabrics has greatly reduced the need for pressing between sewing operations.

The current trends toward automation and deskilling have been very visible in the design of pressing equipment. Many modern presses use suction to hold the parts or complete garments onto the pressing surface or *buck*. Most presses have pneumatic press head closing mechanisms and bucks that are readily interchangeable to handle different garment sizes and styles. The temperature and amount of steam, pressing time, and subsequent vacuum drying time are usually controlled automatically. On such machines, the press operator has time available to load another garment while one is being pressed. The press can have a rotating or reciprocating table with extra bucks that can be loaded and then swung into pressing position. Other designs use a carousel loading system. The results have been major increases in productivity. While it use to take 2 to 10 minutes to hand press a garment, a modern jacket press can handle as many as 80 to 90 jackets an hour with 1 operator.

Once pressed the garments are tagged, folded, and packaged for delivery. In some cases it is necessary to assemble two or more items from different production lots (such as pants and jackets of a suit) to be packaged together. Before packaging, a final inspection is performed and any necessary repairs are made.

**Part II:
Competitive
Environment of the
Textile Industry**

Introduction to Part II

Textile products and apparel constitute one of the major segments of manufacturing industry in the United States. In 1971 textile mill products were responsible for 3.2 percent of the value added at manufacturing establishments and thus were the twelfth largest Standard Industrial Classification (SIC) industry group in terms of value added. In the same year, apparel and other textile products contributed 4.0 percent of the value added and thus ranked ninth among SIC industry groups. Had the data been combined, textile mill products and apparel and other textile products would have been listed as the sixth largest SIC industry group in terms of value added. In 1972 textile mills employed over 950,000 people at 7,203 establishments owned by over 5,500 companies.

The textile mill products industry includes establishments engaged in preparation of textile fibers; manufacture of yarn, thread, and other similar products; manufacture of fabric, carpets, and rugs; dyeing, finishing, and other treatments of textile products; manufacture of knit apparel; and manufacture of other miscellaneous textile products. The apparel and other textile products industry, also known as the "cutting-up" or "needle" trades, produces clothing and fabricates products by cutting and sewing purchased textile fabrics and related materials such as leather, plastics, and furs. Part II is principally, but not exclusively, about the textile mill products industry. Table II-1 gives selected statistics on the textile mill products and apparel industries. Table II-2 contains financial data for selected segments of the textile and apparel industries.

Historically, textile mills were small, family-owned operations; in recent years, large integrated textile manufacturers have increased their significant position in the industry, both through acquisition of smaller mills and through internal growth. Most textile mills, even those owned by large integrated manufacturers, are small- to medium-sized operations located principally in the southeastern and northeastern portions of the United States. Since textile mills are often a major industrial employer in small rural towns, the relative health of the U.S. textile industry has a much stronger impact on specific regions and localities than on the United States as a whole. Table II-3 gives a geographical breakdown of the textile mill products industry. Table II-4 compares the Northeast and the South, the two centers of textile manufacturing activity, and indicates some of the factors behind the growing dominance of the South in textile mill products.

As can be seen from Table II-5, since 1947, growth in textile mill products has lagged behind growth in manufacturing as a whole. As indicated in Figure II-1, after-tax profits for textile mills averaged only 2.5 percent of sales in 1974, compared with 5.5 percent for all manufacturing. This retarded growth, lower profit margin, and the nearly static production of broad-woven cloth indicated in Table II-6, can be attributed in part to several factors:

Table II-1
Statistics for the Textile Mill Products Industry, the Apparel Industry, and Selected Segments of Each, 1967 and 1972

Type of Manufacturer		Companies	Establishments		All Employees		Production Workers			Value Added	Cost of Materials	Value of Shipments
			Total	With over 20 Employees	Number	Payroll	Number	Employee Hours	Wages			
		(number)	(number)	(number)	(thousands)	(million $)	(thousands)	(millions)	(million $)	(million $)		
Textile mill products, Total	1967	—a	7080	4453	929.0	4390.9	828.2	1689.7	3556.5	8153.2	11,741.4	19,815.2
	1972	—a	7203	4505	952.7	6051.9	836.2	1726.0	4807.2	11,718.0	16,505.1	28,071.5
Weaving mills, cotton	1967	218	393	331	202.8	938.4	189.3	398.0	831.5	1624.0	1759.1	3327.7
	1972	190	307	227	121.3	745.2	112.1	235.8	654.9	1256.3	1389.7	2660.6
Weaving mills, synthetics	1967	272	396	312	108.6	528.8	98.3	209.3	445.6	921.6	1365.5	2289.6
	1972	256	412	341	149.7	979.4	134.9	292.7	825.2	1831.6	2062.6	3856.6
Weaving and finishing mills, wool	1967	262	310	217	41.8	216.3	36.6	76.0	170.4	428.6	657.1	1090.0
	1972	178	198	119	19.4	132.1	16.5	34.7	99.0	239.4	217.1	450.1
Knitting mills	1967	2483	2698	1619	240.6	1035.8	213.0	405.9	809.2	1914.1	2627.3	4519.3
	1972	2462	2723	1725	276.5	164.7	240.7	467.2	1263.2	3179.8	4579.4	7703.3
Textile finishing, except wool	1967	590	641	408	73.7	416.3	61.9	133.6	316.7	710.0	1028.3	1735.0
	1972	570	655	432	79.4	563.9	67.3	145.5	436.0	113.9	1518.2	2625.5
Floor covering mills	1967	333	385	209	43.6	227.8	36.0	77.0	165.4	599.3	1161.2	1757.4
	1972	476	529	280	59.9	416.1	48.5	99.8	294.3	1078.2	2116.7	3153.0
Yarn and thread mills	1967	572	768	604	119.2	504.9	110.0	221.8	431.0	946.1	1655.0	2608.6
	1972	594	807	634	147.6	866.1	134.0	280.3	725.8	1579.5	2667.0	4242.7
Apparel and other textile products	1967	—a	26393	12705	1356.7	5582.2	1200.4	2178.6	4340.6	10,064.4		21,326.9
	1972	—a	24438	12226	1368.3	7212.0	1198.3	2161.1	5461.1	13,487.5	14,532.0	27,809.2
Men's and Boys suits and coats	1967	904	1003	649	135.9	641.7	119.9	221.3	509.1	1047.5	862.3	1912.1
	1972	721	856	770	124.8	770.3	108.3	193.7	603.1	1342.6	1064.5	2396.9
Men's and boys' furnishings	1967	2224	2853	1969	344.5	1212.4	313.9	572.6	999.5	2181.2	3459.4	4738.1
	1972	2115	2787	2000	363.3	1692.2	325.4	595.8	1342.6	3241.6	3718.5	6904.7
Women's and misses' outerwear	1967	8978	9416	5615	409.2	1755.8	357.6	634.5	1335.6	3182.5	3377.5	6534.1
	1972	8980	9526	5600	432.6	2269.6	377.7	659.5	1694.1	4101.9	4227.7	8278.0

Source: U.S. Bureau of the Census, *Census of Manufactures*, 1967, Washington, D.C.

Casewriter's Note: The Census Bureau term "establishment" is essentially identical to the more normal term "plant."

aTotals are omitted because they would contain significant double accounting.

Table II-2
Financial Data for Selected Types of Textile and Apparel Firms

	Men's & Boys' Shirts, Collars, Nightwear (N=35)	Broad Woven[a] (N=71)	Dyeing and Finishing[a] (N=32)	Yarn Mills[a] (N=59)
Combined Balance Sheets for Year Ending on or about December 31, 1968				
Assets				
Cash	8.8	5.9	6.9	6.2
Accounts receivable	31.1	16.5	18.9	22.0
Inventory	40.0	27.6	29.4	25.4
Securities	0.0	0.6	1.1	0.6
Other	2.3	1.3	1.6	2.3
Total current assets	82.3	52.0	57.8	56.6
Fixed assets	13.0	42.9	38.3	38.7
Other assets	4.7	5.1	3.9	4.8
Total assets	100.0	100.0	100.0	100.0
Liabilities				
Banks	14.0	4.9	4.0	5.2
Trade	18.1	6.4	14.0	9.1
Taxes	4.4	2.5	3.2	2.3
Other	7.2	6.2	8.8	6.5
Total current liabilities	43.7	19.9	30.0	23.2
Long-term debt	9.3	11.6	5.6	13.3
Total liabilities	53.0	31.5	35.6	26.5
Net worth	47.0	68.4	64.5	63.5
Total liabilities & net worth	100.0	100.0	100.0	100.0
Sales ($000)	199,413	543,630	207,779	487,129
Total assets ($000)	76,210	344,023	111,434	292,835
Combined Income Statements				
Net sales	100.0	100.0	100.0	100.0
C.G.S.	83.2	85.5	82.6	84.6
Gross profit	16.8	14.5	17.4	15.4
Other expense	11.9	8.6	10.5	9.5
profit (BT)	4.9	5.9	6.9	5.8
Current ratio	1.8	2.2	1.9	2.5
Fixed/N.W.	.1	.5	.4	.6
Debt/N.W.	.9	.6	.5	.4
Sales/A.R.[b]	7.6	9.9	8.6	9.2
Cost sales/inv.	5.3	5.2	7.0	6.1
Sales/N.W.	5.6	2.7	3.3	2.6
Percent profit before tax N.W.	15.5	12.7	19.3	14.2
Profit before tax/total assets	8.6	6.2	12.3	8.4

Source: Robert Morris Associates, *Statement Studies*, Charlottesville, Va., 1968.
[a]Cotton, silk, and synthetics.
[b]Days.

Table II-3
Textile Mill Products, Geographical Breakdown, 1967

| | Establishments | | Employees | | | |
Geographic Area	Total (number)	With 20 or More Employees (number)	Total (1,000)	Payroll ($ million)	Value Added by Mfr. ($ million)	Value of Shipments ($ million)
United States, total	7080	4453	929.0	4390.9	8153.2	19,815.2
Northeast region	3799	2093	241.6	1257.6	2275.0	5,186.9
North central region	321	182	30.1	169.1	318.8	677.1
South region	2656	2058	645.7	2902.6	5419.0	13,606.9
West region	304	120	11.3	61.4	140.3	344.0

Source: U.S. Bureau of the Census, *Census of Manufactures,* 1967, Washington, D.C.

Table II-4
Textile Mill Products, Regional Comparison, 1967

Item	Northeast	South	United States, Total
Percent of Establishments with 20 or more employees	55	77	63
Annual wages per employee ($)	5205	4495	4726
Employees per establishment (number)	64	243	131
Value added per establishment ($ million)	.60	2.04	1.15
Value added per employee ($)	9416	8392	8776
Value of shipments per establishment ($ million)	1.37	5.12	2.80

Source: U.S. Bureau of the Census, *Census of Manufactures,* 1967, Washington, D.C.

1. Market changes and necessarily limited flexibility in some textile mills often render capital investments obsolete before the end of their useful life.
2. The proportion of personal consumption expenditures allocated to clothing and accessories fell from 9.4 percent in 1947 to 8.6 percent in 1968.
3. Competition from foreign imports increased, as shown in Figure II-2.
4. Competition from nontextile products, especially plastics and paper, increased.

The relative slippage of textiles compared to the rest of the economy came at a time when, as demonstrated by Figures II-3 and II-4, textiles were becoming

Table II-5

Indices of Production for Textile Mill Products and All Manufactures in United States, 1947-1973

Year	Textile Mill Products	All Manufactures
1947	101	100
1948	105	103
1949	94	97
1950	111	113
1951	107	121
1952	103	125
1953	104	136
1954	95	127
1955	107	140
1956	104	144
1957	98	145
1958	96	133
1959	111	152
1960	107	157
1961	109	158
1962	118	172
1963	119	179
1964	125	191
1965	137	208
1966	145	227
1967	144	229
1968	153	238
1969	163	253
1970	153	241
1971	157	241
1972	169	261
1973	185	286
1974	177	285

Sources: Compiled from U.S. Federal Reserve System data.

more of a bargain with respect to other items. A comparison of the cost structures of textile mill products in 1958 and 1971 is given in Table II-7.

Changes in the types of fibers used have also contributed to the dynamics of the textile industry. Man-made fibers such as rayon, acetate, polyester, nylon, and others have changed the processing methods and possible end products of the textile industry. Figure II-5 shows a breakdown of total fiber consumption by U.S. textile mills.

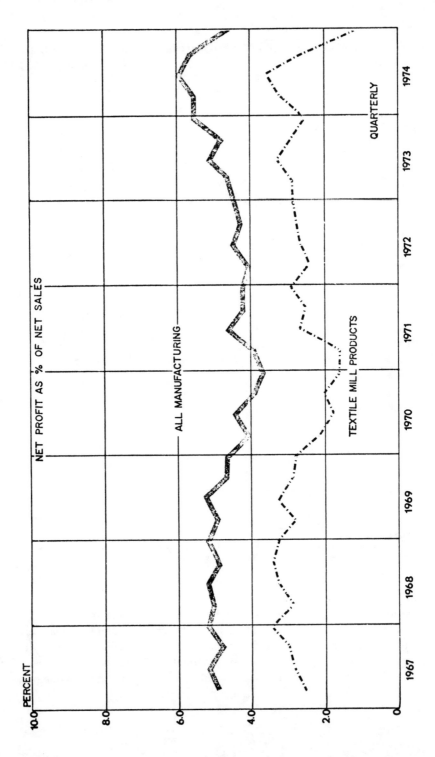

	1967	1968	1969	1970	1971	1972	1973	1974	1973 4TH Q	1974 1ST Q	2ND Q	3RD Q	4TH Q
SALES:[1]													
ALL MANUFACTURING INDUSTRIES[2]	575,427	631,911	694,584	708,810	751,061	849,523	978,594	1,060,961	236,551	242,247	269,621	271,884	277,209
NONDURABLE GOODS	274,782	296,414	328,107	345,705	369,289	413,743	468,835	531,175	113,856	121,598	132,519	137,150	139,908
Textile Mill Products	18,672	20,841	21,780	21,598	22,930	25,616	29,113	31,197	7,577	7,585	8,368	7,595	7,649
Apparel and Related Products	18,170	20,718	22,687	22,011	23,695	28,584	31,974	–	8,176	–	–	–	–
NET PROFITS:[3]													
ALL MANUFACTURING INDUSTRIES	29,008	32,069	33,248	28,572	21,038	36,467	48,134	58,768	13,169	13,509	16,270	15,546	13,443
NONDURABLE GOODS	14,429	15,564	16,372	15,689	16,527	18,019	23,543	34,015	6,977	7,777	6,775	9,328	8,135
Textile Mill Products	540	654	621	413	558	656	831	795	186	239	297	177	82
Apparel and Related Products	420	507	523	426	559	679	655	–	–	–	–	–	–
PROFIT PER DOLLAR OF SALES:[4]													
ALL MANUFACTURING INDUSTRIES	5.0	5.1	4.8	4.0	4.2	4.3	5.0	5.5	5.6	5.6	6.0	5.7	4.8
NONDURABLE GOODS	5.3	5.3	5.0	4.5	4.5	4.4	5.0	6.4	6.1	6.4	6.6	6.8	5.8
Textile Mill Products	2.9	3.1	2.9	1.9	2.4	2.6	2.9	2.5	2.5	3.1	3.5	2.3	1.1
Apparel and Related Products	2.3	2.4	2.3	1.9	2.3	2.3	2.1	–	–	–	–	–	–
NEW PLANT AND EQUITMENT EXPENDITURES[5] PER DOLLAR OF SALES:													
ALL MANUFACTURING INDUSTRIES	5.0	4.5	4.6	4.5	4.0	3.7	3.9	4.3	4.3	4.4	4.2	4.3	4.3
NONDURABLE GOODS	5.3	4.8	4.8	4.7	4.3	3.8	4.0	4.4	4.4	4.4	4.3	4.4	4.4
Textile Mill Products	3.6	2.5	2.9	2.6	2.7	3.0	2.7	2.7	2.7	3.3	2.4	2.6	2.5
PROFIT ON STOCKHOLDERS' EQUITY:													
ALL MANUFACTURING INDUSTRIES	11.7	12.1	11.5	9.3	9.7	10.6	13.1	14.9	14.3	14.3	16.7	15.5	13.2
NONDURABLE GOODS	11.8	11.9	11.5	10.3	10.3	10.5	12.9	17.2	15.3	16.5	12.0	18.5	15.8
Textile Mill Products	7.6	8.8	7.9	5.1	6.6	7.5	9.6	8.2	9.1	10.1	12.0	7.2	3.3
Apparel and Related Products	11.9	12.9	11.9	8.3	11.0	11.9	10.8	–	14.3	–	–	–	–

[1]Sales are net returns, allowances and discount, in millions of dollars. [2]Except newspaper. [3]After federal income taxes, in millions of dollars. [4]Percent or cents. Total for P and E from page 18. Annual data are quarterly averages. Quarterly data at annual rates. [5]Percent. SOURCE: Federal Trade Commission.

Source: Federal Trade Commission 1975.

Figure II-1. Corporate Profit Data (after federal income taxes)

Table II-6
Total Broad-Woven Fabric Production and Mill Consumption of Fiber, 1947-1973

Year	Broadwoven Fabric Production (millions of linear yards)	Mill Fiber Consumption (millions of pounds)
1947	12,371	6,424.9
1948	12,405	6,403.7
1949	10,923	5,445.4
1950	13,091	6,846.4
1951	12,887	6,838.5
1952	12,160	6,440.1
1953	12,994	6,481.5
1954	12,518	6,028.1
1955	13,119	6,709.7
1956	12,931	6,543.5
1957	12,118	6,230.1
1958	11,628	5,967.5
1959	12,414	6,839.1
1960	12,056	6,491.3
1961	11,863	6,533.2
1962	12,301	7,159.9
1963	12,104	7,246.1
1964	12,766	7,782.1
1965	13,431	8,494.4
1966	13,304	9,007.5
1967	12,753	8,982.0
1968	12,698	9,781.7
1969	12,591	9,798.0
1970	11,454	9,557.2
1971	11,147	10,677.1
1972	11,292	11,662.0
1973	11,303	12,474.1
1974	10,721	11,092.0

Sources: U.S. Bureau of the Census, *Census of Manufactures,* 1967, Washington, D.C.; and *Textile Hi-Lights,* June 1974.

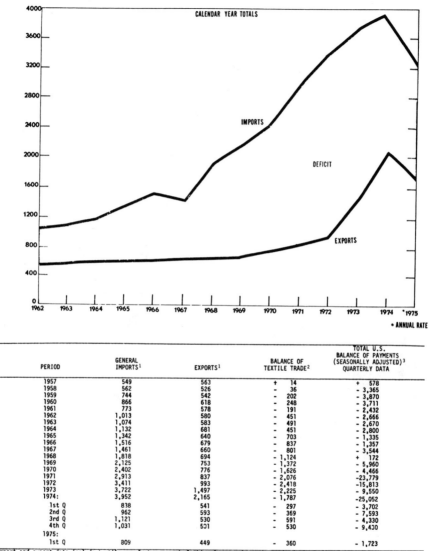

PERIOD	GENERAL IMPORTS[1]	EXPORTS[1]	BALANCE OF TEXTILE TRADE[2]	TOTAL U.S. BALANCE OF PAYMENTS (SEASONALLY ADJUSTED)[3] QUARTERLY DATA
1957	549	563	+ 14	+ 578
1958	562	526	- 36	- 3,365
1959	744	542	- 202	- 3,870
1960	866	618	- 248	- 3,711
1961	773	578	- 191	- 2,432
1962	1,013	580	- 451	- 2,666
1963	1,074	583	- 491	- 2,670
1964	1,132	681	- 451	- 2,800
1965	1,342	640	- 703	- 1,335
1966	1,516	679	- 837	- 1,357
1967	1,461	660	- 801	- 3,544
1968	1,818	694	- 1,124	+ 172
1969	2,125	753	- 1,372	- 5,960
1970	2,402	776	- 1,626	- 4,466
1971	2,913	837	- 2,076	-23,779
1972	3,411	993	- 2,418	-15,813
1973	3,722	1,497	- 2,225	- 9,550
1974:	3,952	2,165	- 1,787	-25,052
1st Q	838	541	- 297	- 3,702
2nd Q	962	593	- 369	- 7,593
3rd Q	1,121	530	- 591	- 4,330
4th Q	1,031	501	- 530	- 9,430
1975:				
1st Q	809	449	- 360	- 1,723

[1]Import and export data include textile manufactures, and clothing (except donated for charity) of all fibers compiled on the basis of the Standard International Trade Classification FT-990. [2]Textile balance of trade represents exports minus imports. Minus sign indicates an excess of imports over exports. [3]Balance of liquidity basis-increase in U. S. official reserve assets and decreases of liquid liabilities to all foreigners excluding allocations of SDR's. Minus sign indicates a deficit in the Balance of Payments. SOURCE: U. S. Department of Commerce.

Source: U.S. Department of Commerce 1976.

Figure II-2. U.S. Textile Trade (millions of dollars)

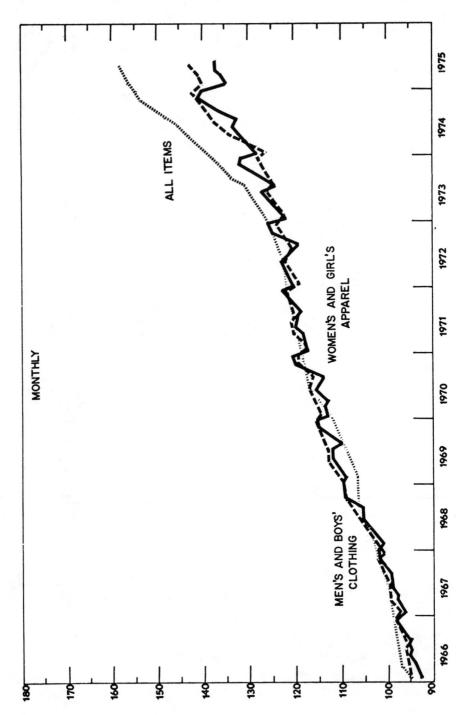

MONTHLY

ALL ITEMS

WOMEN'S AND GIRL'S
APPAREL

MEN'S AND BOYS'
CLOTHING

COMMODITIES AND/OR SERVICES	ANNUAL AVERAGES							1974							1975			
	1968	1969	1970	1971	1972	1973	1974	JUN	JUL	AUG	SEP	OCT	NOV	DEC	JAN	FEB	MAR	APR
All Items[1]	104.2	109.8	116.3	121.3	125.3	133.1	147.7	146.9	148.0	149.9	151.7	153.0	154.3	155.4	156.1	157.2	157.8	158.6
Food	103.6	108.9	114.9	118.4	123.5	141.4	161.7	160.3	160.5	162.8	165.0	166.1	167.8	169.7	170.9	171.6	171.3	171.2
Housing	104.2	100.8	118.9	124.3	129.3	135.0	150.6	149.2	150.9	152.8	154.9	156.7	158.3	159.9	161.2	162.7	163.6	164.7
Transportation	105.0	107.2	112.7	118.6	119.9	123.8	137.7	138.8	140.6	141.3	142.2	142.9	143.4	143.5	143.2	143.5	144.8	146.2
Health and Recreation	105.0	110.3	116.2	122.2	126.1	130.2	140.3	139.4	141.0	142.6	144.0	145.2	146.3	147.5	148.9	150.2	151.1	152.1
Apparel and Upkeep	105.4	111.5	116.1	119.8	122.3	126.8	136.2	135.7	135.3	138.1	139.9	141.1	142.4	141.9	139.4	140.2	140.9	141.3
Miscellaneous Textile Categories:																		
Apparel Less Footwear:[2]	105.7	111.9	116.3	119.9	122.3	126.5	135.7	135.2	134.6	137.6	139.6	140.9	142.2	141.5	137.9	138.5	139.1	139.5
Men's and Boys' Clothing	105.7	112.4	117.1	120.3	121.9	126.4	136.4	137.0	136.0	138.4	140.0	141.4	142.5	142.5	140.0	140.6	141.3	142.2
Women's and Girls' Apparel	105.9	111.7	116.0	120.1	123.0	127.3	134.9	133.6	132.9	136.6	138.8	140.2	141.5	140.0	135.1	135.4	136.1	136.0
Textile Housefurnishings[3]	103.7	106.9	109.2	111.6	113.6	116.2	131.5	129.2	---	---	133.9	---	---	140.1	---	---	140.3	---
Rugs, Soft Surface[4]	102.0	103.5	102.8	102.3	101.5	102.8	111.6	109.4	---	---	114.3	---	---	117.4	---	---	118.1	---

[1] U. S. City Averages for urban wage earners and clerical workers. [2] Included in apparel and upkeep. [3] Included in housing, bath towels, and wool blankets included to 1963, excluded thereafter, red pillows and slipcovers included after 1962. [4] Included in housing; wool and nylon broadloom.
SOURCE: U. S. Department of Labor.

Figure II-3. Consumer Price Index (1967 = 100)

Source: U.S. Department of Labor 1976.

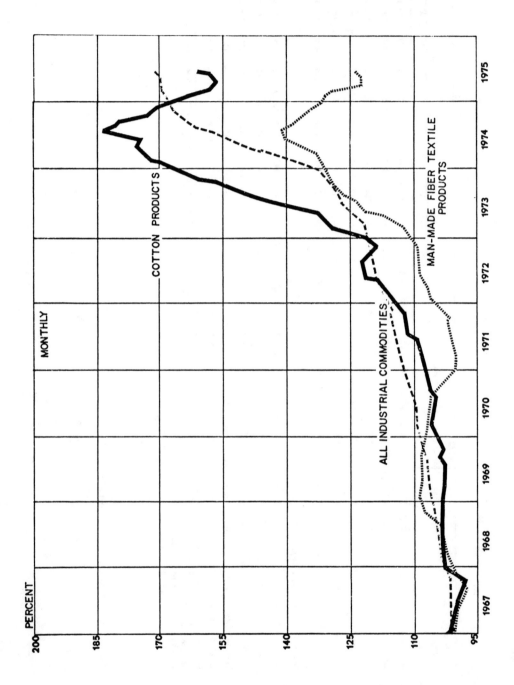

COMMODITY	1968	1969	1970	1971	1972	1973	1974	OCT	1974 NOV	DEC	JAN	FEB	1975 MAR	APR	MAY
INDUSTRIAL COMMODITIES	102.5	106.0	110.0	114.0	117.9	125.9	153.8	164.3	165.8	166.1	167.5	168.4	168.9	169.7	170.3
TEXTILE PRODUCTS & APPAREL	103.7	105.9	107.2	108.6	113.6	123.8	139.1	140.5	139.8	138.4	137.5	136.5	134.3	134.4	135.2
TEXTILE PRODUCTS[1]	104.0	104.6	103.2	103.6	111.6	128.7	147.8	146.8	145.0	142.4	140.2	133.4	134.2	135.2	137.6
COTTON PRODUCTS															
Yarns	104.5	104.5	105.6	110.6	121.8	143.6	175.3	173.4	170.3	165.7	162.0	158.0	156.0	158.1	162.6
Broad Woven Goods	108.1	105.0	100.9	108.2	119.4	145.6	176.2	159.6	154.6	147.1	142.2	136.7	134.5	134.8	139.2
Thread	103.4	103.9	106.1	110.6	122.3	144.3	177.8	178.3	176.0	171.1	167.3	163.3	161.3	163.9	168.6
WOOL PRODUCTS	100.4	101.3	99.4	93.5	99.4	128.2	119.0	112.3	107.3	107.3	103.8	103.8	102.0	103.5	107.0
Yarns	98.9	100.0	100.0	89.8	88.9	105.8	152.6	128.6	129.0	109.4	103.9	103.9	98.5	–	–
Broad Woven Fabrics	100.9	102.5	101.8	99.8	101.6	115.7	114.7	109.0	107.7	107.7	105.4	105.4	106.0	105.3	106.7
MAN-MADE FIBER TEXTILE PRODUCTS	104.9	106.6	103.1	100.3	108.0	121.8	135.8	135.1	134.2	132.3	130.7	129.3	121.7	121.7	123.0
Rayon/Acetate Yarns & Fibers	101.2	101.2	101.9	103.4	108.9	122.2	133.3	145.4	144.8	144.6	143.4	145.0	143.7	144.3	144.7
Noncellulosic Yarns & Fibers	96.0	98.1	97.6	95.7	95.2	97.8	102.1	102.2	101.5	101.1	101.0	98.4	98.5	98.5	97.5
Broad Woven Goods	111.0	115.1	104.3	101.5	116.9	145.5	161.7	154.6	153.4	149.9	146.7	144.7	128.4	128.3	131.6
Knit Goods	99.1	95.2	89.4	92.1	88.4	87.6	114.4	114.4	112.6	105.1	104.7	104.7	98.4	98.1	99.3
APPAREL	103.2	107.2	111.0	112.9	114.8	119.0	129.5	133.1	134.2	133.7	133.8	133.6	133.3	133.0	132.2
Women's, Misses' & Junior's	102.8	106.0	109.0	110.0	111.8	115.4	121.2	123.5	123.8	123.8	123.9	124.0	123.9	123.9	122.4
Men's & Boys'	103.4	108.1	112.5	115.5	117.7	123.2	139.2	144.6	145.7	145.8	145.1	145.4	144.8	144.1	144.0
Infants' & Children's	104.1	108.2	115.5	118.1	119.3	121.7	135.5	137.4	137.4	137.4	136.9	135.9	136.7	137.0	136.3
TEXTILE HOUSE FURNISHINGS	98.1	100.8	103.6	104.2	109.2	113.3	143.1	149.2	149.0	148.4	150.1	150.9	150.9	151.7	151.7
Cotton[2]	105.6	101.2	104.5	105.4	111.2	115.8	150.1	156.5	156.2	155.1	157.1	158.1	158.1	159.0	159.0
Man-Made Fiber or Blends[3]	101.1	103.4	105.4	105.0	106.6	108.6	117.4	123.1	123.1	125.4	125.0	125.0	125.6	125.6	125.6
MISCELLANEOUS TEXTILE PRODUCTS	98.1	104.3	107.0	116.7	125.7	124.7	170.7	172.1	174.5	166.3	167.2	166.1	166.1	155.5	157.1
Jute Woven Goods	97.2	106.5	107.6	124.7	142.0	133.0	181.8	185.5	176.0	160.7	163.8	164.1	162.0	144.3	147.0
Other Misc. Textile Products	98.1	101.0	105.8	108.4	103.7	112.2	153.9	169.3	172.1	172.1	172.1	172.1	172.1	172.1	172.1

¹Excludes hard and bast fibers. ²Sheets, towels, toweling, blanket, bedspread (jacquard weave). ³Blankets. ⁴Burlap; carpet backing fabric.
SOURCE: U. S. Department of Labor.

Figure II-4. Wholesale Price Index (1967 = 100)

Source: U.S. Department of Labor.

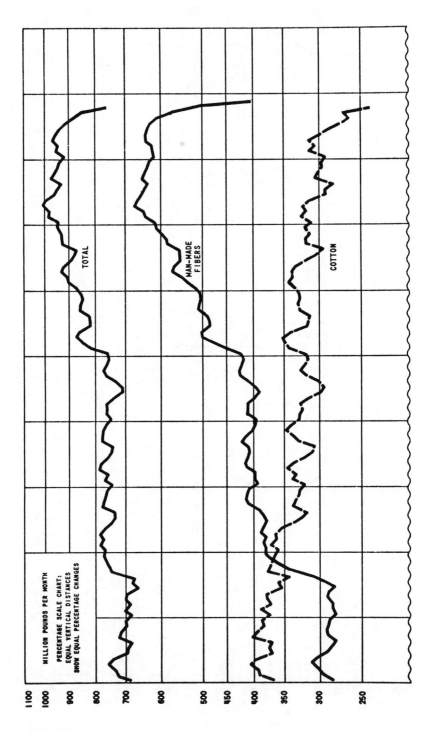

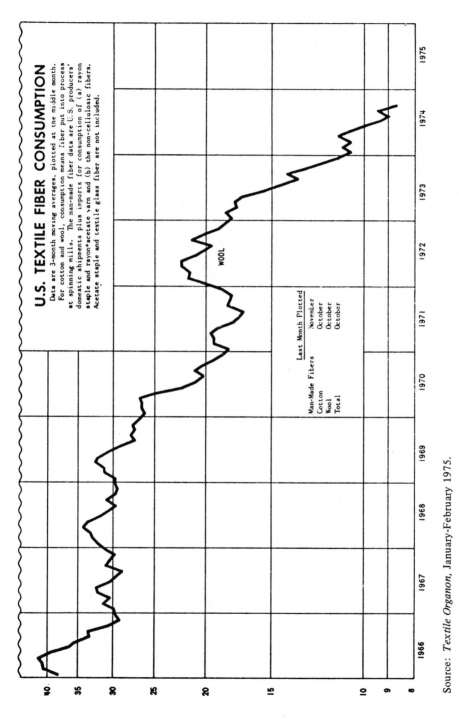

Figure II-5. U.S. Textile Fiber Consumption

Source: *Textile Organon*, January-February 1975.

Table II-7
A Comparison of Cost Structures for Textile Mill Products, 1958 and 1971
(by percentage)

	1971	*1958*
Value of production	100%	100%
Wages to production workers	18	20
Payroll to other employees	5	4
Cost of materials	56	58
Cost of electricity and fuels	2	2
Other costs	19	16

Sources: U.S. Bureau of the Census, *Annual Survey of Manufactures,* 1971, and *Census of Manufactures,* 1958, Washington, D.C.

The Impact of Endogenous Factors on Industry Structure

The textile manufacturing industry can be broken into four parts: (1) raw material preparation; (2) spinning, weaving, knitting, and tufting textile fibers into intermediate and end products; (3) bleaching, dyeing, printing, and finishing intermediate textile products; and (4) cutting and sewing textile goods to produce apparel and other textile end products. Additional topics necessary for an understanding of the structure of the textile industry are: nonwoven fabrics, major textile market segments, merchandising methods for textile products, important service and supply industries for textiles, and finally the integrated textile firm. Figure 4-1 shows the principal structure of the textile industry.

Raw Material Preparation

Raw material preparation for textile manufacture falls into two distinct groups: natural fiber preparation and man-made fiber preparation. The trends in total U.S. textile fiber consumption and in specific types of fibers can be seen in Figure II-5.

The principal natural fibers in use in the United States in the 1960s and early 1970s were cotton and wool. Preparation methods for these two natural fibers differ substantially. Raw cotton is dried to reduce its moisture content to 8 to 10 percent and cleaned to remove dirt, leaves, and bolls. The cotton is then ginned to separate the cotton fibers from the seeds and pressed into 500 pound bales for shipment. All of these operations are normally done in one plant.

Raw wool goes through a different process, called "scouring." After initial removal of large foreign particles, raw wool is scoured to remove the high percentage of natural wax or grease produced by the sheep. After scouring, burrs are removed by a burrpicker, and additional vegetable material by carbonizing. All of these wool operations normally occur at one plant.

These processors of raw wool or raw cotton may be operated either in conjunction with further manufacturing facilities or as independent businesses. They are often located near textile manufacturing plants or sources of raw materials. The independent natural fiber processors compose SIC code 2297. Additional data for independent natural fiber processors is contained in Table 4-1.

Man-made fibers constitute the other major class of fiber raw materials for textile manufacture. Man-made fibers are normally produced by either large

83

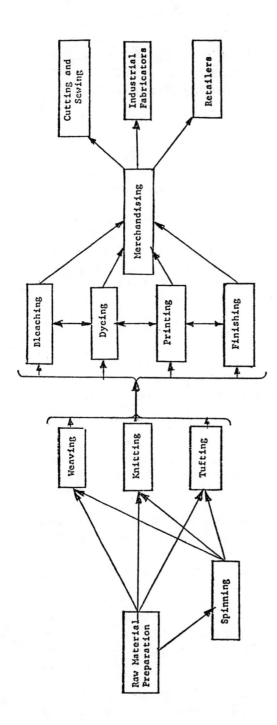

Figure 4-1. Structure of the Textile Industry

Table 4-1

Data for Independent Natural Fiber Processors (SIC 2297), 1967, 1963, and 1958

	1967	1963	1958
Number of companies	65.0	64.0	78.0
Number of establishments	68.0	69.0	81.0
Number of establishments with 20 or more employees	39.0	38.0	46.0
Number of employees (1,000)	5.0	5.8	6.1
Value added by manufacture ($ million)	35.7	45.4	36.1
Value of shipments ($ million)	93.9	119.9	87.6
Percent of establishments corporate owned	78.0	80.0	74.0
Percent of industry shipments by 8 largest companies	75.0	79.0	73.0

Sources: U.S. Bureau of the Census, *Census of Manufactures,* 1958, 1963, and 1967, Washington, D.C.

chemical products companies with wide product lines, small chemical products companies where textile fibers are a principal product, and textile companies themselves. Manufacture of man-made fibers is characterized by relatively large capital investment in single-purpose plant and equipment, significant economies at large production volumes, and relatively high technology. Table 4-2 gives selected data on establishments producing man-made fiber, and Table 4-3 shows man-made fiber production in the period 1960-1974.

Spinning, Weaving, Knitting, and Tufting

Spinning is the process of converting natural or man-made fibers of short lengths into the continuous filaments necessary for further manufacturing processes. Although cotton and woolen spinning mills use distinctly different manufacturing processes, the end-product flexibility of both types of mills has been greatly enhanced by the surge of blended textile products that combine natural and man-made fibers to yield yarns with new and different properties. Table 4-4 contains additional information about spinning mills, such as size, location, and concentration.

Weaving mills produce fabric by interlacing spun or continuous filament yarns so that they cross at right angles. Woven fabrics far exceed the production of all other types of fabrics. Numerical data on weaving mills are presented in Table 4-5. Table 4-6 shows large amounts of raw cotton and other fibers are

Table 4-2
Data for Man-Made Fiber Producers (SIC 2823 and 2824), 1972, 1967, 1963, and 1958

	1972	1967	1963	1958
Number of companies	48	35.0	22.0	19.0
Number of establishments	80	63.0	44.0	40.0
Number of establishments with 20 or more employees	68	55.0	43.0	40.0
Number of employees (1000)	95.3	89.1	71.5	61.3
Value added by manufacture ($ million)	2283.1	1758.6	1333.5	830.0
Value of shipments ($ million)	4229.3	2936.0	2135.0	1411.2
Percent of establishments corporate owned	96.2	96.8	97.7	100.0
Percent of cellulosic fiber shipments by 8 largest cellulosic fiber producing companies	_[a]	99+	100	_[a]
Percent of noncellulosic fiber shipments by 8 largest noncellulosic fiber producing companies	_[a]	94	99	_[a]

Sources: U.S. Bureau of the Census, *Census of Manufactures,* 1972, 1967, 1963, and 1958, Washington, D.C.
[a]Not available.

Table 4-3
Man-Made Production, by Fiber, by Year
(in million pounds)

		Cellulosic Fibers		Noncellulosic Fibers					
Year	Total	Rayon	Acetate	Nylon	Olefin	Acrylic	Polyester	Textile Glass	Other
1961	1995.4	793.2	302.0	475.9	18.9	140.1	77.4	149.3	38.6
1963	2696.7	979.3	369.5	691.5	30.3	209.7	166.6	191.9	57.9
1965	3589.4	1081.8	445.2	939.8	65.6	368.4	305.2	282.3	101.1
1967	4050.2	912.5	475.6	1069.2	118.0	397.7	568.1	308.8	200.3
1969	5605.5	1078.0	498.2	1411.2	202.7	533.0	938.8	501.4	442.2
1971	6151.9	915.1	475.8	1595.3	261.8	545.2	1142.5	468.2	748.0
1973	8354.7	894.6	462.2	2174.7	423.8	742.1	1568.0	688.5	1400.8
1974	8107.3	817.2	381.6	2125.3	463.1	634.0	1517.5	684.2	1484.4

Source: *Textile Organon,* January-February 1974.

consumed by weaving establishments; these data indicate, and field observation confirms, that weaving mills are often backward integrated into yarn spinning. In 1958, over 80 percent of yarn spun on the cotton system (cotton and cotton blends) was produced by establishments for their own use.

Knitting mills produce either knit fabric or knit garments by an interlooping process using one or more pieces of yarn. Table 4-7 clearly shows the rapid rise of both knit fabrics and knit outerwear, in addition to providing general information about knitting mills. Knitting establishments consume insignificant quantities of textile fibers directly as raw materials, which thus indicates that there is essentially no in-house yarn production. In the case of large, integrated textile firms, however, the external yarn shipments may be intracompany shipments from other divisions. Table 4-8 compares the relative importance of knit and woven fabrics shipped in the United States.

In addition to being woven and knitted into fabrics, textile yarns are woven and tufted into floor coverings such as carpets and rugs. Although floor covering mills accounted for only 9 percent of the shipments from all textile mills in 1967, Table 4-9 shows dramatic growth in broadloom carpet shipments between 1960 and 1971, with all of the increases in both dollar value and square yards coming from tufted carpets. Table 4-10 demonstrates the same trend in machinery in place in floor covering mills: Tufting machinery is increasing while weaving looms and other types of carpet and rug machinery are decreasing. Even these statistics do not give the complete picture. Between 1969 and 1970, essentially all the added tufting machines were capable of making carpet 12 feet and more in width; the eliminated machines during this period were for carpet 9 feet and less in width. Thus, the square yard capacity increase in tufted carpets is understated by the change in machinery in place.

Additional data on carpet and rug mills are given in Appendix 4A.

Bleaching, Dyeing, Printing, and Finishing

In 1972 less than 5 percent of the products of weaving operations using cotton, man-made fiber, and silk were made with precolored yarns. The rest emerged in the form called "greige" (pronounced "grey"), a term that is indicative of their often dull grey, unfinished appearance. Except for a small percentage used directly for purposes such as bagging and shoe linings, greige fabric must have its color changed, patterns added, or new physical properties introduced before it is sold to apparel manufacturers or to the public. These desired changes are produced by bleaching, dyeing, printing, and special finishing operations, all of which are performed at textile finishing plants. Finishing operations are performed on knit fabrics and wool fabrics as well, although wool finishing suffered the same decline as the rest of the wool industry in the 1960s and 1970s. (Refer to Figure II-5 for wool consumption data.) This section, therefore,

Table 4-4
Selected Statistics for Classes of Spinning Mills, 1972, 1967, 1963, and 1958

| Year | Companies | Establishments | | All Employees | | Value Added by Mfr. ($ million) | Value of Shipments ($ million) | Percent of Establishments Corporate Owned | Percent of Shipments by 8 Largest Companies |
		Total	With 20 or More Employees	Total (1000)	Payroll ($ million)				
Yarn mills, except wool									
1972	264	424	357	89.6	516.3	867.2	2248.3	97.6	—[a]
1967	256	377	328	74.5	310.5	556.2	1422.5	89.9	31
1963	234	317	284	61.6	208.1	363.2	1067.0	94.0	27
1958	268	356	310	67.8	179.8	292.2	855.4	92.7	—[a]
Throwing and winding mills									
1972	177	212	169	38.0	230.9	477.8	1427.6	95.3	—[a]
1967	159	181	130	18.5	78.6	173.2	568.0	77.3	62
1963	165	180	110	13.6	47.1	93.6	319.3	75.6	59
1958	182	195	119	11.9	37.6	67.6	174.6	79.5	—[a]
Wool yarn mills									
1972	92	98	63	8.3	49.7	92.7	221.4	95.9	—[a]
1967	127	135	107	14.7	66.0	117.9	361.5	86.7	42
1963	136	144	121	17.4	66.5	119.7	422.2	87.5	41
1958	142	150	122	16.0	54.2	91.2	273.6	88.7	—[a]
Thread mills									
1972	61	73	45	11.7	69.2	141.8	345.4	89.0	—[a]
1967	63	75	39	11.4	49.8	98.9	256.6	72.0	81
1963	59	71	36	10.1	37.4	75.8	194.1	84.5	85
1958	70	87	50	11.5	36.5	64.8	178.2	82.6	79

Geographic Patterns in Spinning Mills, 1967 and 1972

Type of Mill	Year	Number of Establishments		
		U.S., Total	Northeast	South
Yarn mills, except wool	1967	377	48	322
	1972	426	61	352
Throwing and winding mills	1967	181	115	63
	1972	212	94	112
Wool yarn mills	1967	135	94	33
	1972	99	55	37
Thread mills	1967	75	47	25
	1972	73	38	29

Sources: U.S. Bureau of the Census, *Census of Manufactures*, 1972, 1967, 1963, and 1958, Washington, D.C.
aNot available.

Table 4-5
Selected Statistics for Classes of Fabric Weaving Mills, 1972, 1967, 1963, and 1958

Year	Companies	Establishments		All Employees		Value Added by Mfr. ($ million)	Value of Shipments ($ million)	Percent of Establishments Corporate Owned	Percent of Shipments by 8 Largest Companies
		Total	With 20 or More Employees	Total (1000)	Payroll ($ million)				
Weaving mills, cotton									
1972		307	227	121.3	745.2	1256.3	2660.6	92.2	—[a]
1967	218	393	331	202.8	938.4	1624.0	3327.7	88.3	48
1963	229	407	350	209.0	771.6	1256.8	3104.1	91.2	46
1958	321	496	395	243.4	724.5	1078.6	2748.6	91.3	40
Weaving mills, synthetics									
1972		412	341	149.7	979.4	1831.6	3856.6	97.3	—[a]
1967	272	396	312	108.6	528.8	921.6	2289.6	84.6	54
1963	277	355	300	88.2	366.0	661.5	1072.3	90.1	48
1958	328	401	310	81.7	276.7	468.6	741.9	89.0	44
Weaving and finishing mills, wool									
1972		198	119	19.4	132.1	239.4	450.1	84.3	—[a]
1967	262	310	217	41.8	216.3	428.6	1090.0	75.8	62
1963	304	361	249	47.4	202.9	386.6	1010.7	82.5	58
1958	411	469	311	56.0	206.1	336.6	929.0	82.5	—[a]
Narrow fabric mills									
1972		376	215	27.1	162.3	289.0	566.2	89.9	—[a]
1967	345	384	220	26.2	121.1	214.4	445.1	71.1	31
1963	350	384	215	23.2	91.9	172.5	349.1	80.2	30
1958	455	488	242	24.6	85.9	142.6	301.5	77.7	26

Geographic Patterns in Weaving Mills, 1967 and 1972

Type of Mill	Year	Number of Establishments		
		U.S., Total	Northeast	South
Weaving mills, cotton	1967	393	78	307
	1972	307	66	223
Weaving mills, synthetics	1967	396	196	190
	1972	412	160	231
Weaving and finishing mills, wool	1967	310	216	52
	1972	198	135	32
Narrow fabric mills	1967	384	258	101
	1972	376	235	111

Sources: U.S. Bureau of the Census, Census of Manufactures, 1972, 1967, 1963, and 1958, Washington, D.C.
aNot available.

Table 4-6

Fibers, Yarn, and Purchased Fabric Consumed by Weaving Mills, 1967 and 1972

Type of Mill	Year	Fibers (million pounds)	Yarn (million pounds)	Purchased Fabric (million linear yards)
Weaving mills, cotton	1967	3379.7	213.9	623.6
	1972	2246.2	235.8	363.1
Weaving mills, synthetics	1967	846.7	617.2	67.0
	1972	1582.1	966.5	279.6
Weaving and finishing mills, wool	1967	252.8	49.7	61.3
	1972	113.3	52.6	7.2
Narrow fabric mills	1967	0	160.1	0
	1972	0	180.2	0

Source: Adapted from U.S. Bureau of the Census, *Census of Manufactures,* 1972, Washington, D.C., by using a conversion factor of 500 pounds per bale of cotton.

concentrates on finishers of woven and knit fabric made of cotton and man-made fibers.

The finishing industry is divided into three groups: commission finishers, converters, and finishing plants that are integrated with other textile manufacturing operations. Commission finishers process cloth belonging to other manufacturers and receive a commission for their services. Converters, on the other hand, buy greige fabric from weaving mills, perform finishing operations, and then market the finished fabric themselves. In the case of finishing plants that are integrated with other textile manufacturing operations of a larger textile company, the plant normally finishes fabric made by its parent company, but in some cases may do contract finishing for outsiders. The methods used by the U.S. Department of Commerce to account for some of these integrated finishers creates a slight bias in the reported census data. If a plant at a given site does only weaving and finishing or only knitting and finishing, it is classed as a weaving or knitting plant, with no mention of the finishing operation. Since these combinations of operations are common, the *Census of Manufactures* data for textile finishers will reflect only those firms where finishing is done at separate plants from other operations and will not be completely representative. Indicative of this bias, 32 percent of the cloth listed as produced by cotton weaving mills was produced in finished, not greige form.

Data on textile finishing mills, which also reflect this bias, are given in Appendix 4B.

Nonwoven Fabric

Nonwoven fabric implies a textile structure produced by bonding and/or interlocking of fibers, accomplished by mechanical, chemical, thermal, or solvent means, or by combinations of these methods. Nonwoven fabric does not include paper or fabrics that are woven, knitted, tufted, or made by felting processes (thus, "nonwoven" is something of a misnomer).

Present uses for nonwoven fabrics include abrasive discs, apparel linings, automotive fabrics, filters, medical supplies, towels, and napkins. Many of these applications are lower-grade items, and many used no textile fibers before the introduction of nonwovens; thus, in the past, nonwoven fabric was no competitive threat to many other textile fabrics. As nonwoven fabric technology improves and relative cost structures change, the market share for nonwoven fabric could significantly increase. Data for production of nonwoven fabrics in the period 1963-1973 is given in Table 4-11.

Merchandising and the Major Textile Market Segments

Merchandising is the textile industry's term meaning wholesale marketing of textile mill products with possible additional processing. Merchandising can be broken into two categories: that for partially manufactured products and that for completed textile products. There are many similarities in the methods used, and sometimes the same agencies are involved in both types of merchandising.

Merchandising partially manufactured goods normally involves either yarn or fabric. Yarn, most of which is an intermediate product to be sold to knitting mills, is merchandised through either direct sales by the textile mill's own sales force, sales to merchants or dealers for sale to ultimate consumers, sales by agents and brokers in major textile marketing centers, or a combination of these methods.

Partially manufactured (i.e., greige) fabric is almost always sold as an intermediate product for further processing, except for the small portion described earlier that is sold to be fabricated in the greige form. Greige fabric for further processing is sold through a variety of methods. It can be sold through agents and brokers (mostly in New York City) to converters, who perform finishing operations on the fabric and then sell it themselves. For industrial purposes, greige fabric is sold either directly to the user or through agents. Greige fabric is also merchandised through wholesalers and jobbers for resale to retailers and others or through the manufacturer's own outlets. Knit fabrics are rarely sold in the greige form.

Completed textile products, such as yarn, piece goods, household furnishings, and apparel are distributed by wholesalers, by the manufacturers' direct sales forces, and by agents and brokers. Wholesalers buy and sell merchandise

Table 4-7
Selected Statistics for Classes of Knitting Mills, 1972, 1967, 1963 and 1958

| Year | Companies | Establishments | | All Employees | | Value Added by Mfr. ($ million) | Value of Shipments ($ million) | Percent of Establishments Corporate Owned | Percent of Shipments by 8 Largest Companies |
		Total	With 20 or More Employees	Total (1000)	Payroll ($ million)				
Women's hosiery, except socks									
1972	256	312	217	49.5	247.4	438.8	984.7	87.8	_b
1967	302	355	257	57.9	230.0	413.0	835.0	75.8	44
1963	363	411	268	51.5	170.9	296.3	606.6	73.2	47
Other hosiery									
1972	375	415	216	32.6	159.7	295.2	600.6	76.9	_b
1967	423	448	290	39.0	136.9	230.7	550.1	65.6	32
1963	504	528	338	43.3	124.1	192.2	451.1	64.4	25
Knit outerwear									
1972	882	917	547	74.4	430.4	799.5	1703.8	86.6	_b
1967	1156	1179	650	73.8	343.5	604.9	1288.0	69.1	22
1963	1175	1185	666	68.6	266.6	463.6	1045.5	73.0	16
1958	1111	1123	633	60.6	204.0	339.9	813.6	70.6	10
Knit underwear									
1972	74	87	74	26.0	134.6	251.5	544.6	88.5	_b
1967	99	113	97	30.7	115.2	201.4	445.3	85.8	54
1963	104	118	104	28.4	95.9	170.7	364.8	89.0	52
1958	133	141	123	29.2	84.8	145.6	310.8	85.0	43
Circular knit									
1972	629	716	430	68.1	492.6	1,036.0	2808.8	96.1	_b

Warp knit								
1972	174	203	155	22.0	159.2	317.8	987.7	97.0	_b
Knit fabric[a]								
1967	489	541	294	36.3	197.5	441.8	1362.2	76.7	24
1963	487	518	243	25.0	117.5	252.9	817.4	84.9	25
1958	336	357	181	18.4	73.9	147.4	487.2	83.8	30
Other knitting mills								
1972	72	73	33	3.9	23.1	41.8	73.1	83.6	_b
1967	61	62	31	3.0	12.7	22.4	38.8	56.5	71
1963	86	88	45	3.6	12.5	20.3	40.7	68.2	50
1958	71	75	38	3.2	9.6	14.5	30.1	72.0	54

Geographical Patterns in Knitting Mills, 1972

	Number of Establishments		
Type of Mill	U.S., Total	Northeast	South
Women's hosiery, except socks	312	62	242
Other hosiery	415	39	370
Knit outerwear	917	703	116
Knit underwear	87	54	29
Knit fabric-circular knit	716	423	259
Knit fabric-warp knit	203	138	61
Other knitting mills	73	44	13

Sources: U.S. Bureau of the Census, *Census of Manufactures*, 1972, 1967, 1963 and 1958, Washington, D.C.

[a]In 1972 reporting, knit fabric was reclassified as warp knit and circular knit.

[b]Not available.

Table 4-8

Comparison of the Value of U.S. Shipments from Weaving and Knitting Mills, 1958-1972

($ million)

	Shipments from	
Year	Weaving Mills	Knitting Mills[a]
1972	7533.4	7703.3
1971	6858.1	6943.4
1970	7076.0	6280.3
1969	7480.2	6194.9
1968	7648.3	5679.7
1967	7152.4	4271.9
1966	6927.3	3643.3
1965	6498.5	3490.7
1964	6120.0	3172.2
1963	6340.2	3048.8
1958	5315.4	_[b]

Sources: U.S. Bureau of the Census, *Census of Manufactures,* 1967 and 1972, Washington, D.C.

[a]Data for 1968-1971 is compiled by using data from U.S. Department of Commerce *Current Business Reports*, Washington, D.C.; for SIC 2257 and 2258 and adjusting to *Census of Manufactures* data.

[b]Not available.

Table 4-9

U.S. Shipments of Broadloom Carpet

(in square yards)

Year	Total	Woven	Tufted
1960	148.2	48.8	99.4
1965	301.9	41.3	260.6
1966	331.3	42.6	288.7
1967	368.6	40.0	328.6
1968	434.6	39.9	394.7
1969	494.7	39.3	455.3
1970	536.4	34.1	502.3
1971	589.8	31.3	558.5
1972	734.9	33.7	701.2

Source: U.S. Bureau of the Census, *Current Industrial Reports,* as quoted in the Carpet and Rug Institute, *Director and Report,* Dalton, Ga., 1973.

Note: *Broadloom* as defined herein includes all woven and knitted carpet and rugs plus tufted roll goods and rugs larger than 4' x 6'.

Casewriter's Note: This broadloom definition accounted for 85.7 percent of all carpet and rugs shipped in the United States in 1971.

Table 4-10
Carpet and Rug Machinery in Place, 1963-1973

Year	Weaving Looms	Tufting Machines	Other[a] Types
1973	1071	2666	1884
1970	1317	2552	1943 (estimated)
1967	1537	2057	2225
1963	2129	2030	2552

Source: U.S. Bureau of the Census, *Census of Manufactures,* 1972, Washington, D.C.
[a]Includes custom carpet tufting machines (420 in 1973), carpet braiding machines (1247 in 1973), carpet knitting machines, and needle punch machines.

Table 4-11
Annual Production of Nonwoven Fabrics

Year	Production (million sq. yds.)
1973	6,479
1972	5,819
1971	4,428

Year	Production (million lbs.)
1970	226
1969	227
1968	199
1967	137
1966	133
1965	129
1963	96

Source: U.S. Department of Commerce, *Current Industrial Reports,* various issues, Washington, D.C.
Casewriter's Note: Between 1970 and 1971, the Department of Commerce changed the method of reporting production from weight to area. Approximate conversion factor based on 1970 data 1 lb. = 19 sq. yds.

that they themselves own. They often buy in large, economical lots, maintain warehouse stocks, and sell to retail outlets through salesmen. They provide credit to customers, delivery and other services, and trade advice. Manufacturers' direct sales forces are often located in major wholesale trade centers; they normally sell large lots of textile goods to major customers. Agents and brokers bring buyers and sellers of textile goods together, for which they receive a fee.

Data on wholesale trade in both partially manufactured and completed textile products are given in Tables 4-12 and 4-13.

As a result of the integration in the textile industry that started in the 1940s (described in more detail later), textile merchandising has undergone some major changes. Since many of the integrative mergers combined fabric forming operations with fabric finishing, there has been less need for merchandisers of intermediate (partially manufactured) textile products. Also many of the large integrated firms have acquired traditional merchandising agencies, thus completing their forward integration through to retail distribution.

In addition to classification by product line and by method of wholesale distribution, the textile market can also be broken down into three major categories of end uses: consumers' goods, industrial goods, and cutters' goods. The same textile product may serve all three market segments at once.

Consumers' goods, which come from manufacturers ready for sale to final consumers, include piece goods, sheets, pillowcases, bedspreads, blankets, tablecloths, napkins, rugs, towels, diapers, hosiery, and knit outerwear and underwear. Industrial goods, most of which are woven fabrics, are sold to businesses outside the textile industry for the manufacture of articles such as sails, tents, bags, upholstery, filters, hoses, tires, rubber footwear, imitation leather, and abrasives. Cutters' goods, which are normally finished fabrics, are sold to firms in the apparel industry for manufacture into clothing and related articles.

Cutting and Sewing

The cutting and sewing, or apparel, industry is the major user of textile mill products. The apparel industry includes establishments that produce clothing and fabricate other products by cutting and sewing purchased textile fabrics and related materials such as leather, plastics, and furs. Establishments in the apparel industry tend to be relatively small, compared to the textile mill products industry; in 1967 the apparel industry had over four times as many plants to produce only about 20 percent more value added. The smaller apparel firms tended to be located near major wholesale and retail trade centers and normally produced higher style garments; the few large apparel plants were usually located in the Southeast and tended to produce low style items, such as work clothes. More data about selected segments of the apparel industry are given in table 4-14.

There are three major types of operations in the apparel industry: manufacturers, jobbers, and contractors. Manufacturers purchase fabric, employ production workers in their own plants to cut and sew garments, and sell the finished products; thus, apparel manufacturers perform all the functions normally associated with manufacturing operations. Apparel jobbers, on the other hand, primarily perform only the entrepreneurial functions of a normal manu-

Table 4-12
Wholesale Trade Textile Mill Products and Apparel, 1967 and 1963

Kind of Business and Type of Operation	Establishments		Sales	
	1967 (number)	1963 (number)	1967 ($ million)	1963 ($ million)
Piece goods (woven fabrics)	3475	3375	9596	7975
Wholesalers	2887	2794	3832	3034
Manufacturers' sales forces	177	191	4082	2634
Agents, brokers	411	390	1682	2307
Men's & Boys' clothing and furnishing	1974		3116	
Wholesalers	1482		1404	
Manufacturers' sales forces	170		1129	
Agents, brokers	322		582	
Women's, children's, infants' clothing	3588	5733	4776	6595
Wholesalers	2610	4260	2212	2753
Manufacturers' sales forces	216	341	1102	1391
Agents, brokers	762	1132	1462	2451

Source: U.S. Bureau of the Census, *Census of Business*, 1967, Washington, D.C.
Casewriter's Note: 1963 data for establishments and sales of men's and boys' clothing and furnishing and women's, children's, and infants' clothing were reported together.

facturing operation, such as buying new materials, designing, and preparing samples, arranging with outside factories (contractors) for the manufacture of their garments from their own materials, and marketing the finished product. A number of jobbers do, however, maintain cutting operations within their own establishments, while other processing (sewing, finishing, and so forth) is done on contract in an outside factory. Apparel contractors employ production workers in their own establishments to process materials owned by others, make products to specifications, and are not involved in the sale of the finished garment. Table 4-15 compares manufacturers, jobbers, and contractors for two segments of the apparel industry.

As indicated earlier, most of the firms in the apparel industry are concentrated near major trade centers. In many segments of the apparel industry, well over 50 percent of the plants are located in three states: New York, New Jersey, and Pennsylvania. Table 4-16 illustrates this trend for two reasonably typical industry segments.

Table 4-13
1967 Wholesale Trade, Textile Mill Products, and Apparel, by Region

Region, Division, and State	Piece Goods		Men's & Boys' Clothing & Furnishings		Women's, Children's, Infants' Clothing	
	Establishments (number)	Sales ($ million)	Establishments (number)	Sales ($ million)	Establishments (number)	Sales ($ million)
U.S., Total	3475	9596	1974	3116	3588	4776
Northeastern states	2593	7745	1026	1695	2207	3381
New England	155	272	106	101	160	204
Middle Atlantic	2438	7472	920	1594	2047	3177
New York state	2217	7222	749	1412	1821	2923
North central states	258	611	324	495	478	470
East north central	188	479	222	345	351	272
West north central	70	132	102	150	127	98
South	319	754	354	561	435	437
South Atlantic	200	513	211	306	253	274
East south central	41	66	59	137	54	55
West south central	78	175	84	118	128	108
West	305	486	270	365	468	488
Mountain	17	8	35	55	26	15
Pacific	288	477	235	310	442	473

Source: U.S. Bureau of the Census, *Census of Business*, 1967, Washington, D.C.

Table 4-14
Apparel and Other Textile Products, Industry Data 1967

Industry Segment	Companies (number)	Establishments		Employees		Value Added by Mfr. ($ million)	Value of Shipments ($ million)
		Total (number)	20 Employees or More (number)	Number	Payroll ($ million)		
Apparel and other textile products, total	24,500	26,393	12,705	1356.7	5582.2	10,064.4	21,326.9
Men's & boys' suits and coats	904	1,003	649	135.9	641.7	1,047.5	1,912.1
Men's & Boys' furnishings	2,224	2,853	1,969	344.5	1212.4	2,181.2	4,738.1
Women's & misses' outerwear	8,978	9,416	5,615	409.2	1755.8	3,182.5	6,534.1
Women's & children's undergarments	1,025	1,213	808	113.5	443.8	867.3	1,780.1
Children's outerwear	1,237	1,334	849	78.5	298.2	537.9	1,127.5
Miscellaneous fabricated textile products	6,857	7,030	1,695	172.7	784.7	1,456.5	3,497.5

Source: U.S. Bureau of the Census, *Census of Manufactures*, 1967, Washington, D.C.

Table 4-15

Comparison of Manufacturers, Jobbers, and Contractors (Independent and Multiplant Company) for Selected Segments of the Apparel Industry, 1967

Item		Total	Manufact.	Jobbers	Indep. Cont.	Mult. C. Cont.
Men's & Boys Suits and Coats						
Establishments, total	(number)	1003.0	399.0	175.0	344.0	85.0
With 1 to 19 employees	(number)	354.0	176.0	100.0	67.0	1.0
With 20 to 99 employees	(number)	328.0	86.0	47.0	175.0	20.0
With 100 or more employees	(number)	321.0	137.0	18.0	102.0	64.0
Employees, average for year	(1000)	135.9	72.4	9.0	30.5	24.0
Payroll	($ million)	641.7	357.0	58.3	126.6	99.8
Cost of materials, etc.	($ million)	862.3	422.0	400.1	23.7	16.5
Value of shipments	($ million)	1912.1	1039.0	547.7	182.9	142.5
Value added by manufacturer	($ million)	1047.5	611.9	147.7	160.4	127.4
Women's & Misses Dresses						
Establishments, total	(number)	5225.0	1870.0	713.0	2642.0	
With 1 to 19 employees	(number)	2127.0	1126.0	411.0	590.0	
With 20 to 99 employees	(number)	2687.0	604.0	268.0	1815.0	
With 100 or more employees	(number)	411.0	140.0	34.0	237.0	
Employees, average for year	(1000)	209.6	64.2	19.3	126.1	
Payroll	($ million)	889.4	282.4	145.4	461.7	
Cost of materials, etc.	($ million)	1507.8	449.2	1012.4	46.1	
Value of shipments	($ million)	3086.3	968.1	1485.7	632.6	
Value added by manufacturer	($ million)	1588.5	522.9	477.0	588.6	

Source: U.S. Bureau of the Census, *Census of Manufactures*, 1967, Washington, D.C.

Table 4-16
Geographical Dispersion of Selected Apparel Industries, 1967

Industry and Geographic Area	Establishments		Employees		Value Added by Mfr. ($ million)	Value of Shipments ($ million)
	Total (number)	20 or More Employees	Number (1000)	Payroll ($ million)		
Men's & boys' suits and coats						
U.S., Total	1003	649	135.9	641.7	1047.5	1912.1
Northeast	668	419	78.0	385.8	611.2	1121.3
North central	116	72	19.7	94.9	164.0	294.4
South	162	129	34.1	141.3	238.8	440.9
West	57	29	4.1	19.7	33.5	55.5
Womens' & misses' dresses						
U.S., Total	5225	3098	209.6	889.4	1558.5	3086.3
Northeast	3755	2346	136.3	603.0	1097.2	2235.3
North central	220	143	16.6	68.3	120.4	214.5
South	547	350	42.0	149.4	230.4	362.1
West	703	259	14.8	68.8	140.5	274.5

Source: U.S. Bureau of the Census, *Census of Manufactures,* 1967, Washington, D.C.

Although the apparel industry is not nearly as concentrated as most of the textile mill products industry, table 4-17 shows a trend toward increasing concentration in the apparel industry as well. Most apparel plants belong to small, single-unit corporations, as indicated by table 4-18. Perhaps because of the needed quick reaction to the apparel market and the difficulties of moving a large organization quickly, there has been relatively little integration in the apparel industry. One exception is United Merchants and Manufacturers, the only firm manufacturing significant quantities of both textiles and apparel. United Merchants and Manufacturers, whose 1973 sales were $847 million, is fully integrated from spinning and weaving through to retailing ready-to-wear apparel via its subsidiary, Robert Hall Clothes, Inc.

Related Industries

There are a number of other industries that are closely linked to the textile industry, either because they supply the essential physical ingredients for textile producers or because they provide necessary services. Included are textile machinery manufacturers, chemical producers, commercial banks and other financial institutions, and dry cleaning establishments.

The textile machinery industry produces such equipment as spinning machines, looms, knitting machines, tufting machines, various finishing

Table 4-17

Percent of Value Accounted for by the Largest Companies in Selected Apparel Industries, 1967 and Earlier Years

		Companies	Value of Shipments		
		Total	Percent Accounted for by		
Industry and Year		(number)	4 Largest Companies	8 Largest Companies	20 Largest Companies
		($ million)			
Men's and boys' suits	1967	904	1912.1	17	27	43
and coats	1963	1031	1526.0	14	23	38
	1958	1275	1260.9	11	19	32
	1954	1255	1140.7	11	18	31
	1947	1761	1412.8	9	15	26
Men's dress shirts	1967	570	1448.2	23	33	50
and nightwear	1963	659	1295.1	22	32	49
	1958	737	942.1	16	26	41
	1954	838	894.0	17	26	40
	1947	922	731.3	19	29	43
Women's & misses'	1967	2058	1776.4	12	15	22
suits and coats	1963	2481	1522.7	8	11	17
	1958	2651	1220.2	3	5	11
	1954	3178	1261.3	3	6	11
Women's & children's	1967	778	1116.8	15	22	37
underwear	1963	978	976.1	11	17	31
	1958	1170	804.9	8	13	24
	1954	1276	770.0	8	13	24
	1947	1467	575.8	6	11	19

Sources: U.S. Bureau of the Census, *Census of Manufactures,* 1967, 1963, 1958, 1954, and 1947, Washington, D.C.

machines, and assorted other textile machinery. Although the textile machinery industry has been the scene of increasing concentration since the early 1960s, growth in the value of U.S.-produced textile machinery shipments averaged less than 4 percent annually between 1964 and 1971. During the same period, imports of textile machinery grew at an average of almost 28 percent annually, with a 41 percent growth rate between 1969 and 1971. More detailed data on the textile machinery industry and its foreign trade status are given in table 4-19.

Another group of crucial suppliers for the textile industry is the chemical producers. Chemical producers supply dyes, bleaches, finishes, coating, plastics, and man-made fibers, among other things. The textile industry typically requires chemical products of high purity and uniform properties.

One of the most important service industries for the textile industry is

Table 4-18

Ownership of Apparel and Other Textile Products Establishments, 1967

Item	Establishments		Employees		Value Added by Mfr. ($ million)	Value of Shipments ($ million)
	Total (number)	20 or More Employees (number)	Number (1000)	Payroll ($ million)		
Apparel and other textile products, total	26393	12705	1356.7	5582.1	10064.4	21326.9
Type of operation:						
Multiunit companies, total	3103	2832	627.0	2517.1	4753.4	10357.9
Corporate ownership or control	3015	2755	616.2	2479.0	4682.7	10223.0
Noncorporate ownership	88	77	10.8	38.1	70.7	134.9
Single unit companies, total	16135	9873	711.1	2986.3	5145.1	10634.5
Corporate ownership or control	12379	8479	626.0	2663.1	4596.7	9664.6
Noncorporate ownership	3756	1374	85.0	323.3	548.4	969.9

Source: U.S. Bureau of the Census, *Census of Manufactures*, 1967, Washington, D.C.

Table 4-19

Value of U.S. Shipments, Exports, Imports, and Apparent Consumption of Textile Machinery, 1964-1971

($ million)

Item	1964	1965	1966	1967	1968	1969	1970	1971
Value of shipments	558.6	664.2	776.5	623.4	592.2	672.0	711.9	728.1
Value of exports	140.3	135.9	156.8	135.7	131.8	141.9	178.5	157.5
Value of imports	59.3	78.0	128.0	131.1	160.9	166.8	220.7	332.8
Apparent consumption	477.6	606.3	747.7	618.8	621.3	696.9	754.1	903.4
Imports as a percent of apparent consumption	12.4	12.9	17.1	21.2	27.2	23.9	29.3	36.8
Exports as a percent of shipments	25.1	20.5	20.2	21.6	22.2	21.1	25.1	21.6

Sources: U.S. Department of Commerce, *Textile Machinery Trends,* 1964-1968; *Annual Survey of Manufactures,* 1969, 1970, 1971; *U.S. Foreign Trade: Exports,* 1969, 1970, 1971; and *U.S. Foreign Trade: Imports,* 1969, 1970, 1971, Washington, D.C.

financial services, especially commercial banking. Financial institutions provide factoring (purchasing accounts receivable for immediate cash), short-term (seasonal) lending, long-term debt financing of plants and equipment, leasing, and management advice.

The dry cleaning industry is also closely allied with the textile and apparel producers. Through extensive contact between industry trade associations, the dry cleaners are kept abreast of new textile products and important aspects of cleaning them.

Appendix 4A:
Selected Data for
Carpet and Rug Mills

Table 4A-1
Textile Finishing Plants, Selected Statistics

	Establishments		All Employees			
Year	Total (number)	With 20 Employees or More	Number (1000)	Payroll ($ million)	Value Added by Manufacture	Value of Shipments
Finishing plants, cotton						
1972	190	114	25.7	176.7	318.6	621.6
1967	216	136	35.7	193.0	313.8	893.9
1963	238	140	42.1	190.5	332.2	869.7
1958	446	174	49.2	189.9	289.1	686.2
Finishing plants, man-made fiber and silk						
1972	255	188	35.2	263.0	503.4	1338.5
1967	233	167	25.7	159.4	271.4	550.2
1963	205	138	19.5	106.0	176.8	323.7
1958	197	132	16.2	74.3	114.8	210.6
Finishing plants, other						
1972	196	125	18.5	122.6	260.0	636.9
1967	192	105	12.3	63.9	124.8	168.0
1963	178	85	9.2	40.4	73.2	206.9
1958	155	79	7.8	28.8	52.0	158.0

Sources: U.S. Bureau of the Census, *Census of Manufactures,* 1972, 1967, 1963, and 1958, Washington, D.C.

Table 4A-2
Geographic Dispersion of Rug and Carpet Mills, 1967 and 1972

		Establishments in		
Type of Mill	Year	U.S., Total	Northeast	South
Woven carpets and rugs	1967	61	24	29
	1972	65	17	33
Tufted carpets and rugs	1967	244	20	178
	1972	381	21	297
Other carpets and rugs	1967	80	39	24
	1972	83	31	38

Sources: U.S. Bureau of the Census, *Census of Manufactures,* 1967 and 1972, Washington, D.C.

Table 4A-3
Carpet and Rug Mills, by Employment Size, 1972 and 1967

Type of Mill	Year	Establishments with Average Employment between								
		1-4	5-9	10-19	20-49	50-99	100-249	250-499	500-999	1000 or More
Woven carpet	1972	26	9	12	1	6	5	2	2	2
and rugs	1967	24	8	5	5	2	8	4	6	1
Tufted carpet	1972	75	28	42	72	42	68	29	17	8
and rugs	1967	49	20	22	35	36	52	12	14	4
Other carpet	1972	33	13	11	12	5	5	4	0	0
and rugs	1967	32	8	8	13	12	4	3	0	0

Sources: U.S. Bureau of the Census, *Census of Manufactures,* 1972 and 1967, Washington, D.C.

Appendix 4B:
Selected Data for
Textile Finishing Mills

Table 4B-1
Selected Statistics for Classes of Finishing Mills, 1972, 1967, 1963, and 1958

Year	Companies	Total	With 20 or More Employees	Total (1000)	Payroll ($ million)	Value Added by Mfr. ($ million)	Value of Shipments ($ million)	Percent of Establishments Corporate Owned	Percent of Shipments by 8 Largest Companies
Finishing plants, cotton									
1972	181	196	115	25.7	177.2	322.1	623.3	92.3	—[a]
1967	202	216	136	35.7	193.0	313.8	893.9	76.4	59
1963	220	238	140	42.1	190.5	332.3	869.7	80.3	59
1958	426	446	174	49.2	189.9	289.1	686.2	80.0	—[a]
Finishing plants, synthetics									
1972	200	259	190	35.5	265.1	527.8	1373.1	96.5	—[a]
1967	212	233	167	25.7	159.4	271.4	550.2	89.7	49
1963	193	205	138	19.5	106.0	176.8	323.7	89.8	44
1958	185	197	132	16.2	74.3	114.8	210.6	91.9	—[a]
Other finishing plants									
1972	189	201	128	18.5	123.6	270.3	637.3	92.5	—[a]
1967	187	192	105	12.3	63.9	124.8	290.9	70.3	44
1963	174	178	85	9.2	40.4	73.2	206.9	79.2	47
1958	149	155	79	7.8	28.8	52.0	158.0	85.2	—[a]

Sources: U.S. Bureau of the Census, *Census of Manufactures*, 1958, 1963, 1967, and 1972, Washington, D.C.
[a]Not available.

Table 4B-2
Concentration and Ownership Trends in Textile Finishing Plants

| | | | Value of Shipments | | |
| | | | | Percent Accounted for | |
Year	Companies (number)	Total ($ million)	4 Largest Companies	8 Largest Companies	Percentage Corporate Owned
Finishing plants, cotton					
1967	202	893.9	42	59	76
1963	220	869.7	45	59	80
Finishing plants, synthetics					
1967	212	550.2	37	49	90
1963	193	323.7	31	44	90
Finishing plants, other					
1967	187	290.9	29	44	70
1963	174	206.9	32	47	79

Sources: U.S. Bureau of the Census, *Census of Manufactures,* 1967 and 1963, Washington, D.C.

Table 4B-3
Regional Dispersion of Finishing Plants

| | Establishments | | 1972 | | | | 1967 | |
	Total (number)	20 or More Employees	Employees Number (1000)	Employees Payroll ($ million)	Value Added by Mfr. ($ million)	Value of Shipments ($ million)	Employees (1000)	Value Added by Mfr. ($ million)
Geographic Area								
Finishing plants, cotton								
U.S., Total	190	114	25.7	176.7	318.6	621.6	35.7	313.8
Northeast	105	56	6.2	50.1	91.5	194.6	7.8	71.4
South	65	52	18.7	122.9	220.2	411.6	27.4	236.6
Finishing plants, man-made fiber and silk								
U.S., Total	255	188	35.2	263.0	503.4	1338.5	25.7	271.4
Northeast	172	130	16.0	135.5	236.8	269.3	2.5+	Not available
North central	6	2	.1	1.0	1.9	3.3	–	–
South	64	52	18.7	123.8	258.1	955.7	10.6	105.6
West	13	4	.3	2.8	6.7	10.2	.5+	Not Available
Finishing plants, other								
U.S., Total	196	125	18.5	122.6	260.0	636.9	12.3	124.8
Northeast	106	62	6.0	43.4	85.9	190.7	2.5+	Not Available
South	75	55	10.0	62.3	140.6	389.6	5.9	55.9

Source: U.S. Bureau of the Census, *Census of Manufactures*, 1972, Washington, D.C.

The Impact of Exogenous Factors on Industry Structure

The Integrated Textile Firm

The U.S. textile industry began as a large number of independent, family-owned mills of small to medium size. Although table 5-1 clearly indicates a trend toward larger, multi-unit operations, table 5-2 shows that there are still many small establishments in operation.

The trend toward merger and integration in the textile industry appears to have been strongly influenced by overall economic conditions—that is, increasing in prosperity and decreasing in depression. Although there have been textile mergers through the history of the industry, the first real wave of mergers occurred during the economic boom that followed World War I. The rate of mergers slowed during the depression beginning in 1921 and surged again through the middle 1920s to a peak in 1929. The deep depression of the early 1930s retarded the merger movement until the early 1940s, when the mergers began again with a somewhat different character. The period 1940-46 marked the beginning of a large series of mergers designed to given the benefits of integration to the companies involved.

There are several factors that greatly influenced the resurgence of textile mergers and the trend toward integration in the early 1940s:

1. Profit margins were kept low by wartime price controls. This had at least two effects. First, the lower prices for textile goods tended to expand demand for them; thus, textile mills were eager to add quickly to their capacity to meet this added demand. Second, the lower profit margins increased the importance of effective cost control over the entire textile manufacturing process; this increased the tendency toward vertical integration.
2. There were generally higher margins on finished textile products. This was a strong incentive for forward integration, particularly among spinning and weaving firms.
3. Many textile executives felt that a full line of textile products was necessary for effective marketing. This promoted horizontal integration.

Textile companies were very aware of these influences on their industry. As a result, vertical integration increased markedly in the period 1940-46. Spinning and weaving firms began to integrate forward by acquiring dyers, finishers,

113

Table 5-1
Selected Data for the Textile Mill Products Industry, 1947-1967

Year	Establishments		All Employees		Value Added by Mfr. ($ million)	Value of Shipments ($ million)
	Total	With 20 or More Employees	Total (1000)	Payroll ($ million)		
1967	7080	4453	929.0	4390.9	8153.2	19815.2
1963	7104	4368	863.2	3385.0	6123.0	15740.5
1958	7675	4617	901.7	2938.1	4851.6	_a
1954	8070	4862	1037.4	3032.5	4748.6	_a
1947	8185	4991	1233.4	2836.2	5340.9	_a

Sources: U.S. Bureau of the Census, *Census of Manufactures*, 1967, 1963, 1958, 1954, and 1947, Washington, D.C.
aNot available.

Table 5-2
Ownership of Textile Mills, 1947-1963

Year	Corporate Owned	Noncorporate Owned			Total Mills
		Individual	Partnership	Other	
1963	5602	1060	398	44	7104
1958	5999	941	726	9	7675
1954	6228	955	886	21	8070
1947	5911	1051	1189	34	8185

Sources: U.S. Bureau of the Census, *Census of Manufactures*, 1963, 1958, 1954, and 1947, Washington, D.C.

selling agents, and converters. At the same time, textile merchandisers, integrated backward by obtaining dyeing, finishing, spinning, and weaving facilities. About half of the cotton spindles that changed hands in this period did so as a result of vertical integration. Horizontal integration also increased between 1940 and 1946. Some of the larger spinning and weaving firms expanded horizontally by acquiring textile companies that specialized in other products. Approximately 18 percent of the textile mergers in this period resulted in horizontal integration. The surge of integrative mergers peaked in 1947 and then slowed through the late 1940s and early 1950s. It started again in 1953 and continued through the rest of the 1950s, except for a minor letup in 1957-58.

As textile companies pursued strategies of horizontal and vertical integration, their size and often their market share increased. By 1958 the fifteen largest textile companies accounted for about a third of both industry sales and industry employment, and 38 firms controlled half of the plant and equipment and all of the major selling agencies. Table 5-3 gives additional data on increasing concentration in selected segments of the textile industry. In spite of this increasing firm size, in 1958 the integrated firms were generally loose consolidations of recently acquired textile mills; this local autonomy was perhaps largely a result of the history of independent, family-owned operations and the fact that many of the former owners stayed on as managers in the acquired firms. In 1958, the Business and Defense Services Administration reported:

... unlike the result in many other industries, in which vertical integration has led to an increasing degree of centralized control, in textiles the managers of each stage of the production process retain a great deal of autonomy, even under single corporate ownership.[1]

As figure 5-1 indicates, the large, integrated textile firms began to capitalize on the benefits gained from integration during the 1950s and 1960s. The increasing concentration indicated by table 5-3 for specific industry segments was occurring as well in the industry as a whole. By 1968, the four largest textile

Table 5-3
Concentration in Selected Segments of the Textile Mill Products Industry

Segment and Year		Companies (number)	Total ($ million)	Value of Shipments Percent Accounted for by	
				4 Largest Companies	8 Largest Companies
Weaving mills, cotton	1967	218	3327.7	30	48
	1963	229	3104.1	30	46
	1958	321	2719.4	25	40
	1954	413	2789.6	18	29
Weaving mills, synthetics	1967	272	2289.6	46	54
	1963	277	1722.4	39	48
	1958	328	1230.7	34	44
	1954	396	1142.6	30	39
Knit outerwear mills	1967	1156	1288.0	15	22
	1963	1175	1045.5	11	16
	1958	1111	744.3	7	10
	1954	1081	544.1	6	10
Knit underwear mills	1967	99	455.3	36	54
	1963	104	364.8	33	52
	1958	133	299.5	28	43
	1954	140	256.3	26	40

Source: U.S. Bureau of the Census, *Census of Manufactures*, 1967, Washington, D.C.

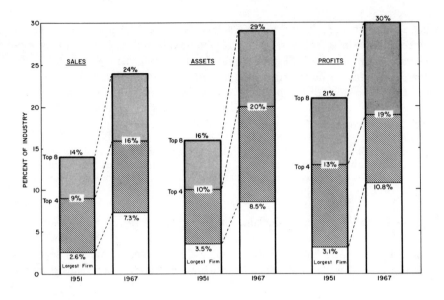

Source: Bureau of Economics, Federal Trade Commission 1968.

Note: Largest firms in each year.

Figure 5-1. Changes in Concentration in the Textile Mill Products Industry, 1951-1967

firms had significantly altered their internal structures and methods of doing business, with a substantial increase in their market share. This trend not only posed serious threats to the future of small, nonintegrated textile mills, but also brought warnings from the Federal Trade Commission:

A continuation of recent trends poses serious problems for the future of competition in the textile industry. Congressional goals of arresting increasing concentration, preserving opportunities for entry, and maintaining the vigor of competition appear to be better served by restraining the unlimited merger activity characteristic of large firms. While the textile industry traditionally has been the center of intense competition and relatively low levels of concentration, there are strong indications that this condition has changed significantly.[2]

During November 1968, the Federal Trade Commission took actions against Burlington Industries that significantly altered the acquisition strategy for the industry. Burlington Industries, clearly the largest integrated textile firm in the United States at that time, had acquired in 1962 Erwin Mills, a major producer of cotton work clothing, sportswear, sheets, and pillowcases. The FTC ruled that Burlington, by acquiring Erwin and several other companies, had eliminated actual or potential competitors. This increased concentration, said the FTC, raised new barriers to entry for future competitors. After some negotiations, Burlington Industries agreed to a Consent Order that they would make no further acquisitions for ten years without prior FTC approval. Later in November 1968, the FTC issued guidelines for textile industry mergers, indicating that mergers falling into any of the following four categories would "raise significant questions of law or policy under Section 7 of the Clayton Act, as amended by the Celler-Kefauver Act" and would invite close examination by the FTC:

1. Any merger between textile mill product firms where the combined sales or assets of the firms exceeds $300 million and the sales or assets of the smaller firm in the merger exceeds $10 million;
2. Any horizontal merger in a textile mill product submarket where (a) the combined firms rank among the top four or (b) have a combined market share of 5 percent or more of any submarket in which the four largest firms account for 35 percent or more of the market;
3. Any vertical merger, either "backward" into the supplying market or "forward" into a purchasing market, where a particular acquisition or a series of acquisitions may involve market shares of 10 percent or more of the relevant market or where the acquisition or series of acquisitions may tend significantly to raise barriers to entry in either market or to disadvantage existing nonintegrated or partially integrated firms in either market by denying them fair access to sources of supply or markets;
4. Any acquisition of a textile mill product firm with sales or assets of $100 million or more and ranking among the four largest producers of a textile mill product by a nontextile mill product firm with sales or assets in excess of $250 million and with a substantial market position in another industry. A substantial market position is defined as being one of the top four sellers of a product or service in which the four largest companies account for 40 percent or more of the market.

It is significant to note that mergers in the four categories are not prohibited; the guidelines do imply that companies contemplating mergers that would fall into one or more categories should seek prior FTC approval. Burlington's reaction to the Consent Order was a changed acquisition strategy. Nontextile acquisitions were made in such fields as furniture, lighting, and decorative accessories; expansion in the U.S. textile market was through internal growth; and overseas operations got new emphasis. In the rest of the industry after November 1968, textile mergers were considered very cautiously, and internal and overseas growth were stressed.

The large, integrated textile firms appear to have certain advantages over the rest of the textile industry. Although some of these advantages are only mixed blessings and although all of them may not be true of a given firm, the advantages of many integrated textile firms are:

1. The have the opportunity to control costs over the entire manufacturing process.
2. They have capable, well-staffed research and development facilities.
3. Due to their research and development capability, they tend to be product and process innovators. New products, with no alternate sources and perhaps with patent protection, can often command higher profit margins than more standardized, widely manufactured products.
4. They have qualified managers, knowledgeable both about textiles and about effective management.
5. They are large enough to tap the major capital markets.
6. They have more staff peysonnel, which increases costs but also partially insulates operating managers from nonoperating problems.
7. Because of their size, they tend to have more market clout than their smaller competitors.

Financial data for several large, integrated textile firms are given in appendix 5A.

Capital Investment and the State of Technology

Compared to most U.S. manufacturing industries, the textile industry is labor intensive, which is typical of the textile industry worldwide. Because of the high cost of U.S. labor, however, the U.S. textile industry is less labor intensive than most foreign textile industries. The U.S. textile industry has an existing low level of fixed assets, and future projections indicate no trend toward improvement. The U.S. Department of Commerce estimated that new capital expenditures per textile employee were $680, while the estimated expenditure per employee in all manufacturing was $1,900.

Not only is there a low level of fixed assets, but also much of the existing textile plants and equipment are obsolete. As reported by the U.S. Senate Committee on Interstate and Foreign Commerce in 1958, more than 75 percent of the textile equipment in use at that time was built before World War II. A similar study of textile machinery in New England in 1959, done by the Federal Reserve Bank of Boston, showed that approximately 20 percent of the equipment then in use was obsolete, that 54 percent should be replaced by 1970, but that only 34 percent would probably be replaced. The same report also showed that 53 percent of the plant floor space was then obsolete, that 77 percent should be replaced by 1970, but that only 24 percent would be replaced.

Two factors, in addition to the nature of textile manufacture, have tended to retard new capital investment in the textile industry. The first is an existing overcapacity in much of the industry; although much of the equipment is old, there is a tendency to avoid buying new equipment when so much is already idle. The second factor retarding capital investment is the instability of the market for textile raw materials and end products. There have been wide fluctuations in the prices for textile fibers; the retail demand for specific textile products can undergo rapid change; and there is vulnerability to imports, particularly among the more standardized products.

Like many other issues in the textile industry, capital investment implies different things for large integrated companies than it does for small, independent operators. The integrated firms normally have on-going capital improvement programs that result in newer facilities based on more modern technology. The integrated mills also have capable research and development staffs to generate internal capital improvements and to evaluate proposed new technologies. For the smaller, nonintegrated firms, there are often no continuing capital improvement programs; major capital expenditures are unusual occurrences. The smaller mills tend to have older, fully depreciated plants and equipment based on technologies that are relatively obsolete. In the decade of the 1960s, about half of all capital investments made in the textile industry were made by the five largest firms.

During the 1960s, there was a significant increase in the rate of capital improvement. This was due, in large part, to a 1961 change in the tax laws affecting the depreciation period for textile machinery. Before 1961, all textile machinery was depreciated over a twenty-five-year period. After 1961, textile companies could write off the cost of most of their machinery in fifteen years, and on some of it in twelve years. Since many small mills had no continuing capital improvement process and since many were already using fully depreciated equipment, the tax law change had much less effect on the smaller mills than on large, integrated producers.

Table 5-4 gives further data on capital investment in the textile industry.

Supply

The textile industry depends very heavily on supplies of certain commodities and other resources, without which it could not function. Among the critical elements that must be supplied to the textile industry are textile fibers, water, textile machinery, chemicals, energy, and labor. These are, of course, tied directly to the technology currently employed.

While U.S. consumption of natural fibers declined through the 1960s and early 1970s, world demand steadily grew. This situation kept world supplies relatively tight, often with wide price fluctuations depending on crop yields. Man-made fiber prices were considerably more stable during the 1960s, but climbed sharply in the 1970s. Much of this rise can be attributed to polyester, which is one of the most popular man-made fibers and which is petroleum-based.

Table 5-4
Annual Capital Investment: Comparison of Textile Mills and All Manufacturing

Year and Item	Textile Mills	All Manufacturing
1967–Capital investment ($ million)	733.1	21,503.0
Per employee ($)	789.0	1,113.0
Percentage of value added	9.0	8.2
Percentage spent on equipment (as opposed to plant)	77.0	73.0
1963–Capital investment	382.4	11,370.0
Per employee	443.0	670.0
Percentage of value added	6.2	5.9
Percentage spent on equipment (as opposed to plant)	82.0	74.0
1958–Capital investment	211.8	9,075.8
Per employee	235.0	590.0
Percentage of value added	4.4	6.4
Percentage spent on equipment (as opposed to plant)	82.0	67.0

Source: U.S. Bureau of the Census, *Census of Manufactures*, 1967, 1963, and 1958, Washington, D.C.

Textile mills require large amounts of fresh water, especially in cleaning and finishing operations. The used water contains relatively large amounts of dyes, finishing chemicals, and cleansers; in 1974, few plants were engaged in recovery of these chemicals for reuse. Water treatment facilities at textile mills in 1973 varied from essentially none at some small mills to extensive systems at many integrated mills. In addition, many textile mills obtained further treatment from nearby municipal water treatment systems. In general, the product mix at a textile mill is not appreciably affected by water use characteristics. Water use data for selected years is given in table 5-5.

The textile industry also needs machinery, chemicals, and various forms of energy to produce textiles. Textile machinery, which was discussed earlier, is being increasingly imported from overseas; (see table 4-19) likewise, much of the research and development in textile machinery is being done outside the United States. From the chemical industry, textile mills obtain dyes, finishes, cleansers, and fibers; these critical raw materials must be of high purity and uniform properties. As an energy consumer, the textile industry does not require disproportionate amounts of energy; however, textile mills, like other manufacturing plants, were hurt by the energy supply shortages and price increases of the early to mid-1970s.

Table 5-5

Water Use in All Manufacturing Industries and in Textile Mill Products

(all water data in billions of gallons)

Industry Group	Year	Fresh Water Intake	Gross Water Used Including Recirculation	Water Discharged Total	Water Discharged Treated Prior to Discharge
All manufacturing industries	1968	12,454	35,701	14,276	4553
	1964	11,177	29,857	13,111	3811
	1959	9,689	26,257	11,445	2666
	1954	9,948	21,042	10,789	1373
Textile mill products	1968	152	328	136	54
	1964	146	269	135	35
	1959	135	182	120	17
	1954	181	211	147	13

Source: U.S. Bureau of the Census, *Census of Manufactures,* 1967, Washington, D.C.

A final critical resource needed for textile manufacture is labor. In 1968, almost 70 percent of all textile workers were employed in the South, due in large part to lower labor costs. While manufacturing employment rose 27 percent between 1947 and 1968, textile employment fell 24 percent. This decrease occurred during a shift from small mills located in the Northeast and South to larger, more efficient, integrated mills in the South. Compared to all manufacturing in 1968, textile factory workers were paid low wages; textile workers were paid $94 per week, while the average manufacturing worker got $30 more. Again compared to all manufacturing, textile workers are not very unionized; 60-65 percent of production workers in most manufacturing industries belong to unions, but in 1966 only 27 percent of textile workers did. There has been a noticeable decline in textile union power as the industry has moved to the South. Additional data on textile workers is given in table 5-6.

Although the textile industry was not hurt as badly as some other industries by resource shortages, textile spokesmen estimated that 1974 industry performance would have been better than the record year in 1973, except for shortages of labor, energy, and fibers.

Demand

Although textile mill profit margins have tended to be about as stable as profits for the rest of manufacturing, they were stable at a consistently lower level, as was shown in figure II-1. Relatively weak markets for textile products in general

Table 5-6

Percentage Distribution by Broad Occupational Group of Workers in All Manufacturing and Textiles, 1968

Occupational Group	Manufacturing	Textiles
Total	100.0	100.0
Professional, technical, and kindred workers	9.6	2.7
Managers, officials, and proprietors	6.2	3.0
Clerical and kindred workers	12.5	8.0
Sales workers	2.4	.9
Craftsmen, foremen, and kindred workers	18.9	12.1
Operatives and kindred workers	43.7	67.3
Service workers	1.5	1.7
Laborers, except farm	5.2	4.2

Source: U.S. Bureau of Labor Statistics, *Bulletin* No. 1635, Washington, D.C.

were indicated by a decline in the percentage of personal consumption expenditures for clothing and accessories from 9.4 percent to 8.6 percent between 1947 and 1968.

Much of the demand for textile mill products is derived from their inclusion in other articles sold to the public. Most of the textile mill products sold in the United States go into apparel, furniture, automobiles, and industrial applications. Although sales of apparel tend to be fairly stable over time, sales of furniture, automobiles, and industrial goods often reflect overall economic conditions, thereby giving a degree of cyclicality to textile producers serving these markets.

During the early 1970s, inventories of textile mill products showed a marked decline, both in absolute level and as a percentage of unfilled orders. During this same period, textile production committed in advance to specific orders rose significantly. These trends reflect both the time lag necessary to increase production and a reluctance to invest in potentially risky inventory. Figure 5-2 illustrates these trends for cotton goods and man-made fiber goods.

Further understanding of textile demand in general, and a comparison of integrated and nonintegrated firms in particular, can be gained from a concept known as the "product life cycle." Sales of successful products often follow similar patterns over time. There is an initial startup period when sales are low, production facilities are being geared up, and marketing efforts emphasize the products' performance characteristics. Following a successful startup phase, there is a period of rapid sales growth, when previous marketing efforts boost demand, competitors emerge, and firms try to maintain and expand their market shares. Greatest profits are often achieved during this period of rapid sales growth. After rapid growth, sales increases slow down as maximum demand is approached. This phase, called "product maturity," is characterized by keen price competition among a larger number of firms and a resulting need for effective cost control.

The large, successful, integrated textile firms tend to concentrate in the startup and rapid growth phases of the product life cycle—that is, by introducing new products spawned by their research and development efforts and producing them until profit margins decline as the product reaches maturity. A few of the integrated textile manufacturers also compete effectively in the product maturity phase, since many integrated manufacturers also have good production cost control.

The smaller, independent textile producers generally do not have the research capability to make major product innovations, so they usually enter the product life cycle during the later stages of rapid sales growth and continue through product maturity. Since their operations are often less efficient, they are at a cost disadvantage compared to the integrated firms, during the portion of the life cycle where production cost is most important. Since transportation costs for textiles are relatively low, small independent textile mills are also threatened by foreign producers; foreign plants in this labor-intensive industry often have significantly lower wage rates.

World Trade in Textiles

In 1971, the entire U.S. balance-of-trade deficit was more than accounted for by the trade deficit in textiles. As was shown in figure II-2, the U.S. imported more textiles than it exported during every year between 1958 and 1973; this occurred after many years of being a net exporter of textiles. This problem in international textile trade can be examined from two perspectives; first, the general conditions that have led to U.S. textile trade deficits and, second, the specific actions of the U.S. government to deal with them.

During the period following World War II, the world textile industry expanded significantly, especially in less industrialized areas such as the Far East. Lacking the capital necessary for many other industries, these underdeveloped countries used their abundant labor resource in the labor-intensive textile industry. Since the lower level of skills required for textile manufacture could be mastered by many local workers and since local wage rates were usually far below the rest of the world, underdeveloped countries were able to manufacture textile products with a much lower labor cost per unit of output. As world textile capacity expanded and competition increased, many previous textile importing countries became first self-sufficient and then net exporters. On the other hand, former textile exporters such as the United States, the United Kingdom, Sweden, France, and Belgium saw export markets shrinking and

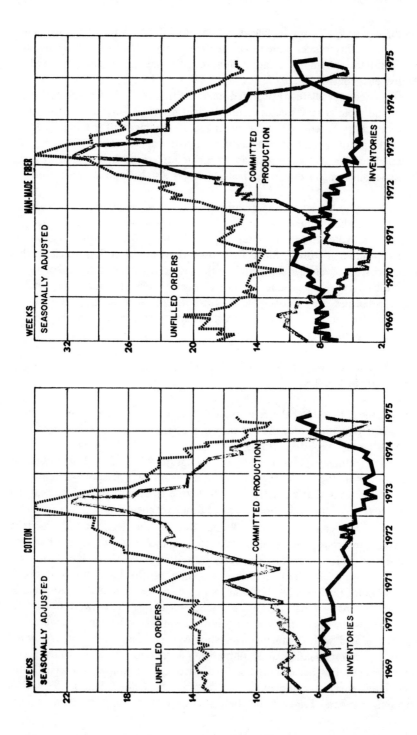

PERIOD	COTTON			PERIOD	MAN-MADE FIBER		
	ORDERS	INVENTORIES	*COMMITTED PRODUCTION		ORDERS	INVENTORIES	*COMMITTED PRODUCTION
1964[1]	12.0	5.0	7.0	1964[1]	21.3	3.6	17.8
1965	19.0	4.2	14.8	1965	18.5	3.0	15.5
1966	21.1	4.0	17.1	1966	16.5	4.9	11.6
1967	14.3	5.0	9.3	1967	15.7	5.3	10.4
1968	12.9	5.3	7.6	1968	18.3	4.9	13.4
1969	13.4	5.4	8.0	1969	17.8	7.9	10.0
1970	13.7	5.4	8.3	1970	14.2	9.3	5.0
1971	15.2	4.9	10.2	1971	16.1	9.0	7.0
1972	19.9	5.1	15.8	1972	22.5	6.6	15.9
1973	20.8	3.1	17.8	1973	30.1	4.6	25.6
1974:	13.8	3.9	9.9	1974:	21.1	6.0	15.1
Apr	16.5	3.1	13.4	Apr	23.1	4.6	18.5
May	14.3	3.1	11.2	May	21.8	4.8	17.0
Jun	14.4	3.1	11.3	Jun	21.4	5.3	16.1
Jul	17.7	4.6	13.1	Jul	24.6	6.7	17.9
Aug	12.0	3.8	8.2	Aug	20.0	6.3	13.7
Sep	11.8	4.0	7.8	Sep	18.3	6.5	11.8
Oct	10.0	4.4	5.5	Oct	16.7	6.9	9.8
Nov	9.9	5.3	4.6	Nov	17.1	8.4	8.7
Dec	11.6	6.9	4.7	Dec	17.8	9.5	8.3
1975:				1975:			
Jan	9.3	6.1	3.2	Jan	15.6	9.5	6.1
Feb	9.1	6.7	2.4	Feb	15.2	9.9	5.3
Mar	11.5	6.9	4.6	Mar	15.9	10.0	5.9
Apr	12.2	6.4	5.8	Apr	16.8	9.0	7.8

*Committed Production is the difference between unfilled orders ratio and the inventories ratio.[1]Table is unadjusted.
SOURCE: American Textile Manufacturers, Inc.

Source: American Textile Manufacturers, Inc.

Figure 5-2. Inventories and Unfilled Orders (in terms of current week's production)

domestic markets being taken by imports. Many of these former net exporters faced potentially massive dislocation as textile activity in small, one-industry towns contracted.

The U.S. government has taken many actions in the past that were intended to ease the plight of the domestic textile industry. In 1962, the United States and eighteen other cotton textile producing nations signed the Long Term Agreement on Cotton Textiles (LTA), a five-year system of quotas on cotton textile products. Under the conditions of the LTA, low labor-cost countries would voluntarily limit their 1962 cotton textiles exports to the United States to the amounts exported in 1961. In 1964-1966, these exports were allowed to rise at 5 percent annually. In the event that these voluntary limits were not observed, the LTA empowered the President of the United States to invoke fixed import quotas against the offending countries.

In 1964 the United States abandoned the two-price system for cotton grown in the United States. Under the abandoned system, the U.S. government fixed the price of domestic cotton at 32 1/2¢ per pound, which was 8 1/2¢ a pound above the world price for raw cotton. The government then paid exporters a subsidy of 8 1/2¢ per pound, thereby allowing them to export at world prices. This enabled foreign textile producers to purchase U.S. cotton at lower prices than U.S. textile producers; consequently, foreign competitors could buy cheap U.S. cotton, manufacture textiles from it abroad in low labor-cost areas, and export them to the United States at prices below those of domestic producers. Under the new system introduced in 1964, the government still set domestic raw cotton prices above world prices (i.e., at 30¢ a pound), but through a system of subsidies to U.S. textile mills, it effectively allowed them to buy U.S. cotton at the world price.

The 1965 Farm Bill altered the cotton price supports again. Under this bill, the support price of domestic raw cotton would be reduced from 30¢ per pound to 21¢ per pound in the first year and to 90 percent of world prices thereafter. The cotton farmers received a subsidy of 9¢ per pound for all cotton sold either domestically or exported. Especially during the first year, this bill was essentially a bookkeeping change, since there was no significant alteration in the effective prices paid by any major purchasers of raw cotton.

During the mid 1960s, a major deficiency (in the eyes of U.S. textile producers) became apparent in the LTA, which covered only cotton textiles. As was shown in figure II-5, cotton consumption in the United States was declining slowly, while consumption of man-made fibers was increasing dramatically. This rise in demand for textile products made from man-made fibers led to increasing pressure from the textile industry for protective agreements covering man-made fibers as well. Negotiations that started seriously in 1969 were successfully concluded in December 1973 in Geneva, Switzerland, with the signing of a comprehensive, long-term, multifiber arrangement (MFA). This multilateral agreement employed a system of quotas by product and by country and created a Surveillance Body to act as mediator in disputes, an important change from the LTA.

In spite of government efforts to stabilize foreign textiles entering the United States, textile imports increased 247 percent between 1963 and 1973.

Notes

1. Business and Defense Services Administration, *Textile Outlook for the Sixties*, p. 18, Washington, D.C., 1960.

2. Federal Trade Commission, *Enforcement Policy with Respect to Mergers in the Textile Mills Products Industry*, Washington, D.C., November 1968, pp. 17-18.

Appendix 5A:
Financial Data for
Large, Integrated
Textile Firms

Table 5A-1

Financial Summary of Eight Major Textile Firms, 1968-1973

Burlington Industries, Inc.
Capital structure as of 3/30/74: Debt, $436.7 million;
preferred stock, none; common stock, 27,262,000 shares

	1968	1969	1970	1971	1972	1973
Earnings per share	3.10	3.01	2.73	1.52	1.86	3.05
Dividends per share	1.25	1.40	1.40	1.40	1.40	1.40
Book value per share	24.29	26.06	27.41	27.63	28.12	29.62
Common shares outstanding (millions)	25.46	26.15	26.34	26.51	26.80	27.26
Avg. P/E ratio	13.6	13.3	13.7	27.9	18.4	10.5
Avg. dividend yield	3.0%	3.5%	3.7%	3.3%	4.1%	4.4%
Sales ($ million)	1619.3	1764.7	1821.5	1727.1	1816.1	2099.8
Operating margin	15.3%	14.5%	13.6%	11.0%	11.3%	13.0%
Net income ($ million)	79.0	78.1	71.4	40.1	49.6	82.4
Net worth ($ million)	618.3	681.3	721.8	732.4	753.5	807.6
Working capital ($ million)	422.2	468.5	500.1	491.4	489.8	586.5
% earned on total capital	10.1%	9.2%	8.1%	5.7%	6.4%	8.8%
% earned on net worth	12.8%	11.5%	9.9%	5.5%	6.6%	10.2%

Dan River, Inc.
Capital structure as of 12/29/73: Debt, $82.2 million;
preferred stock, $6.5 million (292,552 shares);
common stock, 5,589,092 shares

	1968	1969	1970	1971	1972	1973
Earnings per share	1.34	.05	(.24)	(.51)	.65	1.79
Dividends per share	1.20	1.00	.10	0	0	.48
Book value per share	24.17	23.25	22.90	22.42	23.24	24.67
Common shares outstanding (million)	5.62	5.63	5.63	5.63	5.63	5.59
Avg. P/E ratio	17.8	—[a]	—[a]	—[a]	14.8	5.1
Avg. dividend yield	5.0%	5.4%	1.2%	0	0	5.2%

Table 5A-1 (cont.)

Sales ($ million)	285.1	299.6	293.3	312.4	366.6	423.2
Operating margin	9.1%	5.6%	4.5%	4.2%	6.5%	9.1%
Net income ($ million)	7.5	.6	(1.0)	(2.6)	4.0	10.4
Net worth ($ million)	135.8	137.3	135.5	132.7	137.4	144.4
Working capital ($ million)	93.5	97.6	97.3	95.4	111.5	137.1
% earned on total capital	5.6%	2.4%	1.6%	1.1%	3.9%	6.6%
% earned on net worth	5.5%	.4%	—[a]	—[a]	2.9%	7.2%

Mohasco Industries, Inc.
Capital structure as of 12/31/73: Debt, $87.8 million;
preferred stock, none; common stock, 6,350,788 shares

	1968	*1969*	*1970*	*1971*	*1972*	*1973*
Earnings per share	2.05	1.91	1.55	2.07	2.32	2.21
Dividends per share	1.00	1.08	1.10	1.10	1.10	1.18
Book value per share	21.56	22.35	22.66	23.82	24.78	24.73
Common shares outstanding (million)	3.72	4.91	5.12	5.93	6.25	6.35
Avg. P/E ratio	15.9	18.4	15.2	17.2	16.3	9.1
Avg. dividend yield	3.1%	3.1%	4.7%	3.1%	2.9%	5.9%
Sales ($ million)	206.7	312.4	305.9	354.3	431.3	518.0
Operating margin	11.0%	8.4%	8.0%	8.9%	9.0%	9.9%
Net income ($ million)	6.7	9.6	8.0	11.3	14.7	14.2
Net worth ($ million)	85.0	114.1	120.3	145.2	158.6	160.7
Working capital ($ million)	59.0	96.1	96.7	95.6	123.4	134.6
% earned on total capital	7.1%	8.0%	6.6%	7.4%	7.0%	7.6%
% earned on net worth	7.9%	8.4%	6.6%	7.8%	9.3%	8.8%

M. Lowenstein & Sons, Inc.
Capital structure as of 12/31/73: Debt, $118.5 million;
preferred stock, none; common stock, 3,314,092 shares

	1968	*1969*	*1970*	*1971*	*1972*	*1973*
Earnings per share	2.51	2.69	2.58	2.71	2.40	3.10
Dividends per share	.83	.90	.90	.90	.90	.93
Book value per share	37.97	39.73	41.24	42.65	43.56	45.74
Common shares outstanding (million)	3.21	3.22	3.24	3.31	3.31	3.31
Avg. P/E ratio	10.0	9.0	9.4	12.5	10.9	5.6

Table 5A-1 (cont.)

Avg. dividend yield	3.3%	3.7%	3.7%	2.7%	3.5%	5.4%
Sales ($ million)	338.3	376.5	386.6	444.1	470.0	558.5
Operating margin	8.4%	8.5%	8.8%	7.6%	7.1%	7.9%
Net income ($ million)	8.1	8.7	8.3	8.9	7.9	10.3
Net worth ($ million)	121.9	127.8	133.8	141.1	144.2	151.4
Working capital ($ million)	93.9	87.7	84.9	126.5	121.8	164.6
% earned on total capital	6.0%	6.2%	5.8%	6.1%	5.9%	7.1%
% earned on net worth	6.6%	6.8%	6.2%	6.3%	5.5%	6.8%

Springs Mills, Inc.
Capital structure as of 12/29/73: Debt, $106.9 million;
preferred stock, none; common stock, 8,620,311 shares

	1968	*1969*	*1970*	*1971*	*1972*	*1973*
Earnings per share	.22	.82	.72	.98	1.64	2.22
Dividends per share	1.00	1.00	1.00	1.00	.80	.60
Book value per share	29.39	29.18	28.89	28.99	29.75	31.33
Common shares outstanding (million)	8.61	8.62	8.62	8.61	8.60	8.62
Avg. P/E ratio	98.2	22.8	20.3	15.6	9.8	5.9
Avg. dividend yield	4.6%	5.4%	6.9%	6.5%	5.0%	4.6%
Sales ($ million)	253.1	293.3	308.4	325.6	398.9	538.7
Operating margin	5.9%	10.3%	10.4%	11.8%	12.2%	12.3%
Net income ($ million)	1.9	7.1	6.2	8.4	14.2	19.3
Net worth ($ million)	253.0	251.5	249.1	249.6	255.8	270.1
Working capital ($ million)	106.8	116.0	115.9	119.7	127.9	195.0
% earned on total capital	1.3%	3.2%	2.8%	3.6%	5.6%	6.5%
% earned on net worth	.8%	2.8%	2.5%	3.4%	5.6%	7.1%

J.P. Stevens & Co., Inc.
Capital structure as of 11/3/73: Debt, $150.5 million;
preferred stock, none; common stock, 11,634,978 shares

	1968	*1969*	*1970*	*1971*	*1972*	*1973*
Earnings per share	2.52	2.18	.51	(.05)	1.04	2.62
Dividends per share	1.13	1.20	1.20	.98	.75	.81
Book value per share	30.27	31.28	30.62	29.69	29.62	32.09
Common shares outstanding (million)	12.14	12.30	12.27	12.24	12.13	11.64

Table 5A-1 (cont.)

Avg. P/E ratio	9.3	1.2	34.3	—[a]	13.3	5.7
Avg. dividend yield	4.8%	4.5%	6.9%	6.4%	5.5%	5.4%
Sales ($ million)	963.2	1003.0	892.6	861.1	957.7	114.0
Operating margin	10.5%	9.7%	6.0%	4.5%	6.4%	9.2%
Net income ($ million)	30.4	26.6	6.3	(.6)	12.6	30.9
Net worth ($ million)	367.5	384.9	375.7	363.5	359.4	373.4
Working capital ($ million)	326.4	336.3	324.5	302.5	327.3	319.0
% earned on total capital	7.3%	6.4%	2.7%	1.3%	4.0%	7.6%
% earned on net worth	8.3%	6.9%	1.7%	—[a]	3.5%	8.3%

United Merchants and Manufacturers, Inc.
Capital structure as of 6/30/73: Debt, $208.2 million;
preferred stock, none; common stock, 5,968,849 shares

	1968	1969	1970	1971	1972	1973
Earnings per share	4.41	3.92	2.81	2.71	2.50	3.31
Dividends per share	1.20	1.23	1.30	1.30	1.30	1.30
Book value per share	35.92	38.25	39.37	40.38	40.98	43.84
Common shares outstanding (million)	5.93	6.09	6.05	6.09	6.13	5.97
Avg. P/E ratio	7.3	8.9	9.6	9.7	11.0	6.5
Avg. dividend yield	3.7%	3.5%	4.8%	4.9%	4.7%	6.1%
Sales ($ million)	652.0	694.8	708.2	738.4	787.0	847.4
Operating margin	6.7%	6.3%	4.1%	3.8%	2.9%	3.7%
Net income ($ million)	21.0	23.8	17.1	16.4	15.3	20.1
Net worth ($ million)	213.1	232.9	238.2	246.1	251.2	263.0
Working capital ($ million)	207.8	166.3	271.4	321.4	321.7	327.2
% earned on total capital	8.2%	8.5%	6.6%	6.3%	6.5%	7.3%
% earned on net worth	9.9%	10.2%	7.2%	6.7%	6.1%	7.6%

WestPoint-Pepperell, Inc.
Capital structure as of 8/25/73: Debt, $46.4 million;
preferred stock, none; common stock, 4,752,000 shares

	1968	1969	1970	1971	1972	1973
Earnings per share	3.11	2.55	1.82	1.31	2.15	3.75
Dividends per share	2.25	2.00	1.40	1.00	1.00	1.80
Book value per share	38.83	39.37	39.79	40.11	41.38	43.33
Common shares outstanding (million)	4.75	4.75	4.75	4.75	4.75	4.75

Table 5A-1 (cont.)

Avg. P/E ratio	14.7	16.5	12.3	18.3	10.8	6.6
Avg. dividend yield	4.9%	4.8%	6.3%	4.2%	4.3%	4.5%
Sales ($ million)	347.1	372.2	373.9	355.2	408.2	481.7
Operating margin	12.1%	10.9%	9.0%	7.6%	7.9%	9.7%
Net income ($ million)	14.8	12.1	8.7	6.2	10.2	17.8
Net worth ($ million)	184.4	187.0	189.0	190.5	196.6	205.9
Working capital ($ million)	97.5	97.1	101.1	124.5	144.1	152.4
% earned on total capital	8.0%	6.5%	4.6%	3.1%	5.3%	8.5%
% earned on net worth	8.0%	6.5%	4.6%	3.3%	5.2%	8.7%

[a]No meaningful figure.

Part III:
Case Studies

6   **Seneca Mills, Inc.**

In early February 1973, Mr. Daniel Thomas was elected president and treasurer of Seneca Mills, Inc. He replaced Mr. Paul Hamilton, who had been president for over twenty-five years. Mr. Hamilton became chairman of the board of directors and planned to restrict his activities to presiding at meetings and handling two important sales accounts. In the four years prior to 1973, Seneca Mills, a small South Carolina company engaged in the spinning and weaving of fine cotton textiles, had experienced four straight years of operating losses. By February 1973 the situation had deteriorated further. Operating losses for the first six months of the year was expected to be $150,000. Mr. Thomas felt that the company's recent history of losses were the result of changes in the market for woven textiles:

The losses over the past four years have resulted from an erosion of the market for woven fabrics due primarily to the growth of double knits. The resulting overcapacity in weaving has serious cut margins. Now we're facing a decline in demand for all textile products which will further cut margins.

In order to reduce the operating losses, Mr. Thomas felt it would be necessary to reduce working capital requirements, eliminate products that could not produce a profit, retire the less efficient machinery, and concentrate sales activities on a smaller number of customers and products. Three proposals were presently under consideration: increase from a two shift to a three shift operation and use only 50 percent to 60 percent of the 35,000 spindle capacity and 282 of the 705 looms in place; reduce the product line to 30 fabrics and 20 yarns from the current 70 fabrics and 47 yarns; and reduce the workforce from 275 to 130 employees.

Company Background

Seneca Mills, Inc., was a small South Carolina company engaged in the spinning and weaving of fine cotton textiles from blends of cotton and polyester synthetic fibers. The company was founded in 1870 by a group of investors from Atlanta, Georgia. The mill was constructed in Seneca, South Carolina, to produce medium fine cotton grey goods. In the mid 1930s the product line shifted to specialty products and high quality fine cotton goods, and a New

York City sales office was established which engaged in converting operation, selling Seneca cloth in the finished state as well as contracting for grey goods sales. In 1941 the company converted to defense production, manufacturing goods exclusively for the military and a few select civilian accounts.

In 1946 Mr. Paul Hamilton became president. During the next two years both the physical plant and capital structure of the corporation were reorganized. More than $500,000 was invested to improve machinery and operating conditions.

In converting to peacetime activities the management decided to concentrate on the development of specialized fabrics made of worsted, rayon-worsted blends, and fine combed cotton. From 1946 to 1949 most of the Seneca company's sales were in fabrics woven of rayon-wool or cotton-wool blends. These cloths were sold finished to the cutting-up trade by a New York commission agent. The remainder of the mill's volume was cotton grey goods which were sold direct from the mill to converters and cutters-up by a Seneca salesman.

In 1949, the devaluation of the pound sterling permitted the importation of English Viyella cloth at prices below competitive domestic fabrics woven of cotton-wool blends. Problems concerning the company's manufacturing and sales personnel further complicated the situation, and in March 1949 a drop in orders caused the management to shut down the Seneca mill in order to reduce inventory. Intermittent shut downs and losses on liquidation of inventories of rayon-wool blends caused an operating loss of $750,000 in 1949. Cotton sales showed a profit for the year.

By the end of 1949, the mill's sales volume was entirely in cotton grey goods. At that time another New York commission house was taken on to handle cotton sales, in place of the mill's salaried salesman. Operating losses continued until June 1950, when the Korean hostilities brought a sudden improvement in the entire textile industry. As a result, Seneca's profits for July through December 1950 exceeded $115,000.

Government contracts furnished a large share of the mill's sales volume from 1950 to 1953. When the order mix continued to be 60 percent for defense purposes in 1953, however, the relation with the commission agent was terminated and the management reestablished a New York sales office which took over all sales of cotton grey goods in the summer of 1953.

In 1953, a new yarn development, a blend of polyester synthetic fiber and cotton, was brought to the stage where volume production could be achieved. Seneca was the first mill to blend polyester and cotton fibers successfully. To handle sales and merchandising of cloth woven from polyester-cotton blends, the Seneca company contracted with another New York commission house which was to sell the finished cloth to cutters-up for fine shirtings and dress goods.

The polyester blend cotton fabrics proved to be a long-term lucrative market for Seneca, and during most of Mr. Hamilton's tenure as president, the company proved fairly profitable. During the latter part of the 1960s double knit fabrics emerged as a major competition for the apparel market and in 1968 began to seriously effect the woven fabric market share. Operations in 1968 proved marginally profitable and in 1970 showed a loss of nearly $400,000 on sales of slightly over $2 1/2 million. Balance sheet and income statement data for the previous eight years is shown in tables 6-1 and 6-2.

In August 1969, when the aftermath of a hurricane created flooding, everything on the first floor of the mill, including 40 percent of the spindle capacity and most of the power facilities, were destroyed. Facilities lost had a replacement value of nearly $1 1/2 million, and out-of-pocket cost to place the mill in operation totaled nearly $250,000. By 1973 expenditures to repair the

Table 6-1
Comparative Balance Sheets, 1965 to 1972, December 31
(all figures in thousands)

	1965	1966	1967	1968	1969	1970	1971	1972
Assets								
Current assets								
Cash	$ 262	$ 64	$ 78	$ 27	$ 8	$ 6	$ 12	$ 4
Government bonds	15	8	14	3	1	–	–	–
Accounts receivable	276	72	172	280	109	23	29	11
Inventories	652	1,567	1,604	1,502	822	740	912	710
Other	109	114	110	98	90	115	98	104
Total current assets	$1,314	$1,827	$1,978	$1,910	$1,030	$ 884	$1,051	$ 829
Fixed assets–net	$ 538	$ 656	$ 621	$ 694	$ 725	$ 681	$ 662	$ 706
Total assets	$1,852	$2,483	$2,599	$2,604	$1,755	$1,565	$1,713	$1,535
Liabilities								
Secured notes-bank	–	$ 412	$ 194	$ 283	$ –	$ 74	$ 78	$ 76
Due factor (secured)	–	–	148	219	23	55	185	197
Accounts payable	84	132	190	173	144	115	163	160
Miscellaneous	129	123	124	137	143	96	228	165
Total current liabilities	$ 213	$ 668	$ 656	$ 812	$ 310	$ 340	$ 654	$ 598
Mortgage	$ 103	$ 80	$ 48	–	$ –	$ 166	$ 291	$ 332
Preferred stock–6%[a]	$ 669	$ 669	$ 669	$ 669	$ 669	$ 669	$ 669	$ 669
Common stock	11	11	11	11	11	11	11	11
Capital surplus	334	334	334	334	334	334	334	334
Earned surplus	522	721	881	778	431	45	(246)	(409)
Total capital	$1,536	$1,735	$1,895	$1,792	$1,445	$1,059	$ 768	$ 605
Total liabilities	$1,852	$2,483	$2,599	$2,604	$1,755	$1,565	$1,713	$1,535

[a]Cumulative only if earned.

Table 6-2

Comparative Income Statements, 1965 to 1972, Year Ending December 31

(all figures in thousands)

Sales	$3,742	$3,755	$4,139	$3,861	$4,449	$2,504	$3,644	$4,284
Profit (loss) before taxes	785	382	304	6	(275)	(395)	(158)	(177)
Taxes	309	132	95	2	–	–	–	–

manufacturing operations, coupled with accumulated losses from operations of nearly $1 million led to Mr. Thomas' appointment as President.

Mr. Thomas had been with the company since 1965 and represented the fourth generation of his family to be associated with the mill. Seneca Mills' common stock was closely held but occasionally traded over-the-counter. The Hamilton and Thomas families controlled about 75 percent of the common shares.

Marketing

In relating the mill's recent history, Mr. Thomas commented that a major problem was that there had been no continuity of merchandising since before World War II. During 1973 he hoped to effect a reorientation of the Seneca company's merchandising and distribution policies that would lead the way for a reorganization of manufacturing activities and a subsequent return to profitable operations. "As a matter of corporate policy," he added, "a major change in mill balance must originate in sales."

During the postwar years the mill had sold cotton cloth only in the grey, with the exception of goods for the U.S. government and one important civilian customer. Rayon-wool blends, however, had been sold as finished cloth, and this pattern was adopted for polyester-cotton blends in 1953. At the end of 1972 the Seneca management decided to terminate their converting activities and offer only grey goods for sale. It was felt that equivalent profits could be realized while reducing financial requirements by eliminating the month's inventory-in-process at the contract bleachery. Since the agent for polyester-cotton sales had contacts primarily among cutters-up, the Seneca company terminated its relationship with the commission house in December 1972 and began to offer cotton-polyester greige to the converting trade through its New York sales office.

Seneca was a "sheer goods" mill, spinning fine yarns of polyester staple and combed, long-staple cotton and weaving them into high quality cloth for dress goods, shirtings, and light-weight commercial cloths. Average yarn count was 68's, and a high proportion of imported Egyptian cotton was employed. All production was on a job-order basis, thus no finished goods inventory was produced.

Seneca's principal customers were converters selling to the dress goods and shirting trade. The most common cloth constructions sold were voiles, crepes, batistes, broadcloths, oxfords, and fancies for shirts, blouses, and dresses. Consumer demand for these fabrics was highest in spring and summer, therefore mill activity hit its peak in fall and winter. Because Seneca produced "high-end" fabrics, its cloth was used in shirts priced at retail about $8.25 and dresses retailing above $27.50. Two customers that had been served steadily since before the war were both well-known producers of high quality men's shirts. Seneca tried to avoid the competitive markets for "commodity" fabrics such as print cloths and duck. Instead the company concentrated on fine specialities.

A limited number of mills were equipped to compete with Seneca in its field. Large mills found it uneconomical to compete for orders as small as 50,000 yards, and most mills could not readily spin fine yarns. The principal competition came from small weaving mills without yarn facilities and one or two mills similar in size to Seneca's. Although there were a number of companies that competed with Seneca in one way or another, there would be only one or two other mills in direct competition for any given fabric. However, despite the company's apparent separation from the major part of the industry, Seneca's business seemed to be affected by the basic trends in the industry. The effects of a basic change in the market for textiles would be reflected in fluctuations in price and demand for something like 80-square print-cloth, a very competitive item produced in large volume at low cost. The same basic market condition would also be reflected in the demand and therefore the price for high-end goods such as those produced by Seneca.

The textile industry was undergoing a number of changes and the economic outlook was uncertain. Industry production of cotton broad woven goods during 1972 was slightly above 1971. The rate of output prevailing at the end of 1972 was expected to continue until late 1973. Prices were depressed despite industry-wide wage increases at the end of the year.

The company's selling office in Manhattan employed three salesmen, a stylist, and a secretary. Mr. Thomas supervised the operation, spending two days each week in New York. Considerable effort was devoted to the creative aspects of selling, such as originating designs for a customer, translating indefinite customer desires into fabric design and color, or modifying customer designs to permit more economical production. The salesmen worked on a salary and together served approximately fifty customers. Mr. Thomas tried to participate in sales activities at the opening and closing of negotiations with a customer and also helped handle most crisis situations. The stylist participated in any work that involved questions of style or color, usually about 30 percent of the volume handled. Many fabrics developed by the sales office were "confined" patterns offered only to one customer who was given exclusive access to it. Close liaison with mill production officials was required to establish approximate production cost and forecast delivery dates on any order.

The competitive strength of the Seneca company lay in its long history and established reputation as a quality producer of fine goods, plus its continuing ability to produce quality items in small lots at a competitive price. The company's personnel pioneered development of blends of rayon and wool and of polyester and cotton, enabling Seneca to gain a leading position at the introduction of these new items. The management and facilities of the mill were geared to service orders involving low yardages but intricate constructions and high quality. Mr. Thomas felt that inspection of cloth at the Seneca mill was far more careful than typical industry practice.

The company had also developed a reputation as a reliable producer of fabrics that were difficult to weave, in some cases turning out fabrics that could not have been produced at any other mill. By careful production to establish a quality product and careful inspection to maintain that quality, the management continually tried to enhance its reputation in the field.

Manufacturing

Mr. Joseph Chandler, vice-president and mill superintendent, had had more than thirty years of experience in the textile business. Starting as a card room hand in 1942, he had become spinning room second hand by 1949, a yarn mill superintendent in 1961, and superintendent of a combined yarn and weaving mill in 1963. He joined Seneca Mills in June 1965. In addition to extensive work experience in industry, he held a Bachelor's degree in Chemical Engineering, a Bachelor of Law degree, and had studied a correspondence course in textiles. Mr. Chandler remained active in developing new products and processes for textiles; during the 1930s he helped develop a novelty spinning frame; and currently at Seneca he was perfecting a process which he had developed for the improvement of the slashing operations through application of ultrasonic waves.

Mr. Chandler emphasized the importance of correct mill balance for profitable operations. As an example he recalled the operations at a mill where he had worked until joining Seneca. By properly balancing the process flow in the mill, profits were increased rapidly from $200,000 to more than $1 million. He explained that once the balance had been achieved, it was maintained by accepting orders for only those fabrics that would be appropriate to the balanced flow.

There were five important mill departments: Carding, Spinning, Weaving Cloth Inspection, and Mill Maintenance. Each of these departments was headed by an overseer who reported to Mr. Chandler. In addition, a small crew of workers maintained the outside facilities such as mill buildings, land, and other property. These outside costs were segregated from mill costs for accounting purposes. A process flow chart for the carding and spinning operations is given in figure 6-1. Most of the spinning and weaving equipment was over twenty-five

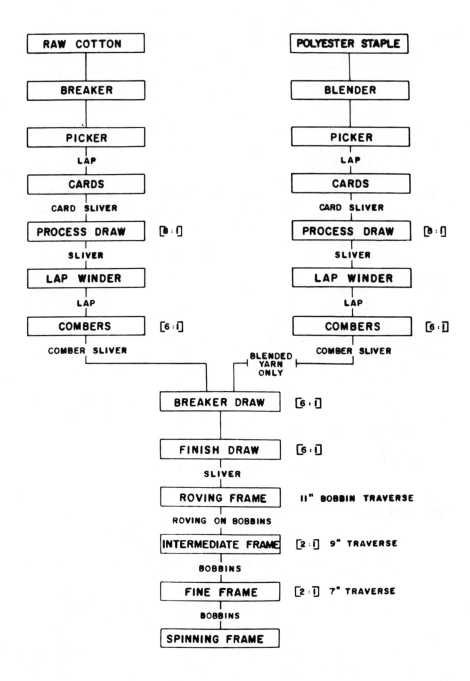

Figure 6-1. Process Flow Chart for Yarn Production

years old which was typical for small weaving firms. The Carding and Spinning Departments together comprised the "yarn mill."

The Carding Department occupied approximately 39,000 square feet of floor space. Breakers were located in the cotton storeroom, and fibers were blown through pipes into the main mill building where the pickers were located. The breakers and pickers were operated only one shift daily, all 64 cards were run three shifts, while the remaining equipment in the department was operated on a two shift basis. Subsequent equipment included 138 drawing heads, 2 lap winders, and 10 combers. The polyester fiber was received in staple form and processed in a manner similar to cotton, although the rates of output were different. One of the four pickers was used solely for polyester staple which was ten carded, drawn, and combed. At the breaker drawing frame after combing, the polyester comber slivers were blended with cotton slivers (usually to result in a blend containing 65 percent polyester and 35 percent cotton. Costs and comparative rates of output per 40-hour machine-week are shown in table 6-3.

The 35,376 spindles in the Spinning Department occupied about 41,000 square feet of space. Additional equipment for winding, twisting, warping, and spooling occupied about 22,000 square feet, and the three slashers occupied another 8,000 square feet. The spinning frames were generally run on a three-shift basis; the other equipment operated one or two shifts, depending upon the mix of products. Only 15,000 spinning spindles were long draft; the remaining 20,000 were regular draft. The yarn mill was felt to be a relatively high-cost operation.

The Weaving Department had 705 looms in place, occupying a total of 62,000 square feet in several areas of the building types and numbers of looms were as follows:

Loom	Number
Draper X-2	555
Box loom	80
Wide Draper	70

All the Draper looms were "plain looms"—that is, only one color; usually natural could be used for the fill yarn. The box looms, however, could handle as many as four different fill yarns and were used for "fancy" constructions such as checks, ginghams, and so forth. Because of this, they cost six to ten cents more per yard to operate. Most of the Draper Model X-2 looms wove 40- or 42-inch cloth. The wide Drapers were looms which had been modified to produce 68-inch and 70-inch cloth, but were otherwise similar to the other Draper models. Forty-two of the Draper X-2's produced 50-inch cloth. After weaving, the cloth was taken to the Cloth Inspection Room, occupying 11,000 square feet of space, where it was carefully inspected, packed, and shipped to the customer.

Table 6-3
Carding Department Costs and Output Rate
(all data for one machine operated forty hours)

		Output in Pounds per Machine for		Cost/Machine		
	Number	Domestic Cotton	Imported Long-Staple Cotton	Polyester	Labor	Overhead
Pickers	4	14,070	11,770	12,235	$79.07	$76.78
Cards	64	300-750	189	292	6.78	6.36
Lap winders	2	11,800	9,520	8,710	22.28	13.52
Combers	10	1,785	1,621	1,960	26.90	15.04

Initial delivery on any cloth order would not come until two or three months after final confirmation of the order. Yarn production and preparation of the loom beams would take eight to ten weeks. If a color was required, two weeks had to be added for yarn dyeing, which was done by an outside firm on contract. A 40-inch loom beam might weigh over 300 pounds and might hold yarn for 2,600 yards of a weave such as 96 x 100 batiste[a] or 1,200 yards for a 102 x 48 poplin. Although all the warp yarn had to be on the beam before any weaving could begin, the fill yarn was usually produced in quantities to match weekly weave requirements. Most orders were delivered 10 percent weekly and thus ran out after ten weeks of weaving. The average loom speed was 186 picks. Loom output depended upon the cloth construction, loom speed, and loom efficiency rate.

The company's production workers were members of an international textile workers' union. The population of Seneca was only a few thousand persons, and the mill was the principal source of employment. In the spring of 1973, however, a large corporation was scheduled to begin manufacturing in a new plant in Seneca which would reportedly employ 200 workers.

All the factory accounting was based on a system of standard costs. Each year, on the basis of machine loadings scheduled and forecast for the next twelve months, the controller prepared budgets for equipment, labor, and overhead. Overhead was split into fixed and variable portions, with fixed costs distributed to mill departments on the basis of plant area occupied, while variable overhead costs were allocated in proportion to direct labor. In 1972 about 60 percent of mill overhead was considered variable. Within each department, labor and overhead costs were apportioned to each machine, with separate rates for labor and overhead expressed in dollars per 40-hour machine-week.

To develop the standard cost for any cloth, the accounting group utilized

---

[a]A batiste was a plain weave of fine yarns of which 96 x 100 would be a typical construction.

the established machine cost rates and technical data on productivity. The yarn manufacturing cost was calculated first, using output rates for the type of fiber to be spun and costs for the machines required. Once the manufacturing cost per pound of yarn had been calculated this way, it was converted to cost per woven yard, based on the yarn weight and cloth construction. Standard labor and overhead costs for slashing, warp drawing, and weaving were then added. Standard weave cost per yard of cloth included a direct charge for the weaver and battery hand based on the actual rates paid those workers, the number of looms they could tend, and the output per loom for the cloth. The weaving overhead expense included a charge for overhead allocated to the department, plus department labor other than weavers and battery hands (such as fixers, changers, and cleaners).

Total manufacturing cost included yarn manufacturing, slashing, drawing-in, and weaving costs, plus the purchase cost of cotton or polyester, dyeing expense, and an allowance for loss on seconds. Purchase cost of fibers ranged from about 40 cents per pound for domestic cotton to approximately 75 cents for imported long-staple cotton, and $1.75 for polyester staple. However, prices for both cotton and polyester were felt to be entering a period of high instability. There was an average loss of 20 percent in yarn production. Mr. Chandler stated that a common "rule of thumb" in most cotton mills was that the cost of an average fabric was one-third for fiber, one-third labor, and one-third overhead.

Each week the standard cost of the week's output was computed and compared with actual expenditures. For each cloth the actual selling price per yard, less the standard cost per yard, multiplied by the yardage delivered, would indicate the standard profit or loss on sales. Each week the total standard profit or loss on sales and the variances between actual and standard labor and overhead costs were reported to the top management. The standard profit was calculated before deductions for interest and selling expenses. Three other important operating figures were reported weekly: loom-weeks worked (loom-hours of operation divided by 40); weaving efficiency (the actual yardage produced divided by maximum potential yardage for the given loom speeds, cloth construction, and hours worked), and percentage of seconds to total yardage produced.

Situation in 1973

A major objective of the management in 1973, was to alleviate the severe financial restrictions which had hampered mill operation for several years. Principal financial support was derived from three sources: a $375,000 mortgage note on all fixed assets payable over eight years, a factoring agreement under which accounts receivable were financed at a cost of 1 percent of face value, and a field warehousing arrangement under which the company was committed, in

December 1972, for 600,000 pounds of cotton worth $300,000 held in a nearby public warehouse. Additional funds could be borrowed at 7 1/2 percent interest under the factoring agreement by pledging inventories other than raw cotton. The company's inventories at the end of the last three years are shown in table 6-4.

Cotton was withdrawn from the bonded field warehouse as needed. The company's lack of adequate cash resources, however, had limited fiber consumption to an average $20,000 weekly during January 1973. The inventory loan from the factor was intended to be used as short-term financing primarily for seasonal needs. It was not intended to exceed peak balances of $150,000.

The operating loss during 1972 had totalled $172,000. Analysis of variances from standard manufacturing costs are shown in table 6-5.

Loom activity each week averaged 1,600 loom-weeks (40-hour basis) until June when it began to drop sharply. Activity leveled off in September at a rate of 1,000 and soon rose to 1,100. Loom efficiency fluctuated little from an 80 percent average, except in November and early December when it dropped briefly to 76 percent. Seconds averaged less than 5 percent each week throughout the year.

Table 6-4
Ending Inventory Values
(thousands)

	1970	1971	1972
Raw material	$ 22	$ 36	$ 10
Work in progress	309	416	396
Greige cloth	208	262	188
Finished cloth	147	153	69
Supplies	54	45	47
Total	$740	$912	$710

Table 6-5
1972 Average Weekly Variance from Standard

	Overhead	Labor
January-March	$2,000	$(1,000)
April-June	2,000	(1,000)
July-September	(3,500)	(2,500)
October-December	(5,000)	(3,000)

Note: ( ) = unfavorable variance.

In May 1973, the Seneca management decided that a complete revision of the company's product mix was necessary to achieve a balance of manufacturing operations and permit profitable operations. Feeling that mill balance was a very important factor in profitable operation, the mill manufacturing staff began a thorough study of more than a dozen alternative schedules for mill operations, estimating revenues and incomes from each proposal. The planned mix of products to be sold included a number of items previously produced plus one new fabric, a poplin cloth for which sales efforts were then in progress. As of January 31, 527 looms were operating on a two-shift basis and weaving 70 different fabrics. Orders being produced on 405 of those looms were scheduled to run out by mid-April but the 42 50-inch Draper X-2 looms and the 80 box looms were scheduled to be in production through August on orders already booked.

Planning at this point was based in large part upon the expectation that the company would book the order for a large volume of poplin cloth. Mr. Thomas himself was currently working with the expected customer for this cloth, a converter who specialized in cloth for uniforms and handled an estimated six million yards of poplin cloth annually. Seneca had submitted a sample of its poplin for testing by the United States Testing Company, and the sample was found to have better abrasion resistance than the cloth currently being used by the converter. Mr. Thomas expected that Seneca could secure a contract calling for delivery of at least 35,250 yards per week at 39 cents per yard.

The poplin cloth would contain 50's two-ply combed cotton yarn in a 102 x 40 construction and therefore was a coarser cloth than that usually produced by Seneca. On this basis, 35,250 yards of cloth would require 7,885 pounds of warp yarn and 3,671 pounds for fill. Although poplin was generally considered to be a "commodity" cloth, as distinguished from the specialty fabrics usually produced by Seneca, the management felt that similar departures from the basic product policy had proven profitable during extraordinary situations in the past.

In preparing the proposals for future operations, the mill overseers estimated the poundage and yardage of material to be handled, and the number of machines, spindles, looms, and other equipment that would be required. Table 6-6 presents the yarn mill and weave room schedules for three of the proposed operating programs. The overseers also prepared detailed schedules of machine operations and labor requirements for each proposal. These schedules were then translated into operating costs. Tables 6-7 and 6-8 present estimated revenues and expenses based on operation of facilities on a three-shift basis, five days per week.

Schedule #2 included a weave schedule identical to that of #1, except that an additional 20,700 yards of poplin would be produced. Yarn production in both instances would be scheduled to match the needs of the weaving department. Because both proposals #1 and #2 seemed to fall short of profitable operations, a new mix of products was set up as proposal #3. Specific differences in the weave schedules can be seen in table 6-6, but it should be

Table 6-6
Comparison of Proposed Weekly Schedules

	Yarn Mill		
	Proposal #1	*Proposal #2*	*Proposal #3*
Warp yarn			
Pounds	14,799	19,333	16,716
Spindles used	10,940	12,888	12,042
No. yarns	11	11	12
Fill yarn			
Pounds	9,112	11,268	10,627
Spindles used	6,708	7,698	6,362
No. yarns	11	11	8
Total pounds yarn spun	23,891	30,601	27,343
Total spindles used	17,648	20,586	18,404

Weave Room

Cloths Included in All Three Proposals

Fourteen fabrics totaling 36,350 yards per week, requiring 42 50-inch Draper X-2 looms and 74 42-inch Draper X-2 looms. Fabrics from this group accounting for 21,700 yards weekly were already in production on January 1973; the fabrics in production included 12,500 yards on 42 50-inch X-2 looms plus 9,200 yards on 27 42-inch X-2 looms.

	Other Cloths Scheduled					
	Proposal #1		*Proposal #2*		*Proposal #3*	
	Yds./wk.	*No. Looms*	*Yds./wk.*	*No. Looms*	*Yds./wk.*	*No. Looms*
Box Loom						
A. Pol. and cot.	–	–	–	–	2,800	9
B. Pol. and cot.	–	–	–	–	4,000	11
C. Pol. and cot.	–	–	–	–	8,800	24
D. Cotton[a]	4,300	16	4,300	16	2,400	9
E. Cotton[a]	2,200	8	2,200	8	3,300	12
F. Cotton[a]	–	–	–	–	700	3
G. Cotton[a]	–	–	–	–	1,400	5
H. Cotton[a]	–	–	–	–	1,900	7
I. Cotton[a]	3,400	16	3,400	16	–	–
Draper E Loom						
J. Cotton	400	2	400	2	–	–
K. Pol. and cot. bat.	29,000	80	20,000	80	–	–
L. Cot. bd. cl. str.	1,200	4	1,200	4	2,800	9
M. Cotton	–	–	–	–	2,800	9
N. Cotton poplin	20,700	40	41,400	80	35,250	68
Subtotals	52,150	166	72,850	206	66,100	166
Totals	88,500	282	109,200	322	102,450	282

[a]In production January 31, 1973.

Table 6-7
Pro Forma Weekly Income Statements and Labor Budgets

	Income Statements		
Sales	Schedule 1	Schedule 2	Schedule 3
Cloth	$49,979	$58,052	$58,272
Waste	1,939	2,145	2,595
Remnant store	946	946	946
Total Sales	$52,864	$61,143	$61,813
Expense			
Labor–direct and indirect	15,880	19,259	16,297
Raw material–fibers	24,238	27,674	23,465
Outside finishing	788	788	788
Yarn dyeing	1,297	1,297	3,199
Overhead	11,421	11,619	11,473
Interest	825	825	825
Factor–1% sales	499	581	583
Sample expense	550	550	450
Brokerage and selling	1,095	1,095	1,095
Profit or (Loss)	($3,729)	(2,545)	$3,638

	Labor Budgets					
	1		2		3	
	Employees	Cost	Employees	Cost	Employees	Cost
Yarn mill	60	$7,572	72	$9,577	56	$4,084
Weave department	40	5,511	48	6,598	46	6,413
Cloth inspection	11	1,337	14	1,624	12	1,440
Mill maintenance	9	1,084	9	1,084	9	1,084
Outside	3	376	3	376	3	376

noted that the major changes were in the volume of poplin cloth and the yardage of fancy cloth to be woven on box looms. Yarn mill output for this proposal also was planned to match weaving requirements. The pro forma income statement for proposal #3 indicated that a $3,600 weekly pretax profit could be attained.

The schedule of operations set forth in proposal #3 was recommended to the management as a means of achieving a profitable mill balance. They planned to begin directing their efforts at achieving such a schedule and hoped to reach that goal by late 1972 by which time the mill would have gone onto three-shift operation. The changes were expected to increase profits both through the more efficient utilization of machinery made possible by balanced mill operations and

Table 6-8
Weekly Overhead Expense

	Average Actual 1972 Cost	1972 Budget	Project 3 Budget
Mill Overhead			
Power purchased	$ 1,971	$ 1,154	$ 1,400
Fuel	540	500	540
General supplies	1,766	2,422	1,525
Repairs	780	1,058	600
Taxes and insurance	1,287	1,500	1,080
General expense	120	231	176
Depreciation	970	769	1,000
Starch and size	480	385	250
Salaries—superintendent and overseers	853	769	908
Salaries—laboratory and health	350	414	283
Payroll tax and benefits	2,893	2,884	1,423
Subtotal	$12,010	$12,086	$ 9,185
General and Administrative			
Salaries—executive	$ 320	$ 481	$ 350
Salaries—office	1,210	1,250	870
Legal and professional	340	288	350
Office supplies and expenses	190	231	150
Telephone and teletype	146	135	100
Travel and entertainment	241	192	100
General	200	172	208
Depreciation—furniture and fixtures	160	163	160
Subtotal	$ 2,807	$ 2,912	$ 2,288
Total	$14,817	$14,998	$11,473

through the limitation of production to the more profitable present products on the most efficient mill machinery. Credit burdens would be eased by the reduction in inventory resulting from change to three-shift operation and the reduction in the volume of activity. Additional funds might also be obtained by selling excess machinery and renting unused mill space.

Mr. Thomas outlined some of the planned modifications in the marketing programs of the company. In the future, the objective of the sales department would be to maintain a balanced mix of profitable products in limited volume. Past efforts, on the other hand, had been directed at building a larger sales volume with the resultant acceptance of many items only for their contribution to fixed costs. In line with the proposed policy changes, the staff of the New York sales office would be reduced to two salesmen and a secretary, while the stylist would be employed part-time on an "as used" basis.

The management felt confident that a reorientation of policies and operations to achieve a balance of mill operations would result in a reversal of the persistent operating losses. Pro forma income statements for the first three months of 1973 based on the transition to schedule #3 were as follows (in thousands):

	January (5 weeks)	February (4 weeks)	March (4 weeks)
Sales	$310	$344	$291
Standard profit[b]	(15)	2.5	0.1
Variances			
Labor	(11)	(6)	(2)
Overhead	(10)	(6)	(2)

[b]Before interest charges and selling costs.

7 WestPoint-Pepperell, Inc. (B)

In 1965 the management of the newly formed WestPoint-Pepperell company was considering what action to take on two major capital investment proposals. One of these called for the expansion and modernization of the existing Shawmut No. 2 mill, which specialized in the production of 100 percent synthetic industrial specialty fabrics. This mill had been started in 1952 by converting the basement and third floor of the old Shawmut mill to the spinning and weaving of industrial synthetics, and in 1964 a finishing department had been added to the mill to make it fully integrated from spinning to finishing. The second proposal called for the building of an entirely new mill for the production of 35 percent cotton-65 percent polyester blend batiste and broadcloth grey fine goods for the apparel markets. The West Point Manufacturing Company had long been a major producer of fine goods and was one of the first companies to manufacture cotton-synthetic blended fine goods in the late 1950s. In 1965, two mills (Shawmut No. 1, with 21,000 spindles and 500 looms, and Wellington, with 35,000 spindles and 750 looms) produced these fabrics. The new plant was to be built at Huguley, Alabama, near the existing mills at Lanett, Shawmut, Langdale, Fairfax, and River View (see WestPoint-Pepperell, Inc. (A)).

Management realized that each of the two proposals would have to be considered in terms of the financial and operational merits that each presented. Beyond this, however, some members of management felt that there were environmental and strategic considerations which, while not having specific bearing upon the immediate operating or financial considerations, might have very important bearing upon the long-range soundness of either investment. It was felt by these individuals that such factors as the international situation in textiles and the changing labor situation in the South should be considered in deciding whether or not the capital investment proposals should be accepted.

The Labor Situation in the Chattahoochee River Valley

When asked by the casewriter why the labor situation in the Chattahoochee River Valley should be a major factor in deciding whether or not a new mill should be located in that area, the vice president in charge of personnel services had this to say:

153

In order to fully understand the current labor situation in this area, you must view the position of the textile industry from an historical perspective. WestPoint-Pepperell and its predecessors have been in this region for over 100 years. It has been the major industrial concern in the Valley, and employer-employee relationships have been excellent through the years. Before the company was here, the area consisted of forests and cotton plantations. As the mills were constructed, transportation problems in those days dictated that towns be built up around the mills. In most cases the company planned and built the towns.

As a consequence, a somewhat paternalistic pattern developed between the company and its employees. Of necessity, the company owned the employees' housing and provided utilities, streets, recreational facilities, and other municipal-type services for the mill communities. Most of the needs of the employees were provided for by the company. It was then, and is today to a lesser extent, common for several members of the same family to work in the same mill.

Throughout the entire South, the textile industry was the major industrial employer, and most of the industry was structured in much the same way as it was right here. Labor was plentiful in the South, and the individual nonagricultural worker in many areas had few alternatives to working in textiles.

After World War II, things began to change. Nontextile industry began to move into the South, bringing with it higher wages, modern working conditions, and a more formal pattern of labor relations. Although there are rare exceptions which persist in a few companies to this day, the traditional textile paternalism began to dissipate in the 1940s and 1950s. In various ways encouragement has been given to an employee's individuality in all areas of his life, while maintaining a genuine employer concern for the employee. For instance, here at WestPoint, the company had disposed of all of its company-owned housing by 1953, by selling to employees at or near book value. Telephone, electric, and most other utilities were disposed of to various utility companies by about 1960.

Since about 1960 our textile wages have increased steadily at a rate of about 5-6 percent a year, but even so, the wage differential between textile and some nontextile wages is considerable. As new industry has moved into the South, the labor supply has gradually tightened to the point where today there no longer exists the labor surplus we had enjoyed for almost 100 years. Today we must compete in the labor market with diverse industrial groups.

Many of our mills were built decades ago, and unlike our more modern facilities have considerable room to improve noise, dust and heat conditions in some areas. If we are to attract the kind of labor we need to operate these mills, we must continue to be alert to every reasonable opportunity for capital expenditure to improve working conditions.

WestPoint-Pepperell and the International
Situation in Textiles

The vice president of corporate development and the president of the industrial division discussed their attitudes toward how the company should react to developments in the import-export situation in textiles.

Although the present administration appears to be favorably inclined towards controlling imports in some way, there is no way to predict when or whether strong action in this direction will be taken. In particular, the Department of State is unlikely to support any sort of unilateral imposition of import quotas, or are any of the countries exporting to this nation going to readily volunteer to curtail their exports. However, we would hope for relief through some reasonable, orderly control of textile imports. The nations exporting to these markets are largely in the Far East, and many of these nations might hurt exporters in other industries if the United States were to attempt to drastically curtail their textile and apparel imports to this country. Also, there is major political involvement in this whole problem on both the national and international scene.

Given this, our company must plan on having to cope with increasing foreign competition. To do so, we must seek future growth in those market segments in which the foreign producers are least competitive. Generally speaking, these segments are the specialty areas. Specialties are sold on the basis of solving a customer's problem and have major service and distribution problems. To these customers price is a secondary consideration. At the other end of the spectrum are the so-called "commodity" fabrics. These are sold almost entirely upon the basis of price, given that the fabric is above certain minimum quality specifications. Most foreign manufacturers can meet these specifications without difficulty, and the simple fact is that in the foreseeable future we are not going to be able to beat them on costs.

Expansion of the Shawmut No. 2 Mill

Background

Historically, one fabric, cotton duck, has contributed more to the success of the West Point Manufacturing Company than has any other. Duck is a heavy fabric, and it is sold primarily to industrial customers and to manufacturers of heavy apparel, such as service uniforms, cook's aprons, etc. In 1965 industrial fabrics made of cotton accounted for a large but decreasing share of the total industrial fabric market (see table 7-1). WestPoint-Pepperell executives believed that the reason for the decline in the use of all cotton fabrics was that industrial customers were highly rational and would use the type of fabric which would most economically meet their needs. Because synthetic fibers were stronger and more durable per unit weight than were all cotton fabrics, industrial consumers could justify their use even if cost per pound of fabric was somewhat higher.

Recognizing the trend away from all cotton, the West Point company had begun the manufacture of all synthetic fabrics on a pilot basis in the late 1940s, and by the mid-1950s a large portion of the Shawmut mill had been converted to the spinning and weaving of 100 percent synthetic fabrics. (The converted portions of the mill were named Shawmut No. 2.) In 1964 a finishing plant for synthetics was added at Shawmut No. 2.

As of January 1, 1965, West Point executives believed that Shawmut No. 2 produced a significant share of all of the nation's synthetic industrial fabrics and that this was a larger share of the market than that possessed by any other firm. At least eighteen other firms held significant shares of the market, including

Table 7-1
Industrial Use of Textile Fibers

	Cotton[a]		Wool		Rayon-Acetate[a]		Other Synthetic[b]		Total
	MM lbs.	%	MM lbs.	%	MM lbs.	%	MM lbs.	%	MM lbs.
1960	614	50	10	.8	300	24	304	25	1128
1961	607	51	10	.8	262	22	316	27	1195
1962	591	47	11	.9	275	22	377	30	1254
1963	575	46	10	.8	261	21	398	32	1244
1964	582	44	8	.6	276	21	464	35	1330
1965	599	42	8	.6	279	19	553	38	1439

Source: *Textile Organon,* January 1968.

[a]In converting either cotton or rayon pounds to yards, a reasonable conversion factor was two yards per pound.

[b]Including nylon, dacron, other polyester, and glass.

many of the largest textile firms, such as J.P. Stevens, Burlington, Callaway, Collins & Aikman, and others, as well as certain nontextile firms such as U.S. Rubber and Firestone. In certain segments of the industrial market, such as spun nylon fabrics and fabrics of very heavy weight, West Point's market share was very substantial. An internal report published early in 1965 stated the following about West Point's market position:

Shawmut No. 2 is the acknowledged leader in the industrial synthetic market. The experience, technical skills, and service which we have offered our customers means that whenever there is a choice our customers choose us. This leadership in synthetic fabrics is a natural outgrowth of our traditional position in cotton fabrics for industry. Our strength in both areas has helped us to continue to be first in the industrial field.

The products developed at Shawmut have been profitable. We believe that similar opportunities for profit will continue to exist in our expanding economy as more users become aware of the superior economics of synthetics. This will be even more apparent as increasing competition among fiber suppliers brings the general price levels of synthetic fibers closer to cotton. The technical service and promotion skills of the fiber producers will also accelerate this growth.

It has become increasingly clear that the capacity of Shawmut No. 2 is not sufficient for us to maintain our position as leaders in this field. On the other hand, the specialized nature of our present product mix is such that it is not logical to add a large number of looms in a short period of time.

One of the basic considerations in any expansion is to be certain that the expansion does not come at the expense of profit margins. To achieve this objective, we feel that it is necessary to allow our present products to find their inherent growth naturally, keeping close contact with our customers to see that a competitive mill does not take away our developments on a price basis.

We feel certain that we can maintain our present share of the market if we do not force our customers to seek other sources because of our inability to supply them. Attached to the end of this report is a letter from a major customer, the Lavinian Specialty Co., on this point [see figure 7-1].

LAVINIAN SPECIALTY COMPANY

85 Via Appia
Rome, New York

Wellington-Sears Company   December 13, 1964
111 West 40th Street
New York, New York

Gentlemen:

A very disturbing situation arose this week, and we thought it appropriate to express our comments directly to you. No information had been given to Bill Beroe to let us know that it would be necessary to book synthetic fabrics from Shawmut further in advance than has been our practice. As a result, when it became time to book orders on the normal pattern, there was considerable difficulty in arriving at a mutually agreeable production schedule. The production dates finally agreed upon will be satisfactory if we do not have a demand beyond our estimates, but there is very little leeway if we should get a peak in demand.

The main problem is not so much letting us know that orders must be placed far in advance of production, but rather is in the fact that we simply cannot make these far-forward estimates. All of these fabrics are used in specialized applications, many for specific customers. Therefore, we cannot estimate many months in advance exactly what orders we will receive. The volume of demand on any specific fabric is extremely variable and completely unpredictable, but in total, we are sure that you will find that over the years we have had a fairly constant volume with Shawmut.

The volume of these specialized fabrics is not large enough that we have ever considered it necessary to have multiple sources of supply and you have had all of the volume since their inception. We have been completely satisfied with your quality and with your pricing and there has never been any reason to develop another source. However, it is essential that we be able to count on production starting within a reasonably short period of time and must work with a source that is in a position to do this. In the past, you have been able to start production in not more than four to six weeks, and while this timing is not completely desirable, it has been completely workable. However, this is about the maximum that we can ever place orders in advance.

It is certainly admirable that you have been able to so completely sell the production of Shawmut, but unless you can find a way to work in our requirements on the four to six weeks advance notice, we will have to develop another source of supply. We do not mean to state this as a threat, but merely as a realistic appraisal of the situation. We have to be in a position to take care of customer demands as they arise, and cannot afford to carry any more inventories than the four to six weeks advance notice requires.

We would prefer continuing to work exclusively with Shawmut on these specialized synthetic fabrics, but unless you can offer the availability required, we shall have to do our best to find someone who can. Your comments will be appreciated.

R. C. de Priam
Vice President-Procurement

R.C.d.P./v

Source: Company records.

Note: Name of customer is disguised.

Figure 7-1. Letter from the Lavinian Specialty Company

The Product

The president of the industrial division explained some of the characteristics of industrial specialty fabrics:

Most of the orders that we receive for synthetic industrial fabrics are for short runs of special design. While orders for fine goods or other apparel-type fabrics might be for hundreds of thousands of yards or more of one type of fabric, orders for industrial specialties rarely exceed 25,000 yards and frequently are for less than 5,000 yards.

The industrial customer generally specifies the type of yarn, fabric construction, and finishing he wants. The finishing processes for synthetics are often of a standardized nature although the opportunity for specializing exists, which gives real product differentiation and market control. Additionally, the spinning of the yarns and the weaving of the fabric is usually quite specialized.

Many of the orders we fill call for the use of filament yarns. These yarns are not spun from fibers by textile mills, but rather are cast into long filament strands from the basic raw material, which in most cases is nylon. This casting is done by the chemical companies such as DuPont and Monsanto, and the yarns arrive here ready to go onto the loom after very little preparation. They do not behave in quite the same way as spun yarns, and consequently they are especially tricky to weave. This is most true of the lighter weight filament yarns. Our closest competition in the industrial synthetics market, J.P. Stevens, is especially good in the handling of these light weight filaments. Our traditional strength lies in spun synthetics and in the weaving of heavy fabrics from both spun and filament yarns. Unlike apparel fabrics, second grade industrial fabrics have no commercial value. They must be disposed of. This makes the task of quality assurance a critical one.

From a marketing point of view, the difference between industrial specialties and apparel fabrics is like that between day and night. Industrial fabrics are made against orders, and to get that initial order it is necessary to work closely with a customer who has a fabric problem and to convince him that you can help to solve his problem. To hold the customer, you must be able to solve his problems, meet his specifications, and get the material to him on time. To market apparel fabrics, in the grey state at least, one must be able to meet delivery time and price. These fabrics are usually of pretty standard design.

The real key to success in industrial fabrics lies in manufacturing. To manufacture these products, one must be constantly dealing with hundreds of yarn sizes and types, many different fabric constructions, frequent changeovers, constant attention to detail. Scheduling problems are a major headache, and because it is hard to make an accurate forecast of demand, it is difficult to anticipate precise raw materials needs. Bottlenecks or low machinery utilizations occur throughout the various processes, and keeping the whole mill in balance is a major problem. Although Shawmut No. 2 is probably one of the most efficient specialty mills in the country, there is lots of room for improvement here.

Another key factor in running this sort of operation is coordination between marketing and manufacturing. The marketing people must be aware of equipment capacity and shortages. Part of the problem of keeping the mill in balance rests on marketing's shoulders—they should, when feasible, try to seek the types of orders that will best balance the mill. However, the marketing people can't turn away or delay orders just because they don't happen to fit well into the mill's schedule at that particular time. The mill people therefore must be kept aware of what is happening in the market and plan accordingly.

Need for Expansion

Realizing that because the demand for synthetic industrial specialties was growing while the capacity of the Shawmut No. 2 mill was fully utilized, WestPoint executives knew that capacity for the production of these products would have to be expanded if Westpoint was to maintain its share of the market. Early in 1965 an internal study was made showing that from 80 to 280 looms would have to be added to the production of industrial synthetics over the next 10 years if WestPoint were to maintain its share of the market (see table 7-2).

Studies by the E.I. du Pont de Nemours Company indicated that the growth rate for synthetic industrial fabrics would be between 9 percent and 15 percent per annum through 1970 (see table 7-3). The same studies indicated that the greatest growth would come in filament-based fabrics. WestPoint executives realized, however, that du Pont, the major supplier of synthetic fibers and filaments to the textile industry, had a vested interest in projecting optimistic growth rates for synthetic fibers and were therefore inclined to believe the du Pont figures to be somewhat exaggerated.

Table 7-2
Additional Number Looms Required at Shawmut #2 to Maintain Market Share

	Cumulative number additional looms required by Shawmut #2 on present product mix to maintain present market share		
	Approx. Annual Growth Rate		
Year	3%	5%	10%
1	8	15	29
2	17	29	59
3	25	44	87
4	33	59	117
5	42	74	146
6	50	89	174
7	59	103	203
8	68	117	231
9	76	132	260
10	84	146	289

Source: Company records.
Note: Figures disguised.

Table 7-3
Forecasts by Du Pont of Particular End Use Industrial Markets
(millions of pounds)

End Use Market	Actual 1963		Forecast 1967		Forecast 1969	
	Nylon	*Poly.*	*Nylon*	*Poly.*	*Nylon*	*Poly.*
V. belts	–	1.5	–	3.8	–	4.5
Conveyors	4.5	.1	6.8	.8	7.5	1.5
Coated fabrics	6.0	.3	9.3	.6	10.5	1.0
Filtration	1.1	.7	1.4	1.4	1.5	1.8
Chafers	1.7	–	3.0	0		
Parachutes, etc.	2.6	–	3.0	–	3.2	–
Other industrials	3.6	1.9	5.6	3.1	6.5	3.8
Total	15.2	4.5	29.1	9.7	29.2[a]	12.6[a]

Source: Company records.
[a]Excluding chafers.

In May of 1965 a proposal was prepared recommending that WestPoint increase its capacity in synthetic industrial fabrics by 150 looms with floor space to add an additional 50 looms at some future date. The new looms would be used entirely for the manufacture of fabrics from filament-type fibers. The proposal called for adding over 57,000 square feet of floor space to the Shawmut mill and for the relocation of 100 existing looms in order to make their operation more efficient.

Tables 7-4 and 7-5 give pertinent details of this proposal.

The Fine Goods Mill Investment Proposal

In 1965, two factors prompted consideration of expansion of fine goods manufacturing capacity. First was a highly optimistic forecast for the growth of cotton-polyester blend fabrics. This forecast, prepared by the E.I. du Pont de Nemours Company, indicated that while the total market for primary fine goods would grow between 1964 and 1969 at the same compound rate as the GNP, the market for polyester blends would grow at a compound rate of 23 percent (with a range of 17 to 37 percent). (See table 7-6.)

The second factor was that much of WestPoint's blended fine goods capacity was located in the Shawmut mill, which also housed the company's growing industrial synthetics operation. Floor space in the Shawmut mill was limited, and the possibilities for adding more floor space to the facility were restricted.

Table 7-4
Shawmut Mill No. 2 Expansion: Capital Expenditure Proposal No. 1007

Summary

Additional production per 144 hours:		
A. 150 New looms	84,000 yards	
B. 100 Looms relocated	9,000 yards	
Total	93,000 yards	
Cost of proposal:		
Machinery and auxiliary equipment, including freight and installation	$928,000	
New building construction	839,000	
Total amount to be capitalized		$1,767,000
Related Expenses		35,000
Deduct Investment Credit		78,000
Net Cost of Proposal		$1,724,000
Working capital	$636,000	
Annual contribution (144-hour week, 50 weeks)		
New looms		$454,980
Relocated looms		48,750
Total		$503,730

Source: Company records.
Note: Figures disguised.

In March 1965, it was indicated that there were only four reasonable alternatives for fine goods expansion:

1. To not expand capacity or build a new plant;
2. To build a new plant but to not expand capacity;
3. To expand capacity by a net total of 300 looms by building a new 800 to 900 loom plant and moving the 500 Shawmut fine goods looms to this new plant;
4. To build a new plant of 600 to 900 looms (having the flexibility to expand to 900 looms if a smaller number were chosen) and retaining the 500 looms at Shawmut.

It was felt that the first alternative would not be adopted by top management if an expansion could be made that would yield at least a 10 percent internal rate of return. Also, the second alternative would be unacceptable to management because it would increase investments and costs without appreciably affecting the basic operating strengths of WestPoint-Pepperell.

Table 7-5

Shawmut Mill No. 2 Expansion: Calculation of Annual Contribution to Be Used in Determining Return on Investment—150 New Looms

Style	Selling Price per Yard	Theoretical Cost per Yard[a]	Contribution to Profits per Yard	Anticipated Yards per Week (5 day)	Contribution to Profits per Week
#1 Grey	60.25¢	48.05¢	12.20¢	4,800	$ 586
#1 Finished	71.65	66.11	15.54	7,200	1,119
#2 (37½") Grey	36.50	29.35	7.15	6,650	475
#2 (37½") Finished	44.10	35.79	8.31	6,650	553
#2 (47") Grey	42.15	37.11	6.04	3,550	214
#2 (47") Finished	51.23	44.22	7.01	3,550	249
#5 Grey	48.85	39.38	9.47	1,720	163
#5 Finished	52.65	46.69	5.96	2,080	124
#6 Grey	46.00	36.98	9.02	9,550	861
#6 Finished	60.25	44.08	16.17	2,350	380
#10 Grey	48.38	46.17	2.21	22,300	493
#11 Grey	72.60	55.70	16.90	3,200	541
#11 Finished	83.53	64.43	19.10	1,480	283
#18 Finished	93.50	76.21	17.29	8,920	1,542
				69,867	$7,583

Annual contribution:

5 day week: $7583 x 50 = $379,150

6 day week: $379,150 x 6/5 = $454,980

Source: Company records.

Note: All figures disguised.

[a]Grey costs include any anticipated increase in fixed expenses due to proposed expansion. No other fixed expenses are included. Finishing costs include no fixed expenses. No depreciation is included in either grey or finishing costs. These costs are to be used only for calculation of return on investment. (Grey costs include 96% of theoretical labor, 47% of overhead, 100% of size, packing, and raw materials, and standard Mill No. 2 defective allowance. No selling or administrative expense is included.)

Alternative number 3 seemed logical if WestPoint-Pepperell wished to expand total capacity by exactly 300 looms, which was the minimum-sized expansion that the marketing department felt should be undertaken. This alternative posed the advantage of allowing the Shawmut mill to be cleared of all fine goods production so that the entire mill could be used for the production of industrial synthetic fabrics. However, if this alternative were to have been adopted, expansion of the manufacturing capacity of industrial synthetics might have been delayed while the new fine goods mill was constructed and the looms were transferred to it. The fourth alternative was the only feasible one if total expansion of fine goods capacity was to be 600 or more looms.

Table 7-6

Du Pont Five-Year Cotton/Synthetic Fine Goods Forecast by Fabric Type and by End Use

(millions of linear yards)

	1964 Actual	*1969 Forecast*	*Change*
Fabric type			
All cotton type apparel fabrics	3,280	3,795	515
Blends:			
All cotton-synthetic blend apparel fabrics	405 (344)	1,140 (797)	735 (453)
Batistes and print cloths	108　(92)	330 (231)	222 (139)
Broadcloth	87　(74)	284 (199)	197 (125)
Lawns and voiles	8　(8)	14　(14)	6　(6)
Filament/spun	37　(37)	67　(67)	30　(30)
Yarn dyes (box loom)	28　(28)	48　(48)	20　(20)
DNC types	40　(40)	65　(65)	25　(25)
Other fine goods	36　(36)	113 (113)	77　(77)
Total fine goods	370 (315)	1,050 (737)	710 (422)
End Use			
Blouses	88　(75)	211 (148)	123　(73)
Dresses	86　(73)	278 (195)	192 (122)
Lingerie and Sleepwear	53　(45)	117　(82)	64　(37)
Dress Shirts	46　(39)	108　(76)	62　(37)
Sport Shirts	62　(53)	148 (104)	86　(51)
Children's and Teen's Wear	35　(30)	189 (132)	154 (102)
Total	370 (315)	1,050 (737)	710 (422)

Source: Company records.

Note: Figures in parentheses are for dacron only.

In the early part of 1966 a set of revised plans was presented to the management of WestPoint-Pepperell for the construction of a new blend mill for the manufacture of fine goods. The plans called for the construction of a modern, one-story, fully air-conditioned structure several miles west of the Shawmut mill which would start production with 650 looms. These looms would be standard Draper X-3's, which allowed the company some degree of flexibility as they could be utilized, with rather minor adjustment, for either industrial or fine goods manufacture. The total area of the mill was designed so that all fiber preparation, spinning, loom preparation, and weaving operations were performed in one huge room. The total estimated cost for the building and site was $3,420,000. The flow of material in the proposed mill was linear—fiber would enter at the back of the mill and grey cloth would leave from the front. The figures and tables in appendix 7A summarize the plans for the proposed new mill.

WestPoint-Pepperell owned no finishing capacity for fine goods fabrics. The combined outputs of all of the company's fine goods mills in 1965 would not support a finishing operation. It was realized that if the new mill were to be built and the Shawmut mill were to sustain output of fine goods, the combined output of all of the company's fine goods mills would be great enough to support a finishing plant if the majority of the production were to be sold finished rather than grey. There was a considerable amount of discussion in the company whether or not the company would have to integrate vertically into finishing for fine goods to meet the increasing competition from other major firms who had vertically integrated their fine goods operations for staple fabrics. These firms included Burlington, Stevens, Springs, and Deering Milliken. If converters were to be squeezed out of the market, it might be necessary for WestPoint-Pepperell to integrate vertically to maintain its distribution. To build a minimum-sized finishing plant that could operate economically might require a fixed investment of at least several million dollars. Some WestPoint-Pepperell executives felt that investment in a finishing plant could be justified on the grounds that the margins on sales of finishing operations would give the company more maneuvering room in pricing. On the other hand, the finishing of apparel-type cloth would cause the company to incur selling, styling, and design expenses and inventory risks that would not be incurred were the company to sell all of its fine apparel fabrics in the grey state.

Appendix 7A:
Summary of Plans for Proposed New WestPoint-Pepperell Mill

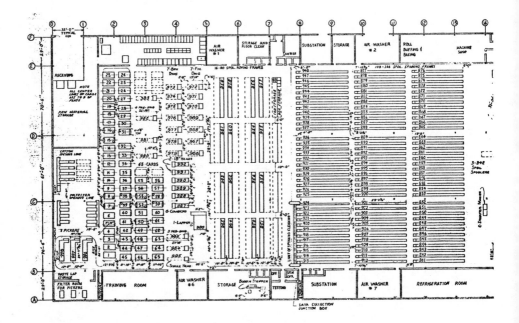

Source: Company records.

Figure 7A-1. Plant Layout

167

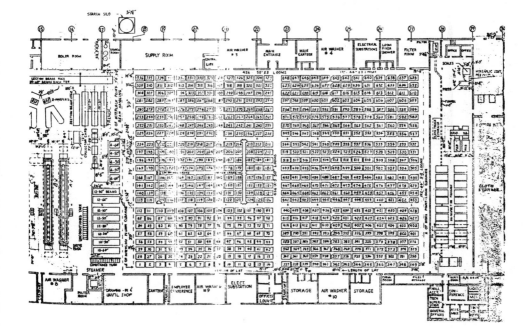

Figure 7A-1 (cont.)

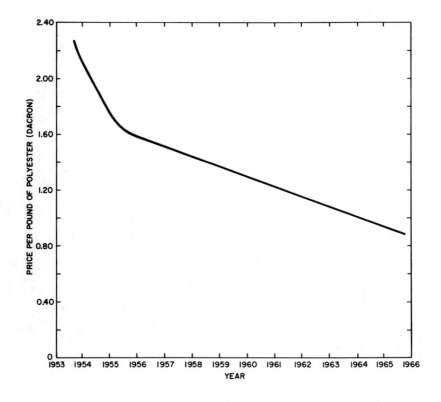

Source: Company records.

Figure 7A-2. Polyester Fiber Price History

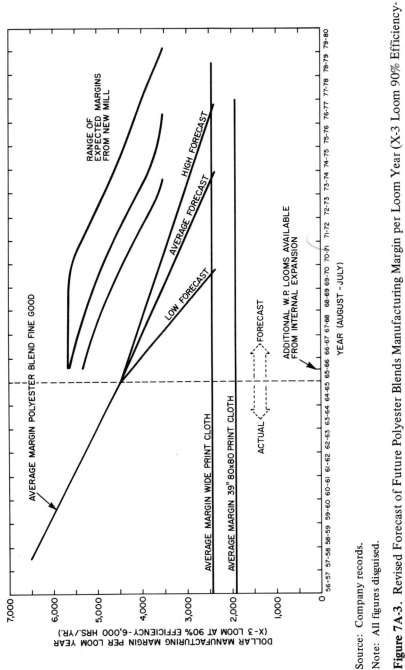

Source: Company records.

Note: All figures disguised.

Figure 7A-3. Revised Forecast of Future Polyester Blends Manufacturing Margin per Loom Year (X-3 Loom 90% Efficiency-6,000 hrs./yr.)

Table 7A-1
Statistics on Proposed Fine Goods Blend Mill

Output: Fine goods apparel fabrics, 65% polyester, 35% cotton
Estimated Annual Sales: $7,622,919 (first year)
$5,860,679 (average year)
Completion date: May 1967
Number of employees: 250
Estimated annual payroll: $1,250,000

Production and machinery status:

Operation	Units	Pounds in Cloth per 144-Hour Week	Waste Factor	Efficiency[a] Factor	Input Capacity (Pounds per Unit per 144-Hour Week)
Picker					
Cotton	1	31,683	.740	.980	43,546
Polyester	2	58,840	.900	.995	32,918
Cards					
Cotton	41	31,683	.780	1.040	986
Polyester	23	58,840	.940	.990	2,769
Predrawing					
Cotton	4	31,683	.790	.760	13,065
Polyester	6	58,840	.940	1.030	10,174
Superlapping					
Cotton only	1	31,683	.790	.600	70,272
Combing					
Cotton only	4	31,683	.940	.980	8,554
Blending					
First	12	90,523	.945	.970	8,179
Second	12	90,523	.945	.970	8,179
Slubbing	1,280	90,523	.950	1.000	74.4
Spinning					
#52 yarn	30,473[b]	78,301	.970	.999	2,649
#60 yarn	5,767[b]	12,222	.970	.999	2,185
Spooling					
#52 yarn	778	78,301	.980	.927	110.8
#60 yarn	151	12,222	.980	.927	89.1
Warping					
#52 yarn only	2	50,622	.980	.560	46,121
Slashing					
#52 yarn only	1	50,622	.980	.730	70,760
Weaving[c]					
Fill	–	39,901	1.000	1.000	39,901
Warp	–	50,622	1.000	1.000	50,622
Size	–	9,123	1.000	1.000	9,123
Total	–	99,646	–	–	99,646

Source: Company records.
Note: All figures disguised.
[a]Efficiency required to keep mill in balance.
[b]Number of spindles.
[c]648 looms.

Table 7A-2
Major Machinery to Be Installed in the Proposed Fine Goods Blend Mill

Process	Major Machinery	Quantity	Total Cost[a]
Opening: cotton	J. Hunter Model BFCV460	4	$ 25,200
Opening: polyester	J. Hunter Model BFS360	8	38,328
Picking: cotton	Hunter-Hergeth Model SW40"	1	27,902
Picking: polyester	Hunter-Hergeth Model SW40"	2	54,573
Cards: cotton	Saco-Pettee 40" cards (used)	43	236,996
Cards: polyester	Saco-Pettee 40" cards (used)	23	126,765
Predrawing: cotton	Ideal Delivery Frame (2 del. per frame)	2	9,880
Predrawing: polyester	Ideal Delivery Frame (2 del. per frame)	4	14,712
Superlapper: cotton[b]	Whitin H-1 Superlapper, 48 ends	1	14,953
Comb: cotton[b]	Saco-Lowell Model 140-A	4	57,816
Blending	Ideal Delivery Frame (2 del. per frame)	12	59,064
Slubbers	Saco-Lowell Rovematics (80 spindles per frame)	16	417,724
Spinning	Roberts Frames, 336 spindles per frame	108	1,279,515
Spooling	Barber Colman "C" type (used)	3	148,384
Warping	Barber Colman 545" x 40"	2	43,819
Slashing	WestPoint–Special design	1	63,403
Weaving	Draper X-3 50" Loom	456	1,100,123
	Draper X-3 48" Loom	192	508,810
Loom winding	Leesons Unifil No. 791	648	594,204
Cloth room	Cloth room and inspection machinery		110,827
Auxiliary	Cans, Bobbins, Mat. Handling, other	—	481,600
Machine shop, office, etc.		—	50,000
Total machinery cost[c]			5,261,739

Source: Company records.

[a]Includes freight, installation, and all minor pieces of machinery.

[b]Polyester does not require superlapping or combing.

[c]Includes allowance for machinery discounts.

Table 7A-3
Summary of Proposed Employees, 5-day Week (Tentative)

Job Number & Classification	Rate per Hour	Jobs per Shift			Total
		1	*2*	*3*	
Carding area					
115 Picker tender	$1.57	1	1	1	3
125 Section man (O/P-slubbers)	2.25	1	1	1	3
145 Card tender	1.80	1	1	1	3
150 Drawing tender	1.80	1	1	1	3
154 Comber lapper tender	1.89	1	1	1	3
156 Slubber tender	2.01	2	2	2	6
178 Overhauler, 1st-gr.-card grinder	2.25	2	–	–	2
Subtotal carding		9	7	7	23
Spinning area					
200 Spinning section man	$2.25	2	2	2	6
216 Roving transferrer	1.66	1	1	1	3
220 Warp doffers	1.96	3	3	3	9
224 Warp spinner	1.89	6	6	6	18
230 Roll picker & cleaner	1.79	2	–	–	2
236 Overhauler, 1st gr.	2.25	1	–	–	1
242 Overhauler, 4th gr.	1.71	1	–	–	1
Subtotal spinning		16	12	12	40
Spooling area					
300 Spooler section man	$2.25	1	1	1	3
302 Spooler tender	1.84	6	6	4	16
307 Spooler yarn man	1.71	1	1	1	3
313 Tailing machine tender & yarn salvager	1.66	1	1	1	3
Subtotal spooling		9	9	7	25
Total Hourly Employees		34	28	26	88
Supervision					
Overseer		1	–	–	1
Shift supervisor		1	1	1	3
Subtotal supervision		2	1	1	4
Total employees (opening-picking through spooling)		36	29	27	92
Warping-weaving area					
337 B.C. warper tender & creeler	$1.86	2	2	–	4
416 Slasher tender	2.00	1	1	1	3

Table 7A-3 (cont.)

Job Number & Classification	Rate per Hour	Jobs per Shift			Total
		1	2	3	
417 Asst. slasher tender	1.71	–	–	1	1
443 Warp drawer	1.81	2	–	–	2
501 Cam loom fixer	2.39	7	7	7	21
502 Unifil fixer	2.39	1	1	–	2
508 Cam weaver	2.10	14	14	14	42
518 Filling distributor	1.71	1	1	1	3
522 Loom blower and oiler	1.71	1	1	1	3
534 Portable tying-in mch. oper.	2.01	2	2	2	6
566 Cloth doffer	1.73	1	1	1	3
576 Smash & pick repairer	1.81	1	1	1	3
Subtotal warping-weaving		33	31	29	93
Supervision					
Overseer		1	–	–	1
Shift supervisor		1	1	1	3
Subtotal supervision		2	1	1	4
Total warping-weaving employees		35	32	30	97
Cloth room area					
608 Shearer operator	$1.77	1	–	–	1
616 Cloth inspector	1.77	20	–	–	20
626 Cloth grader	1.79	4	–	–	4
638 Press operator	1.79	1	–	–	1
– Shearing mch. & press oper.	1.79	–	1	–	1
644 Folder operator	1.79	2	–	–	2
652 Clerk	1.86	1	–	–	1
Subtotal cloth room		29	1	–	30
Supervision					
Shift supervisor		1	–	–	1
Total cloth room employees		30	1	–	31
Total employees (manufacturing area, including supervision)		101	62	57	220
Mechanical and outside					
Machinist, 1st gr.	$2.39	1	–	–	1
Electrician, 1st gr.- Instrument Man	2.39	1	–	–	1
Electrician, 2nd gr.	2.17	–	1	1	2
Service bay filter cleaner	1.48	1	1	–	2

Table 7A-3 (cont.)

Job Number & Classification	Rate per Hour	Jobs per Shift			Total
		1	2	3	
Shop laborer	1.48	1	–	–	1
Janitor and floor cleaner	1.48	1	–	–	1
Roller man and binder coverer	1.89	1	–	–	1
Watchman–weekend	1.67	1	–	–	1
Timekeeper-applicator	2.25	1	–	–	1
Yard and warehouse man	1.48	1	–	–	1
Lift truck operator	1.52	1	–	–	1
Shipping trucker	1.52	1	–	–	1
Subtotal mechanical & outside		11	2	1	14
Supervision					
Plant engineer		1	–	–	1
Shift supervisor		1	–	–	1
Subtotal supervision		2	–	–	2
Total employees mechanical & outside		13	2	1	16
Total plant office and technical		13	–	–	13
Grand total all employees–120 hours		127	64	58	249

Source: Company records.
Note: All figures disguised.

Table 7A-4
Forecast Economics for Proposed Fine Goods Blend Mill

Year	Expected Selling Price (per lb. of grey fabric)	Total Sales ($000s)	Margin ($000s)	Cost (less depreciation[a] ($000s)	Depreciation[b] ($000s)	PBT ($000s)	PAT ($000s)
1	1.53	7,413	4,368	2,008	900	1,460	730
2	1.47	7,148	4,212	2,008	840	1,364	682
3	1.45	7,016	4,134	2,008	780	1,346	673
4	1.39	6,751	3,978	2,008	720	1,250	625
5	1.34	6,486	3,822	2,008	660	1,154	577
6	1.26	6,089	3,588	2,008	600	980	490
7	1.20	5,825	3,432	2,008	540	884	442
8	1.12	5,428	3,198	2,008	480	710	355
9	1.07	5,163	3,042	2,008	420	614	307
10	1.01	4,898	2,886	2,008	360	518	259
11	.98	4,766	2,808	2,008	300	500	250
12	.96	4,633	2,730	2,008	240	482	241
13	.96	4,633	2,730	2,008	180	542	271
14	.96	4,633	2,730	2,008	120	602	301
15	.96	4,633	2,730	2,008	60	662	331

Source: Company records.

Note: All figures disguised.

[a]Includes labor and all out-of-pocket overhead costs.

[b]Total depreciable expense is $7.2 million, depreciated using SOYD over 15 years.

Carpetex Industries

In June 1973 Carpetex Industries was undergoing a major reevaluation of their production and marketing strategy. Carpetex, a major manufacturer of textile products with sales of $265 million (table 8-1 shows five-year summary of financial data) was experiencing three changes in the environment which were expected to have major effects on their ability to maintain their leadershp in the carpet and pile fabrics markets in the future.

1. The automotive industry, which accounted for 20 percent of the company's sales, was changing from loop pile carpeting to cut pile carpeting. Since cut pile carpet required twice the manufacturing time of loop pile carpeting, this would require a 50 percent increase in automotive carpet capacity in order to maintain market share.
2. Material costs, primarily for pile yarn and backing, were expected to increase rapidly over the next two to three years.
3. Small local carpet manufacturing companies were making major inroads into the market for contract and retail carpet. It was felt that these companies were capturing market shares because the proximity of their manufacturing facilities to their local and regional markets allowed them to service customers more effectively.

Company Background

Carpetex Industries was formed in 1955 through the reorganization of Clayton Mills. Clayton Mills had been established in Chambersburg, Pennsylvania, in 1896 by Mr. Charles Clayton, Jr., to manufacture "fine carpets for the distinguished home." The company's original manufacturing facility was devoted to the weaving of velvet and wilton carpets from purchased yarns. In 1923 the company entered the home furnishing fabric market with the manufacture of velvets and other pile fabrics for use in the manufacture of upholstered furniture and draperies. However, this product line never exceeded 10 percent of Clayton Mills' total revenues. The company grew from just under $1 million in 1900 to slightly over $10 million in sales in 1952. In 1952 Clayton Mills market position began to slip as a number of woven carpet manufacturers began to move their product lines into the high price range in reaction to the growth of tufted carpet in the low-priced market. By 1955 sales had slipped to just under $8 million, and

177

Table 8-1
Five-Year Financial Summary
(in millions of dollars)

	1972	1971	1970	1969	1968
Operations					
Net sales	$265.0	$260.7	$241.2	$235.4	$222.5
Earnings before income taxes	18.4	8.7	16.8	11.3	13.4
Income taxes	8.7	3.5	7.9	5.2	6.8
Net earnings	8.6	5.4	8.9	6.1	6.6
Year-end financial position					
Working capital	$ 80.8	$ 57.2	$ 61.4	$ 56.3	$ 58.2
Inventories	76.7	52.9	48.3	47.1	44.0
Property, plant, and equipment—net	70.0	64.2	58.1	53.4	46.7
Short-term debt	17.0	7.0	9.0	7.0	5.0
Long-term debt	45.1	42.0	39.0	36.2	35.4
Shareowners' equity	109.0	81.8	78.4	72.5	68.4
Per share of common stock					
Net earnings	$ 1.80	$ 1.20	$ 1.99	$ 1.38	$ 1.70
Dividends on common stock	1.00	1.00	1.00	1.00	1.00
Shares outstanding at end of year	4,778,000	4,512,000	4,472,000	4,420,000	3,900,000
Other data					
Property additions-gross	$ 10.3	$ 10.8	$ 9.5	$ 11.7	$ 10.7
Depreciation	4.5	4.7	4.8	5.0	4.9
Interest expense	3.4	3.2	3.0	2.8	2.6

production at the three mills in Chambersburg was curtailed. In July of 1955 Charles Clayton Winans became the president of the company, succeeding his grandfather Charles Clayton III. Mr. Winans stated that "the business of Clayton Mills is carpets and the objective of Clayton Mills is to become a leader in the carpet industry." The new president set out to modernize the company. His first step was to use some of the excess of $2 million in cash to purchase a small tufted carpet company, Carpet Textiles, in Dalton, Georgia. Next he reorganized Clayton Mills from a closely held family company into a public company, changing the name to Carpetex Industries. In 1956 35 percent of the common stock was offered to raise $4 million for an expansion program. By 1972 Carpetex had expanded to five plants, all in the Georgia-South Carolina area, producing four major product lines: automotive carpeting, contract and retail carpet, home furnishing fabrics, and specialty apparel fabrics. A sixth plant opened in Detroit, Michigan in 1972 to service the automotive market. All manufacturing at Chambersburg had closed by 1969; however, the company's headquarters were still located in the original mill with all production scheduling, research and development, styling, and market planning located in the three converted Pennsylvania mills.

Product Lines

The breakdown of sales and costs for Carpetex's four product lines is shown in table 8-2. Commercial and retail carpet accounted for the largest portion of sales, but automotive carpet was the leading contributor to the profit.

Table 8-2
Sales and Cost Breakdown, by Product Line
(in millions of dollars)

	Automotive Carpet	Retail[a] & Contract Carpet	Household Furnishing Fabrics	Apparel Fabrics	Total
Sales (million sq. yds.)	22	50.3	12.4	10.5	95.2
Sales (millions of dollars)	$63.00	$152.00	$28.00	$22.00	$265.0
Cost of goods sold					
Material	35.25	100.10	16.6	12.9	164.9
Labor	5.38	7.55	3.8	0.9	17.6
Overhead	8.32	17.50	3.3	3.4	32.5
Total Cost of Goods Sold	$48.95	$125.15	$23.7	$17.2	$215.0
General, sales, & administration expenses plus interest	5.70	20.40	3.1	2.4	31.6
Earnings before taxes	$ 8.35	$ 6.45	$ 1.2	$ 2.4	$ 18.4

[a]Includes 1 million sq. yds. of woven carpet, sold for $10 million, with cost of goods sold of $6.0 million.

Automotive carpet sales in 1972 were $63 million on 22 million square yards. This product contributed $8.35 million to earnings before taxes. Carpetex had a dominant share of the automotive carpet market; the company was primary supplier for the two major manufacturers of automobiles and secondary supplier for the remainder of the American automobile manufacturers. In 1972 Carpetex supplied carpeting for 5 million new cars and replacement carpet for 1 million used cars. Sales for this product line was handled by the vice president of marketing and the director of sales directly with the eleven purchasing vice presidents of the automobile companies and the two major companies which specialized in the auto parts replacement market. Open orders for automotive carpet were negotiated once a year, and ship orders were released against the open order each month according to company needs. The annual orders were reviewed every three months to reevaluate changes in carpet needs which might occur as a result of changes in demand for new cars; however, the annual orders had consistently been within 10 percent of actual sales. Carpets were shipped to customers in a variety of colors, quality, and sizes, cut and ready for installation.

Commercial and retail carpet accounted for $174 million in sales on 50.3 million square yards and contributed $6.45 million to pretax profit. Of this amount, woven carpet accounted for slightly less than $10 million and 1.0 million square yards of sales and $1.1 million of pretax profit. Sales were major national retailers—such as Sears, J.C. Penney—regional discount and department stores—such as Emerson Rug, J. Homestock and Bradlees—wholesale distributors, and building suppliers. The largest customer accounted for slightly over 20 percent of sales, and four customers accounted for over 50 percent of sales. This product line had its own sales force consisting of two national salesmen servicing the national retail and wholesale accounts and eight regional salesmen servicing regional markets through distributors. Forecasting sales in this market was more difficult than automobile carpets, with actual sales fluctuating from 72 percent to 160 percent of forecasts over the past ten years. Sales were highly dependent on the construction industry and consumer sales.

Both *household furnishing fabrics* and *apparel fabrics* were sold through a New York City company which acted as agent for a number of specialty fabric manufacturers. These two product lines both consisted entirely of tufted pile fabrics. The furnishing fabrics were velvets and novelty tufts used by upholstered furniture manufacturers, drapery, and wall covering manufacturers. The apparel fabrics were synthetic furs and other specialty high pile fabrics used by cut-and-sew operations in the manufacture of men's and women's apparel, such as coats, hats, dresses, and accessories.

Manufacturing Process

In 1972, Carpetex still produced both woven and tufted carpets and fabrics. Of these, tufted accounted for over 96 percent of sales for Carpetex. The manufacture of tufted and fabrics consisted of several operations designed to produce a layer of yarn pile or tufts secured to a sheet of material or backing. These operations are shown diagramatically in figure 8-1. The operation of most tufted carpet mills consisted of four segments: tufting, dyeing, finishing and drying.

Although manufacturing for the four major product lines varied somewhat, they were all similar to the basic manufacturing process for retail carpet. The heart of carpet manufacturing was the tufting machine. Yarn, either greige[a] or predyed, spun from wool, cotton, or man-made fibers or from twisted continuous filaments, was normally procured from a yarn mill wound on cones. These cones were mounted on a large metal frame called a "creel." The yarns from the creel were fed individually to the back of a tufting machine into tubes which kept the yarns from getting entangled. These tubes guided the yarns individually into needles (much like sewing machine needles) which were mounted downward on a horizontal bar in the tufting machine. The number of needles in a tufting machine depended upon the "gauge" and width of the machine. Tufting machines existed to manufacture carpet in widths of from 27 inches to over 15 feet. The typical carpet tufting machine had an "efficiency" of 45 percent to 65 percent.[b]

The typical carpet tufting machine producing retail and contract carpet was 15 feet wide. The gauge of a machine was the distance between the points of the needles mounted on the bar. Needle gauges varied from 3/8" to under 5/64". Thus the number of yarns fed into a single tufting machine (and hence the number of cones of yarn mounted on the creel) could vary from 27 (27" wide, 1" gauge), to over 2,880 (15' wide, 1/16" gauge). The wider the machine, the more square yards a single machine could turn out. The finer the gauge, the denser the carpet pile.

The operation of the tufting machine is shown in figure 8-2. A continuous sheet of primary backing made of a woven or nonwoven material was fed under the needle bar from a roll mounted on the back of the machine. The needle bar was raised and lowered, so that the yarn was punched through the backing. A hook was inserted through the loop of yarn thus formed on the underside of the backing, so that as the needle was raised a loop of yarn was created to form the pile. The result was a loop pile rug; to form a cut pile carpet, a knife worked in conjunction with the hook to cut the loops.

The typical loop pile tufting machine operated at speeds of 600 to 800 rpm's—that is, the needle bar went through a complete cycle, to form a row of loops the width of the machine, 600 to 800 times a minute. A cut pile carpet operated at 300 to 400 rpm's.

---

[a]Greige is unfinished (undyed) textiles.

[b]Efficiency was the actual output/theoretical output where theoretical output=(gauge) (speed in rpm) (width). Example, for a 1/8" (.125") gauge, 800 rpm, 12' wide tufter theoretical output — (.125/36) (800) (12/3) yds. 2/min. or 11 sq. yds./min.; at 50 percent efficiency output would be 5.5 sq. yds./min.

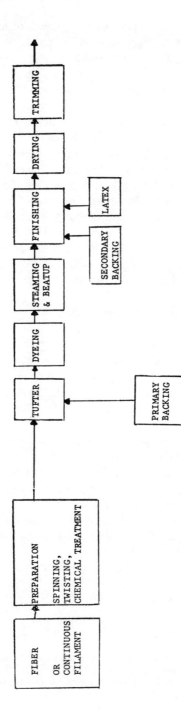

Figure 8-1. Carpet Manufacturing Process

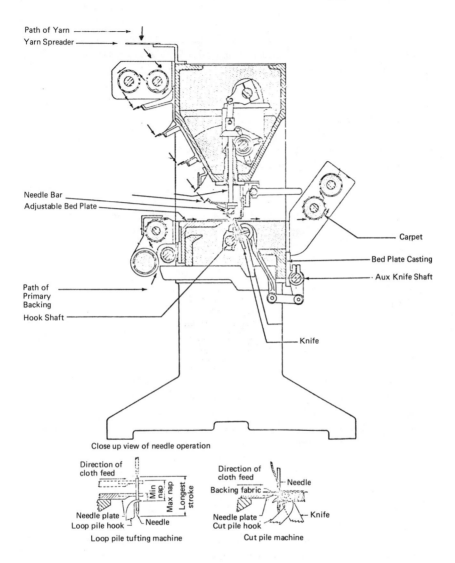

Path of Yarn
Yarn Spreader

Needle Bar
Adjustable Bed Plate

Carpet
Bed Plate Casting
Aux Knife Shaft

Path of
Primary
Backing
Hook Shaft

Knife

Close up view of needle operation

Direction of
cloth feed

Min nap
Max nap
Longest stroke

Needle plate
Loop pile hook
Needle

Loop pile tufting machine

Direction of
cloth feed

Needle

Backing fabric

Needle plate
Cut pile hook
Knife

Cut pile machine

Figure 8-2. Tufting Machine Operation

Once the carpet was tufted, it entered the finishing process. If the yarn had not been predyed, the first step in finishing was to dye the carpet. This was accomplished through beck dyeing, where the carpet was emersed in an open tank containing dye solution, or by printing. In printing, a pattern was transferred to the carpet by a silk screen method. Once the carpet was dyed, it was passed through a steaming and drying process which lifted and separated the fibers (or filaments) in the pile to give the pile fullness.

The carpet was then passed through a finishing process which applied latex to the underside of the primary backing (this gave body and strength to the carpet as well as anchoring the tufts to the primary backing), and the secondary backing was added, with the latex acting as the adhesive agent. The carpet was then dyed, trimmed, and edged as necessary, and inspected before rolling and packing for shipment.

Variation from this manufacturing process for the other three product lines involved the amount of material and types of material used. The typical material content for the four product lines are as follows:

	Automobile Carpet	Retail & Commercial Carpet	Home Furnishing Fabrics	Apparel Fabrics
Filler yarn	1.6 lb.	1.9 lb.	1.0 lb.	.9 -1.9 lb[c]
Primary backing	.3	.3	.2	.2
Latex (or other adhesive)	1.0	1.7	0 to .1	0 to .2
Secondary backing	.5	.6	0 to .2	0 to .2
Total	3.4 lb	4.5 lb.	1.5 lb.	1.5 -2.5 lb

Both primary and secondary backing were purchased as woven synthetic fabrics. The primary backing was woven thin film yarn in the case of the two carpet product lines, and secondary backing was latex or woven cord. Filler yarn ranged from 1/1 to 4/4 yarn, primarily nylon or acrylic.[d] Because of its high usage of yarn, Carpetex was considering the acquisition of a 50,000 spindle yarn manufacturing plant in Williamston, South Carolina.

Existing Facilities

All of the Carpetex production facilities, with the exception of the new Detroit plant, were nonunion, with Carpetex paying above average wages relative to the rest of the carpet industry. The mills were centrally scheduled from corporate headquarters in Chambersburg, Pennsylvania. Schedules were a composite of customer orders and stock orders. In 1972 Carpetex had six primary manufacturing facilities. These facilities, their size, and products are shown in table 8-3.

The issue of capacity was difficult to deal with in the retail carpet industry.

---

[c]Varied widely with type of material; for example, a long haired synthetic fur requires much more filler yarn than a velvet.

[d]Yarn ranged in count from 1 to 4 and in ply from 1 to 4. Actual yarn weight was determined by carpet gauge and pile quality. The finer the gauge, the lighter the yarn required; typically, automotive carpet was 4/2.

Table 8-3
Existing Manufacturing Facilities

	Dalton[a] Ga.		Gadson Ala.	Calhoun Ga.	Rome Ga.	Greenville S.C.	Detroit Michigan
Product	Automobile & retail carpet		Retail and commercial carpet			Furnishing & apparel fabrics	Automobile carpet
Size (thousand sq. ft.)	672		346	330	410	516	120
Book value (million $)	9.6		9.6	7.3	10.4	14.5	4.7
Two-shift capacity (million sq. yds.)	20 (auto)	10 (retail)	25	25	25	25	5.5[b]
Tufting Machines number	20	13	34	34	36	49	5
width (ft.)	12	15	15	15	12-15	3-12	12
gauge (in.)	1/8	3/64-3/16	3/64-3/16	3/64-3/16	3/64-3/16	3/64-1/4	9/64-3/16
1972 Yarn usage million lbs.)	51		23	23	31	34.3	3

aIncluded woven carpet manufacturing comprising 200,000 square feet housing 62 15-foot carpet looms.
bDetroit plant was built with all the equipment necessary to accommodate a total of 18 tufting machines with a 2-shift capacity of 20 million square yards.

A tufting mill, such as the Gadson plant, produced 50 to 100 qualities of carpet, and each quality had an average of about 15 different colors. About 10 percent of the qualities were offered in two different widths (12' and 15'). The balance were offered in 15' widths only. Each type of carpet had different production rates. These variations in production rates created balancing problems. The automotive carpet plant on the other hand was easy to schedule since demand was known well in advance and large runs were possible.

However, automobile carpeting required an additional operation which the other product lines did not; once the carpet was tufted on the 12-foot tufters and finished, it had to be finished into 3' x 3' to 3' x 7' carpets, cut and shaped to fit specific automobiles. Thus both the Dalton and the new Detroit plant required cut-and-sew finishing lines. Typically, a tufting plant requires one finishing line for 18 tufting machines and one dyeback per 4-5 tufting machines. Figure 8-3 shows the layout of the Detroit plant. Although presently containing only five tufters the plant was built to expand to 18 tufters. With the exception of the cut-and-sew operation, this plant is a typical tufting manufacturing unit. In fact the four other Carpetex plants were a twofold duplication of this plant, each consisting of up to 36 tufters, with eight to ten dyebacks and two finishing lines and necessary storage areas for work in process and finished goods.

Changes in the Automobile Carpet Market

In 1972 Carpetex's two major customers decided to upgrade all the carpeting in their automobiles from loop piles to cut pile over the 1973 to 1975 model changes. In 1972 only a few of the luxury models were equipped with cut pile carpet. Because of the known cost structure of the carpet, Carpetex's customers were not willing to absorb more than a 10 percent increase in price for the carpet.

The net impact on Carpetex was: (1) replace all loop pile tufters with cut pile tufters at a cost of $60,000 per tufting machine or modify the existing machines with cutting bars at a cost of approximately $4,000 per machine; and (2) double the number of tufters since cut pile tufters operated at half the speed of loop pile tufters.

This problem was particularly perplexing because Carpetex had just completed the Detroit plant, with the expectation of providing 90 percent of their automotive market from this plant, and the plant was expandable to a maximum of 18 tufting machines. One of Carpetex's machinery suppliers offered an alternative. The supplier had just developed a "supertufter" which operated at twice the speed of existing cut pile tufters. These machines, although not yet on the market, would be available within three months at a cost of $75,000 each. With these new cut pile machines, Carpetex would be able to produce the same amount of carpet as it was able to produce on the old loop pile machines. The company was considering accelerating its expansion of the Detroit plant using these new machines and moving the present five tufters into its four other carpet plants.

Changes in the Yarn Supply Market

Carpetex anticipated yarn price increases averaging 10 percent to 15 percent per year over the next three years. Fifty percent of this increase would be due to fiber prices. Because Carpetex had grown to a point where it purchased over 160 million pounds of yarn, the company was contemplating the manufacture of its own yarn. Mr. Winans explained why the company had not yet integrated backward into the manufacture of their own yarns:

Historically there has been available yarn capacity in the industry which we have been able to utilize. Since we are a large purchaser we have been able to maintain some degree of price and schedule control. However our needs have varied widely in terms of fiber, color and yarn count. These conditions are changing; more of the textile industry is integrating vertically and more and more of our suppliers are marginal producers who have difficulty controlling cost and quality.

In early 1973 an opportunity arose to purchase a 50,000 spindle yarn mill in Williamston, South Carolina, at a cost of $11 million. The mill included all the equipment necessary for the production of up to 35 million pounds of 1 to 4 count yarns from synthetic fibers and filaments. Estimated savings on yarn costs as a result of the Williamston acquisition were expected to be $.0773 per pound. In addition, it was expected that the Williamston mill output could be doubled at a cost of roughly $8 million.

Changes in the Retail Carpet Market

In addition to Carpetex's concentration of retail and contract carpet sales in a few large customers, the company's market was also concentrated geographically, with the northeastern United States accounting for 80 percent of carpet sales. Mr. Winans was concerned about the growth of retail carpet:

For a company of our size we have a small share of the market with less than 7 percent of the $2.6 billion national market. This makes us the sixth largest carpet manufacturer but we are not growing where we should. Look at the West Coast; we have less than 1 percent of that $500 million market and we are losing that to the small local carpet companies. We are at a double disadvantage because we are a large specialized textile company. We can't compete on a local service basis with the small regional carpet companies. At the same time we

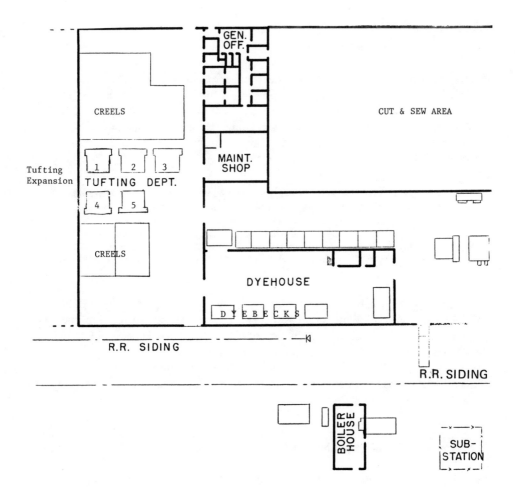

Figure 8-3. Layout for Detroit Plant

189

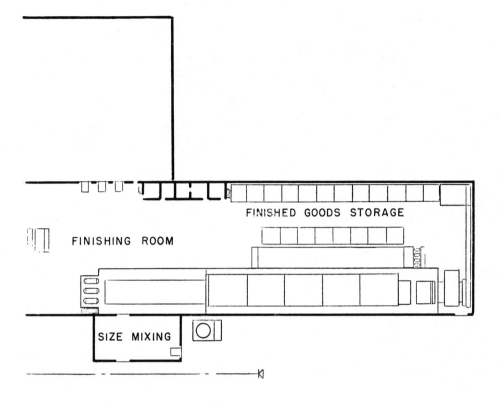

FINISHED GOODS STORAGE

FINISHING ROOM

SIZE MIXING

WATER TANK

NOTE: AREA – 30,000 sq. ft

Figure 8-3 (cont.)

don't have the large national sales force that diversified textile companies such as Burlington and J.P. Stevens have. Even Mohasco is able to integrate their carpet marketing with their furniture marketing.

In the 1950s textile companies started moving their manufacturing to the southeastern United States to take advantage of low labor rates and taxes. We moved along with everyone else. Those advantages have all but disappeared today and such concentration may be a disadvantage with increased transportation costs. It now costs over $.20 a square yard to ship carpet from our Dalton plant to the West Coast and almost $.15 a square yard from Dalton to Detroit.[e] Our problem for the future may be how to diversify geographically as well as integrate vertically.

---

[e]Because of differences in packaging and rate schedules, shipping a cwt. (100 lbs) of carpet cost approximately 1.25 times as much as shipping a cwt. of yarn or a cwt. of backing. Latex could be purchased locally (at about the same price) anywhere in the country.

Texfi Industries, Inc.

In speaking of the early years of his company, Mr. Joseph Hamilton, president of Texfi Industries, Inc., said in July 1970:

Even though many people apparently viewed us as an "infant company" when we started operating in 1963, most of the key personnel involved in starting Texfi actually were fairly experienced in the yarn texturing business. Fred Procter and I had been with Madison Throwing Company, and Louis Cramer was in yarn sales at J.P. Stevens. So we pretty well knew the business of selling textured yarns right from the start.

But from the outset we agreed that we didn't want to stay just in the yarn texturing business, partly because we felt that margins on textured polyester were going to get squeezed in the future. As we got bigger, though, we sold to more and more knitters; so that to integrate forward into knitting would have required us to compete with our own customers and thereby run the risk of losing a significant portion of the market for our textured yarns. Besides that, we have no experience in apparel manufacturing and no background in fashion.

So what we did was form several small operating companies to get us started in both finishing and knitting. We founded Lively Knits, Inc., in April 1966 and Mount Gilead Finishing, Inc., in November 1966 as small pilot operations in knitting and finishing, respectively. We felt, however, that it couldn't be obvious that we were connected with them, so we hired a man and set him up in an employment agency. Besides his regular job of employment recruiting, he would do special recruiting for us to staff these new pilot operations. This way we could hire away some very talented people from places like Burlington and Deering Milliken without their people knowing that we were behind it. We sort of had this big iceberg, but only the tip was showing above the water.

Of course, we had to get new business for these pilot operations. So what we did was to suggest to our customers of textured fibers to try having some of their work done at these new companies. We'd say, "Look, there are a bunch of boys who have started a finishing operation down in Mount Gilead, North Carolina. Why don't you have some of your knitted fabrics finished at their plant?" In response, many customers would send down some piece goods to be dyed, and the boys at Mount Gilead would give it a try. Sometimes it would work out. Sometimes it wouldn't. If it didn't, Mount Gilead would lose the customer, but, of course, such a loss wouldn't hurt Textured Fibers. Gradually, they got things shaken out at Mount Gilead and became pretty good at dyeing.

The same thing was true at Lively Knits. We would suggest to some of the knitters to whom we sold that they send some of their work on a commission basis to a new group down in Fayetteville, North Carolina. It was really wild, because the Lively Knits plant manager usually would ask these customers why they'd bother to buy their yarns from Textured Fibers which, he'd say, really didn't make such a good product anyway. Well, it sounded great, but he about lost us a few customers that way, and we had to tone him down.

In staffing these new operations, we have tended to hire young people from outside the textile industry which is so heavily oriented toward weaving. This way, nobody is committed to doing things any set way, and we've been free to seek "the best way."

In 1968 we raised a substantial amount of money from three insurance companies. Although we knew that eventually we were going to consolidate all of our operations, the insurance companies would not lend us the money until we did. So beginning in 1968 and continuing through early 1969, we consolidated some of the operations by purchasing all of their outstanding stock and converting them into subsidiaries. Later in 1969, when we finally had to make a public issue, we merged all of the companies together and changed the name of the company to Texfi Industries, Inc.

While we were consolidating our financing, we also started up the Fayetteville finishing plant. Now, a finishing operation can really sink your whole company, because it takes a lot of volume to get it going on a profitable basis. Since we were also arranging for new financing at this time, we really ran a double risk in starting up Fayetteville. We bought all the equipment with practically no money down. I remember having to take out a $25,000 mortgage on my own house to raise some of the money for deposits on the new equipment. At the same time, we were still waiting for additional financing so that we could pay for the rest of the equipment, and we practically had the dye becks sitting in our backyard waiting for the new building to go up so that we could start the plant. The machinery manufacturers were threatening to take back all of the equipment unless we paid the bills, but the First National Bank of North Carolina kept promising them that they would get paid. In the meantime, we were trying to arrange the final financing with the insurance companies.

Our start-up strategy was to take huge orders at low price in order to get the finishing plant going, so we just concentrated on basics at the beginning. We, of course, initially had quality problems. But we broke ground in June of 1969, started operations in October, and were operating in the black by January.

Next we bought an operation from Catalina, a division called Kayser-Roth, which makes both single knit and double knit fabrics in two plants out in California. But we haven't had as much luck in taking over established facilities as we have in starting new ones, and we have been losing money on our California operation since we acquired it in October 1969.

Corporate History

Texfi Industries, Inc., was incorporated in Delaware in October 1963 under the name "Textured Fibers, Inc.," for the purpose of texturing raw nylon, acetate, and polyester fibers and selling the textured fiber to knitters. Its corporate name was changed to "Texfi Industries, Inc.," on July 1, 1969, to reflect the changing nature of the company's business.

In 1968 and prior years, Texfi's principal business was texturing synthetic yarns for sales to knitters. However, through the construction and purchase of new facilities, by 1970 the company had evolved into a fully integrated producer of double knit synthetic fabrics, performing all functions between the fiber producer and the apparel manufacturer.

As Texfi evolved from a yarn texturer into an integrated knitter, it has continued to sell intermediate production outside. Thus, a large portion of its textured yarns was consumed by outsider knitters with whom Texfi competed as a knitter of finished fabrics. Similarly, a small portion of its dyeing and finishing operation was done on a commission basis for outside knitters. Appendix 9A contains financial data. The percentage of Texfi's net sales accounted for by its various products and services for five recent fiscal years is as follows:

	1965	1966	1967	1968	1969
Knitted fabrics	1.2%	1.3%	5.4%	23.0%	51.0%
Textured yarns	98.8	98.3	91.5	74.1	46.5
Commission dyeing and finishing	–	–	.5	1.6	2.2
Other	–	.4	2.6	1.3	.3

Table 9-1 summarizes Texfi's divisions and facilities.

Table 9-1
Division and Plant Location

Plant Location	Area (sq. ft.)	Type of Ownership	Type of Operation
Textured Fibers Division			
Liberty, North Carolina	170,000	Owned	Texturing
Sweptsonville, N.C.	70,000	Owned	Texturing
Lumberton, N.C.	128,000	Owned	Texturing and yarn dyeing
Texfi/Lively Knits Division			
Fayetteville, N.C.	60,000	Leased	Knitting
Fayetteville, N.C.	85,600	Owned	Knitting fabric, dyeing, and finishing
Texfi/Knit-One			
Sanford, N.C.	21,000	Owned	Knitting
Mt. Gilead, N.C.	54,000	Leased	Knitting and knit fabric finishing
Texfi/West			
Santa Fe Springs, California	113,580	Leased	Knitting and knit fabric finishing
Ontario, California	57,000	Leased	Knit fabric dyeing and finishing

Manufacturing Facilities

In July 1970 Texfi had recently reorganized into a divisional organizational format, with each division serving separate markets. Tables 9-1 through 9-4 contain data on various manufacturing facilities.

The Textured Fibers Division manufactured and sold textured synthetic yarns of polyester, nylon, and acetate to outside commission knitters and to other Texfi divisions. A new plant which had been completed in Lumberton, North Carolina, in 1969 had modern facilities for both texturizing and yarn dyeing. Yarn-dyed yarns were primarily used in the manufacture of knitted fabrics where more than one color was desired in the finished fabric.

The Texfi/Lively Knits Division knitted, dyed, and finished double knit fabrics for the women's and children's sportswear and dress markets. The Lively Knits Division produced approximately 20 million yards of fabric in 1969.

The Texfi-Knit-One Division made both single and double knit fabrics for the men's and boy's apparel market. This market had historically been very small, but was expected to grow in the future.

The finishing facility in Mount Gilead, North Carolina, processed "wet" or "dry" finished yarn-dyed fabrics after they had been knitted. In the dry finishing process, fabrics made of wool, polyester/wool, acrylics and acetates were steamed, dry cleaned, and stabilized to control shrinkage. In wet finishing, fabrics knitted from polyester and polyester blends were scoured to remove excess oils and then dried and heat set for stabilization.

Although Texfi's various dyeing and finishing services were used in connection with the company's own production of knitted fabrics, capacity was also sold on a commission basis to others.

The Texfi/West Division operated as an integrated manufacturing and sales organization of both yarn- and fabric-dyed knitted cloth to the men's, women's, and children's wear market on the West Coast.

The Lumberton Plant

The Textured Fiber Division's new Lumberton Plant was run by Mr. Bob Barnhill, plant manager, and had a capacity of approximately 195,000 lbs. per week of textured polyester. Table 9-2 details Lumberton's facilities. The plant was modern and air-conditioned and essentially had been running three shifts per day, seven days per week since it began operations in the spring of 1969.

The flow of material in the Lumberton facility was fairly straightforward. Incoming raw yarn of "parent yarn" was stored in the receiving area and marked to differentiate different merges. It was important that yarn from different merges not be mixed in a knitted fabric, since irregularities would show up eventually in the dyeing operation. Yarn wound on returnable sleeves was called

Table 9-2
Lumberton, North Carolina, Facility

Principal Machines		Production Capacity Standard (lbs/wk per machine)	Cost per Machine
Type	Number		
ARCT 440B	6	7,530	$ 80,000
Leesona 555	28	5,520	$ 55,000
Schweiter	30	4,070	$ 13,000
Ratte uptwister	24	2,200	$ 19,000
Assembly winder	13		$ 13,000
Dye kiers		120,000	$500,000 in dye facility
1,000 lb.	2		
750 lb.	2		
300 lbs.	4		
100 lb.	3		
Dryer-extractor	1		
Autoclave	1	240,000	$ 25,000

Source: Casewriter interviews.

Note: Production figures are for 150-denier polyester, 168-hour week for texturing; 144-hour week for all other operations.

"pirns." Yarn wound on cardboard disposable sleeves was called "tubes" or "cheeses." The pirns were usually of the double tapered variety—that is, the yarn is wound on the pirn such that the thickness of the wound yarn tapers upward to maximum thickness in the middle of the pirn. Cheeses, on the other hand, came in as a cylindrical package.

Parent yarn was textured on either of two types of machines: ARCT 440B double heater machines or on Leesona 555 single heater texturing machines. Both of these machines were false twist machines, the difference being that yarn textured on the 440B could be sent directly to the knitter, while yarn textured on the 555 had to be either autoclaved and set, or sent directly to a Schweiter or uptwister before being sent to the knitter.

Textured yarn was of two basic varieties, either set yarn or stretch yarn. In the false twist method of texturing yarn, the raw yarn was first twisted, then heat applied to the twisted yarn, and then the yarn was untwisted. If a stretch yarn was desired, then the yarn was left basically in this state and shipped to the knitter. Stretch yarns were capable of 30 to 40 percent elongation. If a set yarn was desired, however, a second heat treatment had to be applied to the yarn to set, or stabilize, it in its untwisted condition. This left the yarn in a bulky, crinkly condition, but removed the tendency of the polyester to return to its original twisted state. Thus, yarn textured on the ARCT 440B had both heat treatments applied to it and was in a relaxed or stabilized state when it was sent to the knitter.

On the other hand, yarn textured on the Leesona single heater still needed another heat treatment if set yarn was desired. This second heat was applied in the autoclave, or in the dyeing operation, or when the yarn was sent through an uptwister. The uptwister contained a second set of heaters and could also place a small amount of twist in the set yarn. For all practical purposes, however, undyed yarns from either the 440B or the 555 processes were identical.

Yarn to be dyed was wound on a special take-up reel made of wire mesh which allowed the dye liquors to penetrate the yarn package. The reels of textured yarn coming off a 555 were called, "textured packages," and weighed approximately 1 1/2 pounds each. These textured packages were placed on a dye carrier, and the dye carrier placed a load of packages in a dye kettle or "kier." The Lumberton plant had kiers ranging in size from 100 to 1,000 pounds and had the capability of linking two kiers together to form a maximum sized dye lot of 2,000 pounds.

From the kier, the dye lot went to the dryer-extractor. The dye cycle took approximately six hours and used punched tape process control computers to regulate the dyeing process. The process of dyeing the yarns stabilized the textured polyester and served as the second heat treatment. From the dye house, the yarn packages were wound on the Schweiter or uptwister or assembly winder and sent to a knitter.

The final winding operation took place either on a Schweiter, a Ratte uptwister, or an assembly winder. Some knitters preferred their creel packages or iput yarn to the knitting operation in the form of tapered cones. Therefore, the output of the texturing machines had to be rewound into conical form. Other knitters could accept creel packages in cylindrical form but desired them to be a least a certain weight. Thus some knitters wanted only 3 pounds or greater creel packages and would not accept the 1 1/2 pounds packages which were output from the texturing machines.

Mr. Ray Elliott, director of quality control, noted that although the process of manufacturing textured yarn appeared straightforward, in fact, there were many hidden difficultes associated with texturing yarn, especially polyester. Commenting on this aspect of the manufacturing process he stated:

Most of the problems and quality control variations that occur in texturing polyester don't show up until the fabric or the yarn has been dyed. The tension that polyester is subjected to is the key element in the final textured polyester yarn. Maybe the raw polyester that you got from the yarn producer was a little bit un-uniform, so that when it went through the heater banks, it didn't quite texture properly. Well, this yarn won't show up until you dye it, and the dye is absorbed by the yarn in a non-uniform manner, and it will show up in the finished piece of fabric.

Or maybe when you cone the yarn in a Schweiter, you apply a little bit too much, or a little bit too little, tension. This changes the property of the textured yarn just a little bit. This too will show up in the dyed fabric. Since just about all textured yarn is eventually dyed, you are always going to have this problem.

You generally don't have this problem or at least this same type of problem in spun yarns, since much greater variation in the individual staple fibers is required to show up in the finished material. Textured yarns, on the other hand, are made of mono-filament, and this will show up very quickly. Even an operator touching the yarn and putting oil and grease on it can affect the dyeing.

Coning tension is also fairly critical in making the creel packages for the knitting operation. If the yarn is not wound at a correct and uniform tension, when it is taken off the creel package and knitted, it will knit irregularly in the final fabric and show up as a fabric defect, or it might break and cause a run in the fabric. You can run these texturing machines at all different speeds and get a pretty wide range of productivity out of them, but the key factor is to control it and get uniform quality, dyeable textured yarn. A lot of times these defects can be hidden in jacquard-knitted fabric. But in a plain knit, these defects become very obvious.

Mr. Bob Barnhill, plant manager, noted that although the Lumberton plant had been a fairly expensive one to build, it could be expanded at a cost of only approximately $2 per square foot. For example, he could add 14 more ARCT 440B texturing machines fairly easily. The plant was set up with service facilities in the front, but with Porter walls on the back and side for easy expansion. Directly behind the main plant, a new facility of approximately 70,000 square feet was presently being constructed for a new division of Texfi called Texfi/Street. This division was to knit fancy fabric materials and would use textured fibers from the Lumberton plant. Mr. Barnhill noted that his main bottleneck was in getting his salesmen to sell 100 pounds dye lot orders. At present, most of the dyeing orders came in 750 and 1,000 pounds lots.

Lively Knits at Fayetteville

The Lively Knits plant at Fayetteville was Texfi's principal knitting operation, with 150 machines and a capacity of 160,000 pounds of double knit fabric per week based on actual production from the 134 machines presently in use. Tables 9-3 and 9-4 detail the Fayetteville facilities.

Lively Knits knitted about 110,000 to 120,000 pounds per week of internally produced textured yarn and bought 30,000 to 40,000 pounds per week from outside yarn texturers. All of Lively Knits' output was finished at the Fayetteville finishing plant, which, in addition, had 60 to 100 machines doing contract knitting on the outside. Lively Knits had a wide variety of different types of double knit knitting machines. Some of these (such as the Moratronic) cost as much as $45,000 per unit, but the average machine cost approximately $30,000. The plant presently knitted 64 different styles at one time. Lively Knits would accept orders for sample knits only greater than 500 pounds. The

Table 9-3
Lively Knits, Fayetteville Plant

Job Description	Number of Workers		
	Shift 1	2	3
Knitter	31	31	33
Examiner	7	7	6
Needle changer	3	3	3
Wheel builder	2	1	1
Maintenance plus mechanics	10	5	4
	53	47	47
Supervisory, staff		18	
Total plant	165		
Division personnel	32		
Total Fayetteville	197		
Pay Scale			
Knitters, examiners	$2.10/40, $3.15/8, $4.20/Sunday		
Needle changers	$2.26		
Wheel builders	$2.10 - $2.40		
Mechanics	$2.81 - $4.00		
Maintenance	$2.45 - $3.33		
Shift premium	$ .05/hr.		

Source: Plant manager.

Note: 31 new double knit machines were planned to be added by December 1970. Harold Pearson, plant manager, estimated that the following personnel would have to be added: 1 supervisor/shift; 1 knitter/6 machines/shift; 1 examiner/shift; 1 mechanic/2-3 shifts. No expansion of plant would be necessary.

minimum size for regular orders was 5,000 pounds of fabric. Commission knitters typically received $.75 to $.90 per pound for knitting.

In describing the selling of knitted fabrics, Mr. Harold Pearson, plant manager of the Fayetteville facility, made the following comments:

Since we run this plant totally on sold goods, we never knit anything unless we already have an order for it. A salesman will call "order control" and find out how far ahead we are sold up on various machines. He will then negotiate with the customer for delivery of a particular type fabric at a particular date, which he figures he can meet, knowing what machines will be available to knit the fabric at that time. Having gotten an order, he will then notify the plant and will receive a "position on order" and a scheduling on the machines. Texfi will then buy the yarn and texture it. We will knit it and dye it and receive payment as soon as it is sent. The whole yarn delivery, texturing, and knitting process, including finishing, might take us two to three weeks to complete.

Table 9-4
Fayetteville Lively Knits Knitting Facilities

Number	Knitting Machines Type	Feeds	Cut	Diameter
5	Terrot U3P	36	18	30"
46	Morat 18 Cut	48	18	30"
14	Mayer Ilgor	44	18	30"
8	Mayer OVJA	36	24	30"
16	Interlock	24	24	26", 30"
17	Terrot 30"	32	18	30"
13	Morat 24 Cut	48	24	30"
10	Moratronik	36	18	30"
4	Scott and Williams	36	18-22	30"
6	Albi 24"	24	18	24"
6	Albi 30"	36	18	30"
14	Terrot 33"	36	18	33"

This type of delivery obviously would be impossible under the ordinary weaving on a loom, which accounts for the great popularity for knitted fabrics in the fashion field. A weaving loom, for instance, might spend four to six weeks on one single beam. Every day at the end of the day, the New York sales office receives a Telex report from the plant identifying our machine loading and how far in advance each machine position is sold up. Currently, for instance, we have a balance-to-knit backlog of 1,342,222 pounds.

Three to four years ago, when we first got started, we did all of our knitting work on commission. Last year we started knitting some of our own fabrics, which we went out and sold directly. This year, we have complete new lines of fabric representing about 250 to 300 different styles. We have gone from trailing the field to leading the pack.

In mid-1970, Texfi/Lively Knits designers were introducing a completely new line of fashion fabrics for introduction in spring of 1971. Should the introduction prove successful, it would easily absorb the entire knitting output of the Fayetteville plant. However, initial reaction to the lines would not be completely known for some time yet. This program represented a significant departure from the previous methods of commission knitting, where orders would be of a fairly random nature, both in quantity and style requested.

Except for the Interlock machines (which were used primarily for fine nylon double knits), most of the machinery in the plant was of fairly modern design and fairly versatile. Most used different methods of wheels, dials, or cylinders to set the pattern in the knitted fabric. The only exceptions were the Moratronic machines, which had an electronic needle-engaging device run by an optical tape drive. While it would ordinarily take about eight hours to change the setup and the pattern on a regular machine, the tape on the Moratronic could be changed in three minutes. To doff the creels and rethread the feeds on a Moratronic might take an extra half hour. Much of the setup time on conventional double knit machinery could be compressed by setting up a spare set of wheels or dials prior to changeover. When this was done, the changeover would take less than one hour.

Presently, the optical tape for the Moratronic had to be ordered one month to two months in advance, and cost from $125 to $500 apiece. The backlog on the delivery of this type of machine was substantial, and no new orders were being accepted for delivery by the manufacturer before 1973.

In commenting on running a knitting operation, Mr. Pearson, manager of the Fayetteville plant, said:

The salesmen in this business can really kill your plant profit. This is why we don't let salesmen know the actual cost of knitting a fabric. If they had this information, they might be induced to cut the price 5¢ to 10¢ a pound in order to sell it. This is certainly a natural tendency, but one which will leave you without any money at the end of the quarter. Fortunately, we haven't had that problem, since we can get $.15 per pound more than competition because of our higher quality.

On the other hand, a good plant manager can pick up a few extra pennies by buying off-quality yarn. Running off-quality yarn through knitting might cost an extra 2¢ or 3¢ a pound to knit, but yarn can be bought at $1.50 to $1.55 a pound, versus $1.80 to $1.90 per pound on first-quality branded textured yarn. If the plant is run as a cost center (with yarn transferred in at a standard cost), the plant manager is going to lose some efficiency by knitting off-standard yarn, since his knitting cost per pound is going to go up and his plant profit, as indicated in the divisional report, is going to go down.

The real way you compete in knitting is on quality and delivery. When the apparel manufacturer is ready to cut, he wants the fabric there immediately so as to be able to get his garments into the stores as soon as possible. Short lead times on delivery are especially critical in the middle of the season, when some styles and colors might be running much hotter than others.

At the retail level in high-margin fashion goods, the cost of stock-outs is naturally extremely expensive. Therefore, the knitter has to be able to turn on a dime in responding to changes in fashion trends.

We have examiners here who examine 100 percent of the knitted fabric that goes out of the plant. Each roll that they examine has a card attached to it showing the machine the fabric was knitted on; the operator who was in charge of the machine at the time the fabric was knitted; the yarn lot from which the fabric came; the examiner who was inspecting the fabric; and the complete history of the fabric roll to date. As the examiner inspects the fabric, she makes a note on the card concerning every single defect that she finds.

The industry standard for first-quality knitted fabrics is ten defects or less per roll, but we don't let any fabrics go out of the plant at first-quality with more than five defects per roll. Defects might be caused by slubs, runs, broken needles, holes, dropped stitches, and a number of other problems with the yarn and knitting.

In either the texturing process, or in knitting, when a yarn breaks, an operator usually picks it up and ties the two broken ends together. If it is done sloppily, it appears as a large bulge in the course of the fabric. This is a "slub." A needle can drop a stitch, in which case you get a small hole in the fabric. If there is a broken needle, it can cause a run in the fabric. If an examiner spots a run, and the run is less than five inches long, the defect is charged to the machine. Otherwise, if it is longer than five inches, it is charged to the operator. Naturally, needles can break quite frequently, so it is necessary to reneedle before you get killed by broken needles. Since needles cost 30¢ each, it gets pretty expensive to reneedle.

By keeping this kind of data on the knitting machine, on the yarn, and on the knitter, we can track quality defects back to the person, either the knitter, the manufacturer of the yarn, or the fixer of the machine. Beside being able to track quality defects back to a particular person, we can use these cards to save some first-quality merchandise that might ordinarily have to be made into second-quality merchandise. For instance, a long, length-wise run in a tube would ordinarily have to go out as a second, but if the roll of fabric has been flagged to have a long run at such and such a place, the cutter can cut the tube of fabric in the finishing plant so that the cut runs along the length of the run, thereby making it first-quality material.

Additionally, if quality defects are discovered at the finishing end, we can trace them back to the examiner and see whether or not the examiner should have picked up the defect. We can also trace it back to the texturing operation and attach responsibility at that point. So although the system is fairly simple, it is very effective in tracking down and maintaining quality in the knitted fabrics.

Raw Fibers

Harry Cramer, president of the Textured Fibers Division, estimated that the 1970 textured polyester fiber market was running at approximately 130 million pounds per year. Of this total market, he estimated that his division accounted for 15 to 20 percent of total consumption, or 20 to 25 million pounds per year.

There were basically three different grades of raw 150 denier polyester. Depending upon the end use intended for the fiber, a purchaser had considerable latitude in which fibers he purchased. "Off-grade" fiber, not guaranteed for dyeability, could be bought for $.95 to $1.05 per pound; first quality, unbranded, for $1.20 to $1.28 per pound; and branded fiber (such as Dacron), for $1.25 to $1.38 per pound

Because raw fiber prices are subject to change, Cramer felt that Texfi's policy of maintaining "zero inventory" was essential to its profitability. Communications between manufacturing and sales were very frequent, with the plants sending in a daily teletype to New York showing the salesmen the status of the finished goods inventory at the end of the day. During 1969 Textured Fibers Division had inventory turnover of twenty-eight. Besides the effect on maintaining low exposure to a sudden drop in raw materials prices, the zero inventory policy also gave Textured Fibers Division an instantaneous feedback on quality. By maintaining work-in-process inventories at a low level, a bad yarn lot discovered in the dyeing process would obsolete a minimum amount of inventory.

Recent Developments

The double knit business had grown quite substantially in the last two years, with the result that most statistics compiled by the Bureau of the Census, or by industry sources, were out of date. Appendix 7B contains various projections for the future. By the later part of 1969 an equipment shortage existed for double knit knitting machines, in spite of the fact that several manufacturers of such equipment had made significant increases in their plant capacity. Furthermore, one industry source had noted that although there were an estimated 6,000 double knit machines in the United States in 1969, only 3,000 of these machines actually were suitable for modern fashion knitting. Total planned deliveries of new double knit machines were estimated to be an additional 3,000 machines between 1969 and 1971. Texfi itself had made purchase commitments for 400 new machines during this period at a cost of approximately $40,000 per machine. This would be in addition to the approximately 320 double knit machines which Texfi currently operates, including those at the Kayser-Roth facility in California. For many machines, such as the Moratronic, additional deliveries could not be secured before 1972.

Sales of double knit fabric, especially those made of polyester and spun polyester blends, were expected to maintain an exceptionally strong growth trend throughout the 1970s. *American Fabrics* magazine, for example, had called knits "the multimillion dollar baby" in its summer 1969 issue. Most industry sources were expecting significant penetration of men's wear—especially the men's tailored clothing market—as soon as a significant number of 24-cut machines became available.

Recognizing their need to build a strong base of management for future profitable growth, Mr. Joseph Hamilton, president of the corporation, recently invited the management consulting firm of McKinsey & Company to make a study of Texfi Industries, Inc. Two broad areas to be investigated by McKinsey were: (1) executive compensation, and (2) product line profitability analysis. In this context Mr. Fred Procter, vice president and controller, stated:

The men in the plant want to be measured for their performance. At present, we only have an informal bonus system to compensate the men. Hopefully, in the future, we will be able to institute a more equitable system based on plant profitability and return on investment. The men want recognition for their outstanding efforts, and I agree with them.

The second area to be investigated by McKinsey & Company—analysis of the profitability of each product—reflected the hope that by analyzing the contribution of any particular fabric, some maximization of contribution per machine hour could be achieved through a more rational marketing and scheduling approach.

Appendix 9A:
Texfi Industries, Inc.,
Financial Data

Table 9A-1
Sales and Earnings

	Three Months Ended		Six Months Ended	
	May 1, 1970	*May 1, 1969*	*May 1, 1970*	*May 1, 1969*
Net sales	$22,220,784	$12,065,319	$40,619,313	$24,508,777
Income before income taxes	$ 2,221,061	$ 753,300	$ 3,883,375	$ 1,470,204
Income taxes	1,109,802	310,335	1,926,224	637,829
Net income	$ 1,111,259	$ 442,965	$ 1,957,151	$ 832,375
Average shares of common stock outstanding	1,968,597	1,571,000	1,852,114	1,498,750
Earnings per share of common stock	$.56	$.28	$1.06	$.56

Note: 1. Net sales for 1969 periods reflect minor reclassification to conform with 1970 presentation. Net income for the six months ended May 1, 1969, has been reduced by $6,548 resulting from a pooling adjustment.

2. Federal investment tax credit applied as a reduction of the provision for federal income taxes for the three and six months ended May 1, 1970, was $77,209 ($.04 per share) and $151,722 ($.08 per share) and for the three and six months ended May 1, 1969 was $106,385 ($.07 per share) and $196,853 ($0.13 per share).

3. The above amounts are subject to year end audit.

	Financial Position	
	May 1, 1970	*October 31, 1969*
Current assets	$29,225,469	$21,616,229
Current liabilities	12,427,592	15,626,402
Working capital	16,797,877	5,989,827
Property, plant and equipment, net	27,233,997	23,910,601
Total assets	58,013,746	47,096,052
Long-term debt	17,565,572	15,522,206
Common shareholders' equity	26,033,412	14,239,279
Book value per share of common stock	$ 12.19	$ 8.20

Table 9A-2
Balance Sheet, October 31, 1969 and 1968

Assets		
	1969	*1968*
Current assets		
Cash	$ 974,811	$ 3,926,480
Receivables		
Trade:		
Factors, less advances of $900,000 in 1969 and $1,371,000 in 1968	10,114,748	4,474,025
Customers, less allowances of $250,316 in 1969 and $265,036 in 1968 for doubtful accounts	3,838,998	3,508,061
Other	565,204	151,003
Refundable taxes on income	577,107	
Inventories	5,346,961	2,544,582
Prepaid expenses	198,400	95,047
Total current assets	21,616,229	14,699,198
Property, plant, and equipment—at cost		
Land and land improvements	443,578	285,685
Buildings	4,792,240	2,105,622
Machinery, equipment, etc.	22,281,563	10,773,638
Leasehold improvements	1,161,730	56,402
Construction in progress	244,287	2,069,036
Less accumulated depreciation and amortization	5,012,797	2,956,834
Property, plant and equipment, net	23,910,601	12,333,549
Advance payments on purchases of machinery	855,592	36,851
Deferred charges, etc.	713,630	283,413
Total	$47,096,052	$27,353,011
Liabilities		
Current liabilities		
Notes payable, banks and other	$ 6,900,000	$ 2,021,788
Current maturities of long-term debt	1,921,041	1,924,756
Accounts payable	5,512,252	4,806,028
Accrued liabilities	1,166,228	478,739
Accrued income taxes	126,881	1,668,269
Total current liabilities	15,626,402	10,899,580
Deferred Income Taxes	1,708,165	981,374
Long-term debt	15,522,206	9,814,200
Shareholders' Equity		

Table 9A-2 (cont.)

Common stock, $1 par value–authorized, 5,000,000 shares; outstanding, 1,735,630 shares in 1969 and 1,408,500 shares in 1968	1,735,630	1,408,500
Additional paid-in capital	8,241,598	1,819,575
Retained earnings	4,262,051	2,429,782
Shareholders' equity	14,239,279	5,657,857
Total	$47,096,052	$27,353,011

Note: See Notes to Financial Statements.

Table 9A-3
Operating Data

	1965	1966	1967	1968	1969
Net sales	$10,892,301	$14,720,215	$26,793,993	$46,559,064	$59,534,091
Other revenues	1,876	4,605	14,811	79,381	40,439
Total revenues	$10,894,177	$14,724,820	$26,808,804	$46,638,445	$59,574,530
Costs and expenses					
Cost of goods sold	$10,041,348	$13,650,865	$23,289,914	$39,246,175	$50,555,407
Selling, G & A	405,031	491,666	1,230,732	2,188,893	4,779,090
Interest expense	138,391	237,025	455,729	805,742	1,382,948
Miscellaneous	943	2,119	29,349	1,258	55,704
Total	$10,585,713	$14,381,675	$25,005,724	$43,242,068	$56,773,149
Income before tax	308,464	343,145	1,803,080	4,396,377	2,801,381
Income tax					
Current	361	261	597,911	1,806,564	242,321
Deferred	117,900	135,299	217,698	306,816	726,791
Total	$ 118,261	$ 135,560	$ 815,609	$ 2,113,380	$ 969,112
Net income	$ 190,203	$ 207,585	$ 987,471	$ 2,282,997	$ 1,832,269
Average shares common	690,150	886,838	1,141,400	1,193,733	1,612,690
Earnings per share	$.18	$.18	$.86	$1.91	$1.14
Depreciation and amortization	263,037	426,329	729,946	1,207,361	2,260,868

Table 9A-4
Financial Position at Year End

	1965	1966	1967	1968	1969
Current assets	$2,683,924	$3,788,513	$ 8,322,303	$14,699,198	$21,616,229
Current liabilities	1,994,498	3,020,849	5,968,909	10,899,580	15,626,402
Working capital	689,426	767,664	2,353,394	3,799,618	5,989,827
Property, plant and equipment, net	2,269,752	4,040,189	7,131,174	12,333,549	23,910,601
Total assets	4,958,808	7,834,824	15,522,156	27,353,011	47,096,052
Long-term debt	2,361,419	3,695,290	7,004,008	9,814,200	15,522,206
Common shareholders' equity	305,198	683,846	1,729,317	5,657,587	14,239,279
Book value per share common	.44	.66	1.48	4.02	8.20
P, P&E, gross—approx.	2,500,000	4,900,000	8,500,000	15,290,383	28,923,398

Note: 1. All years give effect to acquisitions accounted for as pooling of interests.
2. Earnings per share are after deduction of preferred dividend requirements in 1965-1968.

Notes to Statement of Income

A. The Company purchased all of the capital stock of Throwing Corporation of America in March 1967 and its accounts have been included in the foregoing statement since the date of acquisition. Net sales of this company were $5,696,886 for the period from the date of purchase to November 2, 1967, and $10,391,055 for the fiscal year ended October 31, 1968.

On October 31, 1968 the Company acquired all of the outstanding stock of Lively Knits, Inc., and on that date, Mt. Gilead Finishing Corp. and Greenhurst Fabrics, Inc., were merged into the Company. Two-thirds of the capital stock of Knitmoor Fabrics, Inc., was acquired upon its organization in December 1967 and the remaining one-third interest was acquired in December 1968. On March 4, 1969, the Company acquired all of the outstanding stock of Polikoff Textiles, Inc. Such transactions have been accounted for as poolings of interests, and accordingly the foregoing statement includes the accounts of these companies since the dates of their incorporation as follows: Polikoff Textiles, Inc., November 17, 1964; Lively Knits, Inc., April 4, 1966; Mt. Gilead Finishing Corp., November 3, 1966; Greenhurst Fabrics, Inc., July 17, 1967; and Knitmoor Fabrics, Inc., December 27, 1967. During the fiscal year ended October 31, 1969, all of its remaining subsidiary companies were merged into the Company. The following is a reconcilement of net sales and net income as originally reported with amounts shown in the foregoing statement:

| | *Fiscal Year* | | | |
	1965	1966	1967	1968
Net sales:				
As originally reported	$10,762,303	$14,473,478	$24,933,198	$37,379,861
Pooled companies	129,998	253,617	2,276,033	12,261,371
Less intercompany sales		(6,880)	(415,238)	(3,082,168)
As shown above	$10,892,301	$14,720,215	$26,793,993	$46,559,064
Net income:				
As originally reported (after adjustment for change in depreciation practices–Note C)	$ 189,189	$ 220,983	$ 672,910	$ 1,522,651
Pooled companies (loss)	1,014	(13,398)	314,561	760,346
As shown above	$ 190,203	$ 207,585	$ 987,471	$ 2,282,997

Net sales and net income for the year ended October 31, 1969 include $1,554,401 and $31,930, respectively, for Polikoff Textiles, Inc., for the period prior to its acquisition by the Company.

During 1969 the Company changed its fiscal year to end on the Friday nearest October 31; previously its fiscal year ended on the Thursday nearest October 31 (usually 52 weeks). Accordingly, the five fiscal years shown above ended on October 28, 1965; October 27, 1966; November 2, 1967 (53 weeks); October 31, 1968; and October 31, 1969.

B. Federal investment tax credits, applied as reductions of federal income taxes currently payable in the foregoing statement, were as follows: $40,562 ($.06 per share) in 1965; $44,495 ($.05 per share), in 1966; $106,740 ($.09 per share) in 1967; $332,167 ($.28 per share) in 1968; and $629,992 ($.39 per share) in 1969. Of the 1969 amount, approximately $283,000 will be used to reduce federal income taxes payable and the remainder will be carried back to obtain a refund of taxes paid in prior years.

At October 31, 1969, unused investment tax credits of $66,477 are available as a carryover for reduction of federal income taxes payable in future years.

As a result of recent legislation, the investment tax credit will no longer be available as to equipment ordered after April 18, 1969. On the basis of purchase commitments entered into prior to that date, the Company believes it will be entitled to approximately $960,000 of investment credits when the equipment is received and placed in service which is scheduled principally during the fiscal years ending October 31, 1970, and 1971. The utilization of these anticipated credits is dependent upon future earnings and certain other limitations.

C. During 1968 the Company changed the useful lives and the method of computing depreciation of certain depreciable assets as explained in Note 4 to the financial statements. The foregoing statement for 1965 through 1967 was restated to give rectroactive effect to adjustments arising from such changes. These changes had the effect of increasing net income by $38,957 ($.06 per share) in 1965, $130,416 ($.15 per share) in 1966, $178,479 ($.16 per share) in 1967, and approximately $272,000 ($.23 per share) in 1968.

D. Earnings per share are computed based on the weighted average number of shares of common stock outstanding during each period, after retroactive adjustment for the 600 for 1 stock split in October 1968 and shares issued in acquisitions accounted for as poolings of interests. Stock options granted have not been included in computing earnings per share as the dilutive effect would not be material. No dividends have been declared or paid on the common stock during the periods shown above.

Preferred stock dividend requirements deducted from net income in computing earnings per share of common stock are as follows: four fiscal years 1965 through 1968—$63,693, $43,936, $6,000, and $6,000. These amounts include fixed annual dividends at the rate of $6,000 in each year. The fiscal years 1965 and 1966 include participating dividends of $57,693 and $37,936, respectively (per share of common stock: 1965—$.09; and 1966—$.04), declared and paid in the subsequent year. The participating dividend requirements based on certain net profits for the fiscal year ended November 2, 1967, would have been $256,061 if the preferred stock had not been purchased and retired; if such dividend had been declared, earnings per share of common stock would have been $.64 per share of that year. The purchase and retirement of the preferred stock on October 30, 1968, resulted in elimination of the participating dividend requirements for the year ended October 31, 1968.

The increases in net sales in the fiscal years ended November 2, 1967, October 31, 1968, and October 31, 1969, were due primarily to (a) a substantial increase in production capacity in each year, (b) the purchase on May 2, 1969, of knitting and finishing facilities in California, (c) inclusion of sales of Throwing Corporation of America, purchased in 1967, for eight months of the 1967 fiscal year and for the entire 1968 and 1969 fiscal years, and (d) changing the major portion of knitting operations in 1968 from contract knitting on a commission basis to knitting apparel fabrics for sale to customers. The decline in the Company's income before income taxes in the 1969 fiscal year as compared to the 1968 fiscal year is attributable principally to depressed prices for textured yarns in fiscal 1969 as compared to the historically high levels prevailing throughout fiscal 1968, to increases in selling, administrative and general expenses as the Company increased its management and selling personnel in response to the additional capacity and scope of the knitting and dyeing and finishing operations which the Company inaugurated in fiscal 1969 and to increased interest expense. The effect of these factors on net income was offset in part by the increase in available investment tax credits referred to in Note B. During fiscal 1969 the Company acquired knitting and finishing facilities in California and commenced texturing and yarn dyeing operations at Lumberton, North Carolina, and fabric dyeing and finishing at Fayetteville, North Carolina, and Ontario, California. A portion of the costs of commencing these new operations was deferred. See Note 5 on financial statements. The Company's knitting, dyeing and finishing operations in California have operated at a loss from the beginning of such operations through the three-month period ended January 30, 1970.

Notes to Financial Statements

(For the Three Fiscal Years Ended October 31, 1969)

1. Basis of Financial Statements

    The accompanying financial statements include the accounts of Texfi Industries, Inc. (the "Company") and its subsidiaries, all of which were merged into the Company during the fiscal years ended October 31, 1968 and 1969. All material intercompany sales and other transactions were eliminated.

    On October 31, 1968, all the outstanding capital stock of Lively Knits, Inc., was acquired in exchange for 330,750 shares of previously unissued common stock. On that date Mt. Gilead Finishing Corp. and Greenhurst Fabrics, Inc., were merged into the Company and 90,000 and 29,250 shares, respectively, of previously unissued common stock were issued in accordance with terms of the merger agreement. Two-thirds of the capital stock of Knitmoor Fabrics, Inc., was acquired upon its organization in December 1967 and in December 1968 the remaining one-third interest was acquired in exchange for 4,000 shares of the Company's common stock. On March 4, 1969, all of the outstanding capital stock of Polikoff Textiles, Inc., was acquired in exchange for 48,000 shares of previously unissued common stock. These transactions were accounted for as poolings of interests.

    As of March 2, 1967, the Company purchased all of the outstanding capital stock of Throwing Corporation of America at a cost which was $541,339 in excess of the underlying book value of the net assets of date of acquisition. Of that amount, $483,822 was allocated to property, plant and equipment and $57,517 to intangible assets. Amounts allocated to depreciable assets are being depreciated over the lives of the related assets; amounts allocated to intangibles are being amortized over five years.

2. Receivable from Factors

    Certain trade accounts receivable are sold, without recourse for credit losses, to Meinhard-Commercial Corporation and Rosenthal & Rosenthal, Inc., commercial factors.

3. Inventories

    Inventories are stated in the accompanying balance sheet at the lower of cost or market. The cost of raw materials and supplies and the cost of raw material content of goods in process and finished goods are computed on the first-in, first-out basis; labor and manufacturing expenses included in inventories are based on average costs.

    Inventories used in the computations of cost of goods sold for the three fiscal years ended October 31, 1969 were as follows:

	October 27, 1966	November 2, 1967	October 31, 1968	October 31, 1969
Finished goods	$ 556,730	$ 219,069	$ 228,107	$ 816,577
Goods in process	329,089	492,821	1,715,751	2,063,582
Raw materials and supplies	401,155	733,462	600,724	2,466,802
Total	$1,286,974	$1,445,352	$2,544,582	$5,346,961

4. Depreciation and Maintenance Policy

    Depreciation has been computed by the Company using the straight-line method for financial statement purposes and the declining balance method for income tax purposes. Depreciation of certain assets had been computed utilizing the declining balance method for both financial statement and income tax purposes prior to November 3, 1967. As of that date, the method of computing depreciation as to substantially all property was changed to the straight-line method for financial statement purposes only, and the Company lengthened from 5 to 8 years the lives used in computing depreciation for its major processing equipment. Retroactive effect has been given in the accompanying statements to the change in the method of computing depreciation and the change in useful lives, and to deferred income taxes resulting from depreciation for income tax purposes having exceeded depreciation for financial statement purposes. See Note C to statement of income.

A summary of the estimated lives used in computing depreciation and amortization is as follows:

	Years
Land improvements	5-15
Buildings	15-50
Machinery and equipment	4-15
Office furniture and equipment	3-10
Automobiles and trucks	3-7
Leasehold improvements	2-25

Upon the retirement or disposal of any item of property, the cost is deducted from the property account and accumulated depreciation is deducted from accumulated depreciation. Any profit or loss on the disposal is credited or charged to income. Maintenance and repairs are charged to expense, and renewals or betterments are capitalized.

5. Deferred Charges, etc.
Deferred charges at October 31, 1969 include $322,148 representing the unamortized portion of costs incurred in the startup of operations at new plants. Such costs are being amortized over periods of up to two years. These costs have been deducted currently for income tax purposes and appropriate provisions have been made for deferred income taxes.

6. Notes Payable and Long-Term Debt
Long-term debt at October 31, 1969 consists of the following:

Lease-purchase contracts, 4 3/4% to 7 1/2% due quarterly to 1973	$ 2,582,531
Equipment obligations:	
Conditional purchase contracts, 6% and 8 1/2%, due quarterly and monthly to 1971	399,163
Bank, 8%, due 1973	177,498
Banks, 4% to 5 1/2%, due 1971 to 1974 (due in monthly or quarterly installments plus interest computed on the original amount of the loan)	2,470,875
Mortgage loans, 6%, due monthly and annually to 1976-1981	509,305
Promissory notes, 7 7/8%, due in annual installments from 1972 to 1983	10,500,000
Other note, 9 1/2%, due quarterly in varying installments to 1971	303,875
Subordinated promissory note, 7 1/2%, due in annual installments of $50,000 commencing April 30, 1980	500,000
Total	17,443,247
Less current maturities	1,921,041
Remainder—due after one year	$15,522,206

Table 9A-5
Sales by Inside-Outside Production
(million)

Year	Mill Production	Purchased Yarns	Total Sales
1964	—	—	$ 3.8
1965	6.8	4.0	10.8
1966	10.7	3.8	14.5
1967	23.0	2.0	25.0
1968	35.0	3.0	37.4

Table 9A-6
Additions to Fixed Assets
(in millions)

Year	Total	Yarn Division	East Coast	West Coast	Corp.
1964-65	$ 2.6	$ 2.6			
1966	2.2	2.1	$ .1		
1967	4.1	3.1	1.0		
1968	6.3	2.9	3.4		
1969	13.6	5.1	2.7	$5.8	$.4
	$28.8	$15.1	$7.4	$5.8	$.4

Appendix 9B:
Forecasts for the Yarn
Texturing Business

Table 9B-1
Texturing Capacity Forecasts

Method of Texturing	By End of 1969 (million lbs.)	
	Previous Forecast	Current Forecast
False twist	240	295
Other	60	105
	300	400

Source: Du Pont, January 1970.

Table 9B-2
Textured Yarn Forecasts

(millions of pounds)

	1968	1969	1970	1973	1974
Throwster textured					
Nylon	148	140	163	200	208
Polyester	60	90	124	195	205
Acetate	30	30	30	25	25
Other	7	8	10	12	14
Total	245	268	327	432	452
Fiber produced textured					
Nylon	9	15	20	68	90
Polyester	–	+	1	15	25
Acetate	6	6	6	5	5
Other	1	1	2	2	3
Total	16	22	29	90	123
Grand Total	261	290	356	522	575

Source: Du Pont, January 1970.

Table 9B-3
Textured Yarn Forecast by End Use
(million lbs.)

End Use	Nylon			Polyester		
	1969	*1970*	*1974*	*1969*	*1970*	*1974*
Hosiery	39	55	88	–	–	–
Socks	28	29	34	–	–	–
Warp Knit	6	9	25	1	3	20
Circular Knit	67	74	112	80	108	175
Broadwoven	8	8	26	8	12	27
Upholstery & Misc.	7	8	13	1	2	8
Total	155	183	298	90	125	230

Source: Du Pont, January 1970.

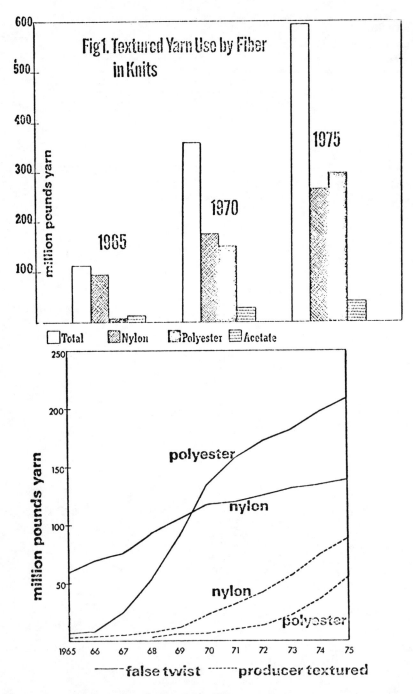

Source: *Modern Knitting Management*, June 1970.

Figure 9B-1. Projection of Textured Yarn Use, by Fiber

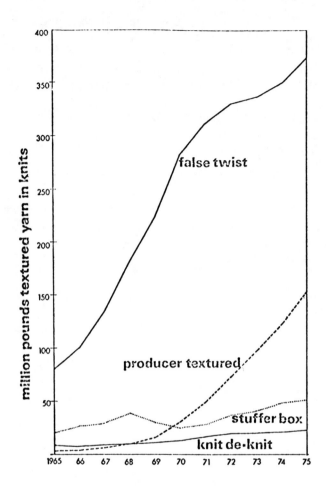

Source: *Modern Knitting Management*, June 1970.

Figure 9B-2. Projection of Textured Yarn, by Method

About the Author

Richard Paul Olsen is professor of business administration at Institut pour l'Etude des Méthodes de Direction de l'Entreprise (IMEDE) in Lausanne, Switzerland. He was formerly an assistant professor at Harvard University Graduate School of Business Administration. Professor Olsen received the A.B. from Rutgers University, the M.B.A. from the University of Southern Mississippi, and the D.B.A. from the Harvard Business School. He has been consultant in management of technology, operations management and new ventures to companies in the United States, Canada, and Europe.

Professor Olsen is the author of many articles and cases in the area of management of technology and operations management. He is coauthor of *Operations Management: Text and Cases* (Richard D. Irwin, 1975), and is currently engaged in research concerning the introduction of new process technology in electronics and textiles.